FOLLOW THE LEADER

DOG TRAINING MANUAL

A Practical Guide and Philosophy for Training Your Pet Dog

By Gary Miller, C.P.D.T.

Underdog Books

Miami, Florida
2001

Printed in the United States of America
ISBN: 1-891231-63-4

Library of Congress Control Number:
2001096001

Underdog Books

Published by Underdog Books
21741 SW 97th Court
Miami, Florida 33190

Acknowledgements

Writing a book is hard, really hard. I never thought that it would be easy exactly but I know I did not fully appreciate the enormity of the project when I first started. I do not think that anyone could ever write a book such as this without a good deal of help. Although it is my name that is listed as the author, many others contributed to this book in a variety of ways, both directly and indirectly. I would like to acknowledge those who played a part in this endeavor and express my sincere gratitude to them. I would like to thank several people in particular: My wife, Louise, because without her support it would not have been possible for me to complete this book. My two sons, Jason and Brian. Their time and expert technical help with my computer requirements were invaluable. My parents, for their encouragement, ideas (e.g., the little devil dog) and constructive comments on the manuscript inspired me to complete this project. Tonya Sturrup, for her professional advice and input on dog training and suggestions on how to best communicate ideas to dog owners. Kathy Waddell, for her editorial review and advice on my rather "creative" use of punctuation and grammar. And finally, all the positive reinforcement trainers, many of whom do not even know me, but who have influenced me and reaffirmed my commitment to the positive style of dog training.

Many of the photographs in this book were made possible by contributions and help from a number of people. I wish to acknowledge and express my gratitude to everyone for his or her generosity and help. Photographers and contributors: Jason Miller, Tonya Sturrup, Karen Cooprider and Gary Miller.

All cartoons drawn by the author, Gary Miller.

Dedication

To my dog, Happy Jumping "Jack" Rabbit, for showing me the power of positive reinforcement.

V

Contents

Preface

With ever-increasing frequency dogs are becoming more intimately integrated in normal everyday human society. There is a tremendous difference in the way most people view dogs today as compared to thirty or forty years ago. Only a few short decades ago most dogs lived outdoors and were relegated to living in a doghouse in the backyard. Their status in the family unit was not especially high and they were kept primarily for utilitarian purposes.

Today, a majority of dogs are kept, or at least allowed to live a good portion of their lives, inside the family home. Their purpose has more to do with companionship than utility and they are often viewed as adopted family members. As rural populations shrink and a more urban way of life dominates our society, our attitudes towards animals, and dogs in particular, have changed dramatically.

The irony is that dogs are banned from most public places and yet they are more popular than they have ever been in the past. Through necessity dogs have had to adapt to more stringent and restrictive rules that come with urban living. Their ability to live in modern, urban human society does not come naturally however. Dogs must (and can) learn rules that allow them to coexist with human beings. Because dogs must live with human beings, and not the other way around, it is important that dog owners teach their dog the rules.

As any good teacher knows, a student cannot learn unless they are sufficiently motivated. This book is an instructional guide for dog owners on how to motivate their dog. With the easy to use principles outlined in this book, virtually anyone can teach their dog the essential rules for living in a human society. This book is written for the average dog owner who wants to train their "pet dog." Many books are concerned with teaching competition style obedience, which is usually not necessary or very practical for the typical dog owner.

The Follow The Leader method of training is a humane, simple, common sense yet scientifically proven method for training dogs (and other animals). It will give you the tools and knowledge for effectively teaching your dog in a way that is fun for both you and your pet. It eliminates the need to physically dominate your dog. It will strengthen and elevate the bond or friendship that you have with your dog. It will give you greater insight into how your dog sees the world. You may even gain a new respect for your dog, while your dog will definitely learn a new respect for you.

This book offers pet owners an alternative to traditional, outdated methods for dog training. It refutes and points out the flaws in long-established rules for "dominance" or "alpha" type training and theory. Difficulties in training can often be attributed to these misguided and counterproductive methods.

The methods outlined in this book are based on simple, yet powerful learning principles that have been scientifically proven. In spite of this scientific foundation, I have intentionally avoided as much technical jargon and theory as possible. This undoubtedly will leave me open to some criticism from the scientific community but I hope to gain the appreciation of the average pet owner who simply wants to train his or her dog. The most important aspect of Follow The Leader dog training is not the science behind it but rather that it is humane, effective and practical.

Introduction

The domestic dog holds the distinction of being the most common household pet in the world. In spite of its ubiquity, many owners do not really understand their dog. As a professional dog trainer, I have found that my job primarily deals with training dog owners, not dogs. Understanding natural behavior and what really motivates a dog is an underlying principle for most training. I nearly always find myself explaining to owners how their dog views the world. Once an owner begins to understand their dog, training becomes much easier. As the training progresses, the quality of life for both the dog and the dog owner invariably improves. Enhancing the quality of life for dogs and owners was one of my primary motivations for writing this book. I feel confident that I have been able to make a difference in the dog/human relationship of my private clients over the past few years. My hope is that this book, with its wider range of distribution, will help improve the quality of life for even more dogs and their "people."

In the broadest of terms there are essentially two different categories of training.[1] Both types take advantage of how dogs and other animals learn but are actually the antithesis of one another. A wide variety of terms are used to denote each category. On the one hand we have aversive techniques, often called force, correction or negative training. On the other hand there are appetitive techniques, more often called motivational, reinforcement or positive training. All of these terms may be used interchangeably throughout this book.

Both aversive and appetitive training can be used to change, alter or develop behaviors. In fact, aversive training has been the primary method used by professional dog trainers for many years. It is undeniable that aversive training can be used effectively under certain circumstance to train dogs. However, there has been, and continues to be, a tremendous transformation in training methods during the last decade. Change was slow at first but as more trainers became better informed, a ground swell began developing that is shifting predominantly aversive styles of dog training to more appetitive styles.

There are still quite a few "old style" trainers who make extensive use of aversive training techniques. Unfortunately, it is sometimes difficult to change old habits. More unfortunate is that the general public seems to be even further behind the times. There is wide spread belief that the only way to train your dog is to physically dominate him/her.[2] Domination is accomplished through pushing, pulling and punishing the dog until it does what the handler wants. Physical domination is commonly aided by the liberal use of leashes, choke chains or even shock collars.

A lot of aversive type training techniques came out of WWII when dogs were first utilized extensively by the United States military. Many of the military trainers became civilian trainers after the war. They set the standard for training that was passed on to

---

[1] It is not necessary for dog owners to become experts in "learning theory" or other technical aspects of animal behavior. It would be easy to get caught up in long explanations of "classical conditioning or operant conditioning" and other scientific terms. A more generalized and simplified approach is taken here. However, for those interested in the more technical aspects of animal behavior, see the referenced literature at the end of this book.

[2] From this point on I will simply use either "him" or "her" randomly, and without prejudice, throughout the rest of this book in order to avoid the awkward "him/her" or "he/she" notation.

others as the pet dog became increasingly popular. Very little changed in dog training for many years.

If, for the moment, we ignore the issue of ethics or humane treatment, one of the most serious problems with aversive training is that it is difficult to use effectively unless one is extremely well practiced. Timing is important in any kind of training but it becomes crucial when using aversive techniques. Experienced trainers may have the skills for such crucial timing; however, the average dog owner does not.

Stress is an important part of learning. Not enough stress and the dog is not likely to be motivated enough to learn. Too much, and the dog may shut down and not be able to learn. The trick is to stay in between these two extremes. Aversive training works at a very high level of stress. It is very easy to apply too much pressure on a dog. Too much pressure not only results in no learning but also can make the animal afraid and even aggressive. Reinforcement training works at the other end of the stress scale. If there is not enough stress, the animal will not learn, but at least there are no harmful side effects. Scientific research has shown that optimum learning (for any animal) is more likely to occur under low rather than high stress.

Whether you are training a dog, cat, chicken, child or your spouse, the principles are virtually the same. All animals learn in the same way. Anyone interested in exactly what these principles are for learning should refer to the suggested reading and reference section of this book. Knowledge of animal behavior can provide valuable insights for application to any training program. In essence, the most effective way to train your dog (or boss, employees, boyfriend, girlfriend, brother, sister, etc.) is with appetitive methods.

Until the 1900's there was effectively no scientific research in the area of animal behavior. At first, few scientists believed that the pragmatic study of animal behavior was possible or even beneficial. Eventually, psychologists and other scientists began to accept animal behavior science as a credible discipline during the 1950's and 1960's. The science of "ethology" was born.

Behavior "therapy" for dogs was first introduced in the sixties but was widely regarded as ridiculous by most people. However, behavior therapy began to be taken more seriously in the early 70's. Then, by the 1990's most veterinary schools were incorporating "behavioral medicine" as a standard part of the veterinary curriculum.

Today, more and more colleges offer specialties at the PhD level in "clinical animal behavior" and the number of practitioners in the pet therapy field is growing. Yet the general public is still somewhat skeptical about "pet psychologists," a regrettable term that came out of the sixties pop culture. The popular term is actually quite inaccurate. Professionals who specialize in behavior modification of pets are more accurately called "applied animal behaviorists."

Scientific research on wolves and other wild canids (members of the dog family) has been extensive. But, until recently, very little scientific study had been conducted on the behavior of the domestic dog. However, there were a few important exceptions[3]. This early work correlated the findings of wolf studies with dog behavior. Armed with this new scientific research, many trainers began to base their training techniques on these correlations. The result was a special emphasis on establishing dominance or alpha position when training a dog. Dominance theory became the new paradigm in dog training.

---

[3] Notable exceptions are Lorenz (1954), Scott & Fuller (1965) and Fox (1978).

I believe that the "wolf pack" behavior theory has only limited relevance in dog training. My disputation is that many dog trainers have misinterpreted wolf pack behavior and incorrectly applied it to dog training. For one thing, after careful analysis of the research, one finds that there are some significant differences between adult dog and adult wolf behavior. Dogs are not wolves (although, as we will see, they are closely related biologically) and in my opinion, humans are not necessarily perceived strictly as "pack" members by a dog.

I contend that the only reason many professionals are successful in training dogs using alpha or dominance philosophy is because they can end up doing the right thing but for the wrong reason. However, this only holds true for reinforcement training. When aversive training is combined with the dominance paradigm it can result in the abusive treatment of many dogs at the hands of some misguided individuals.

While the practice of aversive training is in retreat, the dominance theory persists. The problem is that as long as dominance theory is still bandied about, aversive trainers can use it as justification for their harsh, militaristic treatment of dogs. In this book I intend to convince you that there is an important difference between being dominant and being your dog's leader.

I encourage readers of this book to read other books as well. To that end, I have included a list of suggested reading at the end of this book and a reference section to more technical literature. If something in this book does not seem to be working for you and your dog, try a different approach. Arguably, the only creature more adaptable than a dog is a human being. I believe the onus falls upon us, as human beings, to be ready and willing to modify (adapt) our training techniques to suit each individual dog, not the other way around.

It is doubtful that any one book could possibly provide every answer for every training problem. While this book does not pretend to provide every answer to dog training, it will impart practical and useful knowledge to the reader for developing a suitable training philosophy that will benefit every dog owner and his or her dog. It contains specific training techniques as a guide and it also provides a well-defined, humane viewpoint for evaluating any other dog training technique.

Note to readers: I have gone to great lengths to avoid as many technical terms as possible; however, the use of some of the "vernacular" was inevitable. Most technical terms are defined when they are first introduced but if you forget or it becomes unclear, refer to the glossary at the end of this book for clarification. In my attempt to minimize technical terms it was sometimes necessary to use more generalized or less accurate terminology. Therefore, the definitions that are given in the glossary reflect how the term is used in this book but may not be accepted universally as technically correct.

Part I

The Philosophy

Chapter 1
The Follow The Leader Concept

Appetitive training is the essence behind the Follow The Leader concept. Whatever you choose to call it, motivational training, reinforcement training or positive training, it is the mechanism that promotes learning in a humane, practical and effective way. However, there is a little more to the Follow The Leader concept than that.

The domestic dog is aptly named *Canis familiaris* by scientists. Becoming <u>familiar</u> with your dog is an important part of the overall Follow The Leader philosophy. Being familiar means to have some insight into your dog's needs and view of the world. This insight will help you and your dog during training. You may also find that it will elevate your respect for your dog and strengthen your bond (friendship).

The name Follow The Leader itself comes from one of the underlying philosophies of the concept, which is to make yourself the focus of your dog's attention. **You need to be the most interesting thing in the environment.** If your dog learns to focus on you and look to you for all its needs, then you automatically become the leader. Using the methods outlined in this book you can easily establish yourself as your dog's leader, which is the same as being your dogs best friend.

Establishing leadership does not require punishment or any harsh treatment of your dog. In fact, I believe that these techniques are counterproductive. You can establish your leadership position through kindness, which will in turn lead to a lasting, mutually satisfying relationship with your dog.

A leader (or friend) must **earn** the position. Earning the position will require some work and commitment on the part of the owner. Those who are not willing to put in the work or commitment should reconsider owning a dog. Dog ownership comes with responsibilities and obligations. The responsible pet owner must be willing and able to provide adequate food, shelter, medical care, socialization and training for their dog. In addition to these, a responsible dog owner must also maintain reproductive control over their dog.

- Feeding -
Proper nutrition is an essential part of being a responsible pet owner. You should carefully research the nutritional needs of your dog and follow your veterinarian's advice. Buying and feeding your dog the cheapest dog food is not only bad for your dog it will probably end up costing you more due to medical problems that will stem from poor nutrition (see *Food For Thought,* Chapter 14).

- Shelter -
Your dog should have access to adequate shelter to be comfortable and safe. The responsible dog owner must provide protection from the weather and a secure containment area such as a fenced yard. Dogs must never be allowed to run loose without direct supervision. Dogs that are allowed to wander create public health and nuisance problems. They are also vulnerable to numerous hazards that could injure or kill them.

-Medical -

Providing medical care is part of being a responsible dog owner. Dog owners should take their pets to the veterinarian on a regular basis and follow the veterinarian's advice carefully. Inoculations for distemper, rabies and other preventive medicines (e.g. heartworm tablets) have to be administered on a regular basis according to the advice of your veterinarian.

- Socialization -

Regular socialization is the responsibility of the dog owner. Too many dogs are relegated to the backyard once their novelty wears off. There, they are largely ignored. Dogs are social creatures, just as we are, and need regular social contact in order to remain healthy. A dog should become part of the family.

- Training -

In order to become part of the family, the dog needs to be trained. Dogs are capable of behaving in a manner that is acceptable to human society but they must be taught the rules. It is unfair to expect dogs to automatically know how we want them to behave. It is our responsibility to train them.

- Reproduction -

Responsible dog owners must maintain control of the reproductive activities of their dog. There are an estimated 53 million dogs in the United States alone. It is estimated that as many as 9 million dogs are euthanized (killed) by U.S. animal shelters and pounds each year. This does not take into account the millions of abandoned dogs that die a slow agonizing death due to disease or malnutrition. Obviously there is an overpopulation of dogs in the United States. There are simply more dogs than there are homes willing to take care of them.

There are numerous reasons people allow their dogs to breed. Reasons run from accidents to simple indifference, from educational to financial. Some of the most common reasons owners allow their dogs to have puppies is because they believe that in order for their dog to have a "fulfilled life" dogs should be allowed to have at least one litter. Another common reason is that owners want their children to "experience the miracle of birth." Still, others think that it might be a good way to make money.

The reality is that millions of dogs are killed every year in animal shelters. These dogs did not have a fulfilling life. Dogs can lead a perfectly happy life without ever giving birth. As for the educational experience of watching the miracle of birth, perhaps it should be balanced by experiencing the needless tragedy of death due to overpopulation. No one has ever gotten rich breeding dogs and the moment a person starts breeding for money, their priorities change, no matter how much they loved dogs originally.

The desire to allow our dogs to reproduce or witnessing puppies being born and raised by their mother is understandable. I personally find it hard to imagine anyone who is not emotionally moved by a young puppy. However, responsible dog owners must rise above their emotions and take an objective view for the sake of our dogs.

The bottom line is that most pet dogs should be spayed or neutered. It suffices to say that for those who do decide to breed their dog must do so responsibly. Do not rush into the decision and do a lot of research. Be prepared for all the obligations that come from breeding your dog. Irresponsible breeders have ruined many breeds by breeding genetically flawed animals. Breeding is not something that should be done without considerable thought and planning. Responsibilities go well beyond standing around at the entrance to the local supermarket with a box full of puppies looking for people who will take one on impulse.

The only legitimate reason to breed a dog is to improve the breed. If you are doing it for any other reason, you are being irresponsible. Before breeding, consider carefully and be honest with yourself. In most cases you should get your dog neutered or spayed. Veterinarians usually recommend that it be done at a young age. Your dog will actually be healthier as a result and you will have done your part in curbing the overpopulation of dogs.[4]

---

[4] Ask your veterinarian about getting your dog spayed or neutered. The chances of getting many types of cancer are actually reduced in dogs that are spayed or neutered. It can also make your dog a better pet by reducing aggression and the desire to wander. Forget about the myths you hear that it causes dogs to get fat. Too much food makes dogs fat! Many people do not realize that as a dog ages and becomes less active, it does not require as much food.

Chapter 2
Keys to Effective Training

There are four key elements to effectively training your dog. All four of these elements are interrelated. Taken all together, they define the relationship you will have with your dog, which can be good, bad, or something in between.

The first key element for effective training is to understand your dog. One of the most common mistakes owners make is that they often treat their dog as if it were a furry, four-legged, child with an admittedly lovable but slightly dim-witted kind of mentality. Owners who try to "elevate" their dog to human status are really not doing them justice. Dogs deserve to be respected for the amazing creatures that they are. True understanding comes through objective observation and interpretation of natural dog behavior. It is important for dog owners to avoid anthropomorphic (the assigning of human characteristics to a non-human species) thinking when dealing with their dog. An academic degree in animal behavior is not required to have a basic understanding of dog behavior. Dog behavior (as compared to human behavior) is actually quite straightforward.

The second key element to effective training is communication. This does not mean being able to discuss the latest trends in the dog food market with your pet but if you are demanding a particular behavior from your dog then you must be able to communicate what you want. Dogs already know how to do almost everything you want them to do. Sit, down, stay and come are the most common behaviors that we ask of our dog. The dog already knows how to do all of these, but we must have an effective communication system for letting our dog know just when we want each of these behaviors to occur. It has been my experience that dogs "learn to learn" and your dog will learn progressively faster if you perfect your ability to communicate to him what you want.

Like any good communication system it should always be a two-way affair. It is not only important to be able to let your dog know what you want, it is also important to know what your dog is trying to communicate to you. Your dog will communicate primarily through body language. To be a good dog trainer you will need to recognize signals from your dog.

That brings us to our third key element, which is leadership. Dogs are highly social. All social groups require a leader. A dog will instinctively follow an established leader or, if there is no perceived leader, they will assume the role themselves. Once a dog accepts a leader it does not usually challenge the position. Conversely, be aware that a dog already established in a leadership position does not give up its role easily. The choice becomes whether you follow your dog or your dog follows you. I would certainly suggest the latter.

Bonding is the fourth key element. Bonding connects you and your dog in a cooperative relationship. It is a kind of psychological glue that can only be enhanced by the other three elements but it best comes about through trust. Being consistent and fair at all times will quickly earn you the trust of your dog. And you will learn to trust your dog in return. The human/canine bond is probably the most common and certainly one of the strongest interspecies bond possible. Bonding is an important yet often overlooked component in training a dog.

The four key elements: understanding, communication, leadership and bonding combine to give you powerful, effective tools for training. These fundamental elements promote a satisfying, happy and mutually beneficial relationship between you and your dog.

Chapter 3
Understanding Your Dog

Before you can fully bond, communicate with or lead your dog, you must first understand him. To do this you have to throw away any anthropomorphic views you may have and look at dogs with an objective respect that these fascinating animals deserve. The social behavior of dogs and humans can appear to be similar, therefore endearing them to us, but often dogs can have a completely different motivation for a particular behavior. As a dog trainer I have observed a kind of Rorschach syndrome among many pet dog owners. Like looking at inkblots or clouds, some owners make interpretations of their dog's behavior to fit their own feelings. For example, a dog owner may be having difficulty getting their dog to sit at one of my beginning obedience class sessions. I have had them tell me something like "my dog knows how to sit, he just isn't behaving very well right now because he is mad at me for taking away his favorite toy before we left home." What is really happening is that the owner is feeling guilty for not letting his dog have his favorite toy. It is most likely that the dog is just distracted because it is in a new environment and is too busy exploring to pay attention to his owner, or maybe because it has not been taught to sit in a different context, i.e. a strange environment. The fact is, dogs live pretty much in the here and now and do not hold grudges. Only humans do that!

This is not to say that dogs do not have feelings or emotions. I have observed animal behavior for many years with what I hope is an objective point of view. My personal opinion is that many animals do appear to experience true emotions and most certainly dogs have some of the most well developed emotions. Clearly dogs experience a range of emotions. Their emotions may not be as complex as human emotions but we have much in common. As mammals, we share many common evolutionary characteristics with dogs. Both human beings and dogs are social creatures as well and have certain common social needs. And in the case of the dog we even share pretty much the same environment. It should not be difficult to believe that human and dog emotions could have at least some basic commonality.

A human has a much more complex brain structure than a dog, so it is unlikely that dog emotions would be as complex as our own. Dog emotions and feelings are in a way more basic or "pure" if you prefer. Perhaps an analogy would make this clear. Think of emotions as being primary colors. These are "pure" colors, but you can make many other colors by mixing them together. The brain is responsible for mixing these colors. The human brain is capable of mixing many different colors, whereas a dog's brain is limited to mixing only a few variations, but they both share the same primary colors to begin with.

However, even if we have common emotional states, this does not mean that we view the world in the same way. To begin with, a dog experiences the world quite differently from human beings. We perceive the world mostly through visual input. A dog probably perceives the world mostly by olfactory input. For a dog, the loss of its sense of smell could have nearly as much of a disorienting affect as a human losing their vision. There are profound differences in the way the world is perceived by dogs and humans. The information is not only different in the way it is gathered, but also processed in vastly different brain structures. The significance of things in the world are altogether different between dogs and human beings. The emotions and feelings of a dog will be motivated and elicited for many different reasons than those of human beings. Although the domestic dog often displays human-like behaviors there are frequently underlying fundamental differences. Our human bias' can easily make us misinterpret what we see.

One way to understand a dog is to study its wild relatives where there is little or no human influence. The majority of experts agree that dogs most likely came from wolves. In fact, modern dogs can still breed freely with wolves, producing viable young. By strict definition, wolves and dogs are of the same species. Biologically, dogs are really a domesticated variation of the wolf. As we will see later, domestication produces surprisingly significant side effects on the genetics that control behavior and appearance in a wolf.

The extraordinary malleability of wolf genes has allowed for the tremendous variation in dog morphology (physical appearance) but the mind of the dog (with some notable exceptions) is still remarkably similar to the wolf. The study of wolves can indeed give us important insights into dog behavior, whether it is a Pekingese, Dachshund or German Shepard dog. However, we must be very careful about how these studies are interpreted and applied to dog training. When comparing dogs and wolves, it is as important to keep in mind the sometime subtle differences, as it is the similarities.

Dogs and wolves are pack animals. On a fundamental level, the social behavior of dogs is not greatly different from that of their wild ancestor the wolf. The differences are mostly a matter of degree rather than any real disparity. Within the social setting of a wolf pack there is a well-defined "pecking order." Wolves establish a hierarchy where each member of the pack has a particular social position. Position in the hierarchy entitles the individual to a proportionate amount of access to certain resources. These resources can be defined primarily as food, shelter and sex but not necessarily in that order. At the top of the hierarchy is the so-called "alpha" member of a wolf pack who has primary access to these resources. Like their wild relatives, dogs also want access to these same resources. Dogs also form hierarchies but, unlike the wolf, the structure tends to be more dynamic or less rigid.

The rather inflexible social hierarchy structure of wolves has important survival value. In a wolf pack only the dominant or alpha female comes into estrus. And only the alpha male mates with her. Dominant wolves in the wild are generally the fittest of the pack. Thus wolf packs have a system whereby only those individuals who are in alpha positions (fittest) get a chance to pass on their (superior) genes to ensure the survival of the species[5].

Domestic dogs do not have the same survival pressures as the wolf. Firm social hierarchies are not necessary for a dog's survival. Indeed, extensive studies on domestic dogs show that dominance "status" in the pack can be somewhat fluid. Depending on the situation a dog can show dominance in one situation but change to a subordinate roll in

---

[5] This brings up at least two interesting side points. One point is even though the alpha male and female are the fittest they still need a social system of cooperation to help them and their offspring to survive. The entire pack helps in the rearing and care of the young. The other point is that if only dominant individuals produce offspring wouldn't there be a strong genetic pressure towards producing more and more alpha type wolves? Obviously, there can only be so many alpha positions. The answer is in two key areas that have an impact on the development of the domestic dog. Part of the answer is in the malleability of the genes, which allows for great variation and the other is that social position is not controlled exclusively by genetics.

another. Nevertheless, the remnants of a fundamental hierarchy system continue to exist during pack behavior in dogs. Most dog behaviorists seem to believe that dogs will consider humans as fellow pack members if they are properly socialized as puppies.[6] I am not sure that this is strictly true but I do agree that socialized dogs will treat you **as if** you were a pack member.

All social behavior of the dog, whether it is directed towards other dogs or other species, is genetically limited. During social interactions with people, dogs only have certain mechanisms available in their behavioral repertoire. They cannot behave in any other manner.

Genetic limitations restrict all species, including human beings. One cannot expect a cat, for example, to wag its tail and pant like a dog in a greeting gesture towards its owner. Even if a kitten is "adopted" by a nursing, mother dog the kitten will never behave the same as a dog. Cats simply do not have the genetic make-up for such behavior. At the same time, the nursing, mother dog will treat the adopted kitten exactly the same as the rest of her puppies. The mother dog simply cannot treat the kitten in any other fashion. By the same reasoning, dogs cannot treat human beings in anyway except **as if** they were pack members. But this does not mean that they necessarily perceive a human being as a strange, two-legged dog. I personally believe a dog knows the difference.[7]

Whether dogs consider people real pack members or not, owners can establish themselves as a leader. Thanks to their genetic encoding dogs are willing to follow a leader. A leader in this context is really a best friend, not a boss, not a bully but a best friend. Being your dog's leader should not be considered a dominance issue.

If you as an owner can become your dog's best friend you will automatically establish leadership, which is one of the fundamental key elements to effective training and a prerequisite for controlling much of your dog's behavior. How you can establish yourself as leader is discussed in chapter five and demonstrated throughout much of this book.

Dogs are highly social because they inherited their genes from wolf ancestors who are highly social. Social cooperation among wolves does not involve a moral code. It is based purely on survival. The rigors of surviving in the wild put certain demands on all animals. A more cooperative social behavior among wolf ancestors proved beneficial as a means for meeting some of these demands. An individual's chances of survival were increased

---

[6] Socializing is a term often used by dog trainers to denote a kind of acclimation to things in the environment. At a very early and critical stage puppies are "imprinted" with information that will predetermine how they perceive things (threat or non-threat) in the environment for the rest of their lives. During the socialization period puppies can also be socialized to accept almost any kind of animal (e.g. rabbits, ducks, other dogs, humans, etc.). This important critical period will be discussed in more detail in later chapters.

[7] In chapter two I stated that many owners treat their dog "as if" it were a human child. That is not to say owners really think that their dog is a child; consciously they know the difference. But sub-consciously we all can easily ignore the differences. It simply takes less effort not to think about it and then just act according to our own inherent human social instincts. Our familiarity with them facilitates our tendency to sometimes treat dogs as if they were human. We are able to relate more closely to a dog than, let us say, an alligator because of our shared social patterns. We are able to recognize and relate to social patterns of dogs and they are able to recognize and relate to social patterns in human beings. Debates rage over the exact level of consciousness that is possessed by a dog (or other animals). But if you accept that a dog has at least some conscious thought, as I certainly do, then you can understand why I believe that perhaps consciously they know we are not a dog but because more of their behavior is controlled by sub-conscious mechanisms, they can not treat us any differently than they would another member of their species.

when they cooperated with the other members of the pack. Wolves that did not inherit genes that promoted a more social temperament were not as likely to survive or get a chance to pass on their own genes to future generations.

Strong social behavior has become genetically programmed into each and every wolf. Very similar programming exists in dogs. But *natural* selection is no longer a primary factor for dog survival. Human beings determine what genetic traits are to be passed on to the next generation. This is why good, responsible breeders will always look at more than just the appearance of a dog before breeding them. Temperament, which is largely a measure of how social a dog is, should always be taken into consideration. Dogs with deficient temperaments should not be bred. These dogs do not only make poor pets, they can be dangerous.[8]

In later chapters we will discuss specific ways to use some of our knowledge of wolf/dog behavior to our advantage. A thorough discussion of wolf/dog behavior would require an entire book (probably several) dedicated solely to the subject. Such detailed knowledge would be helpful to serious dog trainers, but it is not really necessary for the average pet dog owner. Anyone interested in more detailed information can refer to the reference section at the end of this book.

---

[8] There is a great debate concerning "nature vs. nurture." With any given dog it is difficult to know whether a poor temperament was created by genes or caused by under-socialization at some critical stage. Chances are, there is a complex interrelationship between both nature and nurture. Regardless of which is more important nature (i.e. genetics) cannot be ignored. Just as a precaution the prudent breeder would never breed a dog with a poor temperament.

Chapter 4
Communicating With Your Dog

Communication among wolves is accomplished mainly through body language. Dogs also communicate with each other through various postures and movements. Some breeds are limited in their communication owing to physical modifications that are characteristic of their breed. Drooping ears, curly tails, long fur and docked tails are all examples of physical modifications that can affect the communication ability of a dog. It has been suggested that dogs are no longer as dependent on body language as the wolf. Nevertheless, all dogs still use a wide variety of body postures for communication.

It is useful for the dog owner to be able to recognize at least some of these body postures or "signals." We can divide these signals into categories: calming[9], submissive, fear and aggression. There may very well be other categories but these are the most important to us as dog owners and trainers.

Categorizing behaviors is useful for our understanding, but one should never lose sight of the fact that dogs have a dynamic range of responses. There can be a great deal of interplay between different signals but careful observation can reveal volumes about the emotional state of a dog. Recognizing these signals and understanding what your dog is communicating can be an invaluable aid in training.

Often overlooked but very revealing body language signals are the so-called "calming signals." Dogs exhibit calming signals in an effort to placate or to head off potentially aggressive situations with other dogs (and people). Calming signals are not quite the same as submissive gestures. The purpose of calming signals is kind of like a dog's way of saying, "I don't want to fight, let's just remain calm, no threat here." These are different from submissive signals. Submissive signals are usually more obsequious and obvious, perhaps the equivalent of throwing oneself at the feet of a powerful over-lord.

Dogs use calming signals all the time. We may miss them simply because we don't recognize them or more importantly, we misinterpret them. Specific calming signals are things like looking away, blinking the eyes, yawning, shaking, stretching, scratching, licking the lips, sniffing the ground or a slight drop of the head. If you own a dog or have been around them you have seen these behaviors many times. They are especially evident when a new or strange dog approaches or if someone new is in your house. Calming signals will also be exhibited to the dog owner under various circumstances.

An example of a misinterpretation of a calming signal is the case where an owner comes home to find the pillow from the couch torn to shreds and littering the floor. Unless the person is a very good actor, they become agitated, even if they are trying to remain calm. The dog will notice that the owner is not his usual happy self and will often begin to exhibit calming signals. Typical calming signals in this instance are for the dog to look away and drop the head or appear to look "guilty." Owners will often misinterpret the behavior and become convinced that the dog knows he has done something wrong and feels guilty. It is doubtful that dogs ever feel guilty. Guilt is one of those complex

---

[9] Body postures that are used by wolves to attenuate aggression between pack members are called "cut off signals" by wolf behaviorists. Well-known Norwegian dog behaviorist, Turid Rugaas, coined the term "calming signals" to signify similar postures of dogs.

emotions that require some sense of ethics or moral judgment. It is doubtful that dogs think in such complex terms. The dog is simply reacting to what may be very subtle signals of anger in the only way it knows how in an attempt to "calm" the owner.[10]

Submissive signals are usually more demonstrative and easier to recognize than calming signals. Some of the more common submissive signals are pronounced lowering the head and ears, licking the mouth or face of another dog (or human) or rolling over on the back. Puppies or young dogs at the approach of an adult dog demonstrate these signals most often. They also offer the same behaviors to humans. Submissive signals not only indicate a reluctance to fight, but acknowledge uncontested dominance.

At the other end of the spectrum from calming and submissive signals are fear and aggression. These signals can range from subtle to overt. Aggressive postures or warning signals include staring, erect ears and showing the teeth. Fearful postures are typically raised hackles (piloerection), tucked tail, cringing and avoidance (moving away). It is not uncommon to see a mixture of signals involving both fear and aggression.

Knowing and recognizing the body language of dogs is helpful in many aspects of training. For example, if a specific training technique is inadvertently causing stress, your dog will show this through calming or fear signals. This would be an indication that you should try a different approach. Owners (trainers) should always be aware of their dog's emotional state, especially while training.

Learning the body language of dogs is not difficult. It can be fun and interesting. Try observing dogs and watch for signals that they give to one another. Go to parks or other areas where dogs might be present and watch the interactions. Study how they behave toward other dogs as well as people. Look for the subtle body signals displayed during any social interaction.

Common signals include staring, looking away by turning the head or sometimes just the eyes, turning the whole body sideways or away, licking the nose, yawning, sitting, bowing, casually sniffing the ground, various tail positions and movements, casual scratching, various ear positions, etc. One small word of caution may be in order. Try not to over analyze every behavior. To paraphrase Sigmund Freud, sometimes a scratch is only a scratch.

While it is important for us to recognize and understand the body language of dogs, it is perhaps more important to realize that dogs quickly learn to read slight changes in our body language. Dogs are no doubt better at reading body language than we are. Body language and signals can become an important training tool. If you use hand gestures or other signals when training, your dog will learn these cues much more quickly. (Continued on page 20)

---

[10] If this is not the first time a dog has made a mess and the owner has gotten angry about past transgressions on the part of the dog, then the dog may be reacting because it knows that whenever there is a mess the owner gets mad. It still does not mean the dog "knows" it has done something wrong. Right and wrong are human values and have no meaning to a dog. A dog can understand consequences if properly linked to a behavior or circumstance but not right and wrong.

Dog Talk

At first glance, the two photographs below may simply appear to be three dogs passively lying down together on the lawn but their body language tells a different story.

Right: Note the dogs on the right and left. The dog on the right is giving the dog on the left a challenging stare with ears erect and lips taught. The dog on the left offers some classic "calming signals," which in this case are yawning, head tilted down and ears dropped.

Left: This photograph was taken immediately after the one above. The dogs on the left and right have now turn heads away from each other. This is an indication that neither dog wants to take issue with the other and "calm" has returned. Note that the dog in the center has remained completely neutral throughout the entire exchange.

When giving signals to a dog it turns out that small gestures are better than big or exaggerated ones. Small gestures leave less room for variation, so they are more consistent and clear to your dog. By presenting an otherwise neutral body language and giving only one clear signal at a time, we can be more effective in teaching a dog what we want.[11]

A dog will learn to read its owner's natural body language very quickly. It gives a dog important clues as to what is going to happen next. Dogs are sometimes thought to be psychic. In many cases the so-called psychic abilities can be explained simply by the fact that a dog can read the unintentional body language of its owner. Even if a dog is not psychic, its ability to notice minutiae in human behavior can be nothing short of astounding. Examples of their talents are found from ordinary every day acts, such as knowing when we are getting ready to take them to the park to the extraordinary, like dogs that can actually tell when a person is going to have an epileptic seizure.[12]

As human beings, our preferred means of communication is verbal. Dogs have very good hearing, but communicate only a minimum amount of information using auditory signals. Fortunately for us, dogs are quite adaptable and are able to learn the meaning of certain verbal commands from us. Most dog owners are more comfortable giving verbal commands to their dog. This is fine as long as the sound of each command is distinct. If you had a dog named Rover you would probably find it difficult to teach him a command such as "over" to convey your desire for him to leap over something. But, if you used the command "jump" there would be no difficulty at all.

As you will see, I like to teach dogs using signals first. Verbal commands can always be added later. I feel it makes learning much easier for most dogs. For most dogs words are just noise that you are making and have little meaning. If you talk a lot to your dog it will become even more difficult for her to pick out significant sounds. Body language or signals have significant meaning to a dog and are very easy to discern.

---

[11] Many "novelty" trainers are expert at teaching animals to respond to the faintest signal. Dogs, parrots and even horses have been taught to perform in a way that make them appear to have amazing cognitive abilities, like math. One of the most famous was a horse called Clever Hans. Clever Hans and his owner became quite famous early in the 1900's as a result of the apparent ability of Hans to solve mathematical problems. His owner would write out a math problem and hold it up for Hans to see. To answer, Hans would dutifully tap his foot an appropriate number of times. So amazing was this mathematically gifted horse that reportedly a number of scientists decided to conduct a series of tests to see just how clever Clever Hans really was. After a battery of carefully designed tests, it was determined that Hans was very clever indeed. But rather than being able to do math, as many people thought, including his owner, Clever Hans was actually responding to apparently unintentional signals to get food rewards for giving correct answers. Without realizing it, the owner would lower his eyebrows when he would give Hans a math problem. Hans knew to begin tapping his foot. As soon as Hans reached the right number his owner would lift his eyebrows, probably in surprise, and Hans would stop tapping to get his reward. If you think about it, this story has many implications, both positive and negative, for dog owners. Most dogs are at least as astute as Clever Hans in discerning faint signals. This ability can be exploited for training, but beware of inadvertent or unintentional signals that you could be teaching your dog.

[12] Dogs, called assistance dogs, have been trained to help owners afflicted with certain diseases such as epilepsy and diabetes. It is known, for example, that epileptic seizures are often preceded by certain symptomatic changes in behavior. Epileptics themselves often do not recognize these symptoms until it is too late. Some dogs can recognize early symptoms even before trained medical personnel. These dogs can be trained to alert their owners to an impending seizure. Once alerted the patient can then quickly take precautionary measures to prevent injury during a seizure. Similarly, assistance dogs have also aided diabetics but may alert in response to olfactory cues when body chemistry changes.

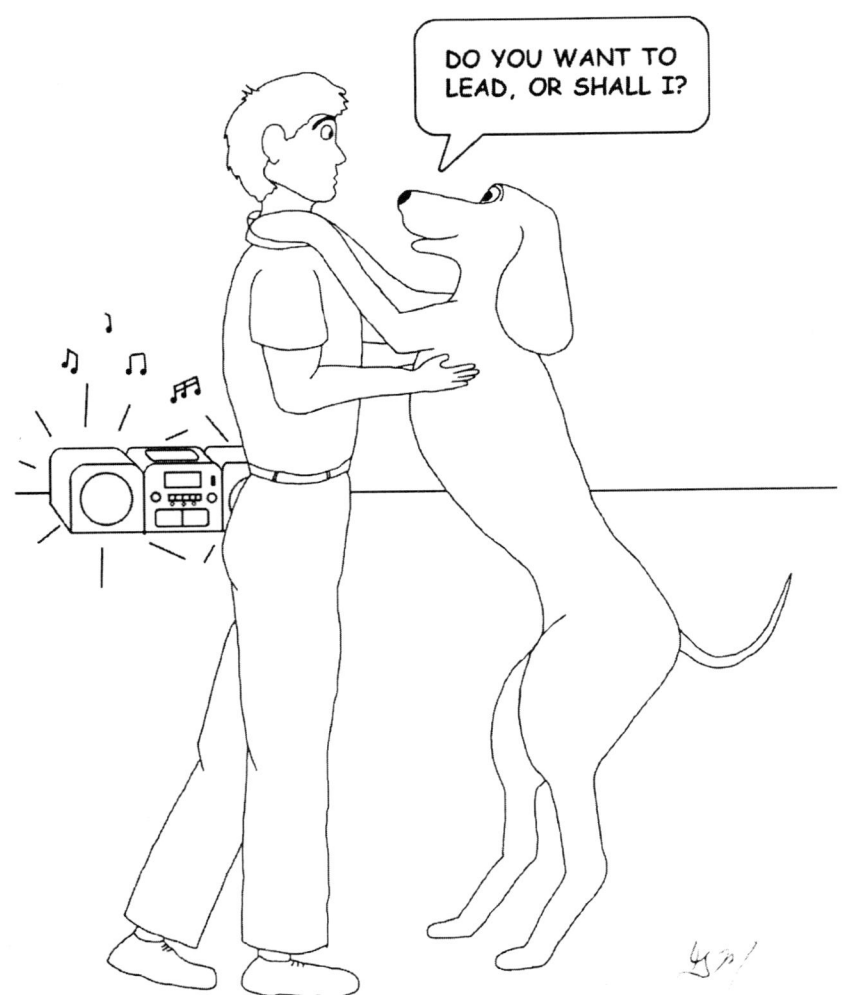

Chapter 5
Leadership

Often, one of the more poorly understood and underestimated aspects of dog training is leadership. An effective training program begins with establishing the dog owner (handler) as the leader. Establishing a leadership role with your dog is one of the cornerstones of the Follow The Leader training philosophy.

How you become a leader to your dog is also important. Sadly, many people (even a lot of professional trainers) believe that leadership can be established by physically overpowering your dog. Your every command is followed by some physical manipulation or punishment if the dog does not comply. A dog is subjugated to the handler's will by physically pushing or pulling on the dog. A handler helps to ensure physical victory by using various types of devices such as collars that cause discomfort or pain for the dog.

Owners believe that they must "dominate" their dog or it will not do as they command. According to the rules for this dominance technique the handler swiftly punishes dogs that show any resistance. If a dog decides to fight back, it is immediately "strung-up" or held off the ground by the leash with a choke collar. Regrettably, many dogs suffer from this kind of abuse every day by unthinking dog owners or trainers. Physical dominance techniques have been a popular method for gaining control over dogs for a long time.

Fortunately, most modern dog trainers are realizing the flaws in the theory of physical dominance and are now moving away from these methods. More humane means are easier, more effective and safer for both the dog and dog owner. Unfortunately, much of the general dog owning public still adhere to the old school thinking of being "dominant." There is a tremendous difference between dominating your dog and being your dog's leader. As you will learn, you can become your dog's leader without resorting to physical dominance.

Drawbacks to physical dominance methods are that they are best initiated while the dog is still a puppy so it cannot resist. This method of establishing leadership can sometimes be risky if employed on an adult dog, particularly a large or aggressive type.[13] It can also establish an adversarial relationship between you and your dog rather than a cooperative one. Trained in this way, dogs frequently will comply only as long as it believes the handler is able to enforce the command. When conditioned to submit to physical dominance, dogs often become only reluctantly obedient. They can be particularly difficult to control in "off leash" situations.

---

[13] A popular, but ill-advised, "solution" to aggressive or even recalcitrant behavior of a dog is to perform a maneuver called an "alpha roll." If a dog exhibits hostile or obstinate behavior, the handler is supposed to immediately roll the dog over on its back, grab the loose skin around the neck, put his face close to the dog's, show his teeth and growl menacingly. The idea is to simulate how a dominant pack member would put a subordinate in check. One of the serious flaws in this concept is that under natural conditions the subordinate would *voluntarily* roll on its back to show submission to the more dominant pack member. A dominant pack member never actually forces another member to roll on its back and expose its stomach. The "alpha roll" can be a very dangerous maneuver. An aggressive or even seriously fearful dog may bite the handler in the face in self-defense. **Never** try to perform an "alpha roll" on a dog!

There are alternative ways of establishing leadership using non-aversive means. One is by controlling the environment, not the dog. Some of the easiest things in the environment for us to control are desirable resources. Resources include food, shelter, play objects, play opportunities and even sex (reproductive opportunities). If we can teach our dog that nearly everything that he wants comes only from us, we will have little difficulty establishing leadership. This is an important concept.

Although it is done through a different means, controlling resources is exactly what the dominant wolf does in the pack. Each individual within the pack has a certain status in a hierarchy. The exact position in the hierarchy determines how much access each member gets to available resources. As a dog owner, you will simply need to control access to resources and anything your dog wants. There is no reason to be threatening, harsh or cruel to establish a leadership position with a dog. Just make sure that you always control (most) of the everyday things your dogs wants, e.g. food, toys, access to the outside, access to come inside, going for a ride in the car, going for a walk, etc. Whatever your dog wants should be in your control. If you control most everything your dog wants you will automatically become the leader.

Holbrook Jackson said, "Man is a dog's idea of what God should be." Perhaps there is some unintended wisdom in this humorous and anthropomorphic quote. Of course dogs cannot think like human beings, but in this case it may be helpful to "translate" what is going on in a dog's head into human terms for the sake of understanding. The idea of playing "God" with your dog is actually an appropriate analogy. We are able to do things that, for a dog, must be quite unfathomable. As humans we can perform a variety of "miracles" like make balls move through the air, make doors open, cause automobiles to move, grant food at will and create water. Dogs depend on us for such miracles.

Simply put, to get a dog do to what you want, just maintain control over those things that your dog wants and give them to him only when he does what you ask. A specific example would be that before he gets his dinner your dog must "wait" in a sit position and look straight into your eyes until you give him the command to eat. Another example is in order for your dog to go outside to play he must sit patiently by the door while you open it and give the command to go. Still another example is if your dog wants to run and chase a ball that you have, she must first "heel" along side you in a specific position with eyes on yours before you throw the ball.

The idea is to make your dog look to you for everything it wants. The dog owner should, in the eyes of the dog, control the whole environment and therefore control the dog. Control is not gained through physically overpowering the dog. It is gained through mentally overpowering the dog. The result is a dog that will find you quite fascinating and will be eager to "follow the leader."

The mechanics of becoming a leader to your dog will be discussed in detail in later chapters. It is a concept that permeates all training exercises. It is an important concept to understand and to bear in mind while training and interacting with your dog. At first it may require a lot of conscience thought and effort on your part, especially if you have always been taught to use physical control, but it can become very simple and effortless with a little practice.

Follow The Leader

Throughout this book, notice how the author's dogs watch him almost all the time. The author has firmly established his leadership position with both of his dogs without ever using force. Establishing leadership by controlling resources is easy and highly effective. There is no need for a physical contest to assert dominance. In the photo above the author is about to throw a "monkey's fist" for his dog Pepper. Pepper does not look at the toy; she looks at her "leader" for permission to chase it.

Chapter 6
Bonding

Bonding is a natural process that does not take a great deal of effort. Because of the basic nature of a dog, bonding can take place without any conscious thought on the part of the dog owner. Bonding takes place among wolves in order to promote cooperative behavior and minimize hostilities between pack members. It has a similar effect on the human/dog relationship. Bonding promotes cooperation between the dog and its human handler. Bonding allows a handler to maintain control as long as he or she is firmly established in a leadership position.

The bonding instinct is what keeps the pack together. Wolves use a wide variety of mechanisms to strengthen bonds within the pack such as resource sharing, play and to a limited degree, mutual grooming. Cooperative behaviors such as hunting and caring for the young within a pack also help promote stronger bonding.

By the way, none of these behaviors for bonding involve petting. We as primates use petting as part of our bonding behavior. Most dogs learn to like petting, but it is not natural for them. In fact, our dogs would still form a close bond to us if we never petted them. However, most of us would not feel as close to our dogs if we did not pet them. Petting has more to do with our needs than those of the dog. Don't worry, I am not advocating that you should never pet your dog, but as you will see later, there are proper times and ways to pet your dog. The most important point here is that there are other ways to bond with your dog and it is those things that we must learn to emphasize in our daily interactions.

The more time you spend with your dog the more closely you will be bonded. Those owners who put their dog in the backyard and have only limited contact will never form a close bond. The more time you spend with your dog the more closely you will bond. Quality time can help make up for the lack of quantity to some degree. The positive training methods in this book are examples of quality time.

Human beings, wolves and of course dogs, are all capable of forming strong bonds not only with a conspecific (a member of its own species) but between different species as well. A lone wolf finds survival difficult and, for obvious reasons, gets few chances to pass on its genes. Wolves with "social" genes are more likely to pass those characteristics on to future generations.

Originally, the dog inherited its predisposition to bonding from its wolf ancestors. Because human owners find bonding with their dog beneficial, breeders have actively maintained (and perhaps enhanced) the tendency through selective breeding. Dogs not only <u>can</u> bond, they <u>need</u> to bond. It is both our obligation and benefit to provide the opportunity to bond with us.

Bonding among wolves facilitates a cooperative effort with each other and is the key to individual survival. This same genetic tendency for bonding is strongly inherited by modern dogs. It happens to benefit dogs and human owners in a mutually satisfying relationship. The value of bonding as a training aid is inestimable.

An important, underlying sub-factor of bonding is trust. As your dog learns to trust you the bond gets stronger. Conversely, each time your dog learns to mistrust you, your bond weakens. A dog will learn to mistrust its owner when it is punished, especially when the punishment is not linked to any particular behavior (from the dog's point of view). It is very difficult to establish a bond based on trust when punishment methods are employed during training.

Positive, reward based training is the best way for a dog learn to trust its owner. The more trust a dog has in its owner the stronger the bond and a strong bond equals effective training. Dogs that are closely bonded to their owners will often learn more quickly. This happens because the dog will be more attentive. An attentive dog will respond more readily to commands.

An interesting side affect is that not only does the dog learn to trust its owner, but the owner learns to trust their dog as well. The bond is psychologically based, but is known to produce physiological benefits for pet owners. Reportedly, as a group, owners of pets live happier, healthier and longer lives than non-pet owners. Interactions with pets tend to lower blood pressure and heart rates of owners (I can only assume that this would apply to the owners of relatively well behaved dogs).

A bond can take place between a dog of any age and its owner. In other words, whether a new owner gets a puppy or full-grown dog, a strong bond can be forged. However, there is a "critical period" that occurs early in the life of your dog that has a profound affect on its ability to bond with people in general. The process whereby your puppy learns how to react towards people (also other dogs and things in the environment) is known as *socialization*. It is an extremely important part of your puppy's development and its significance should not be underestimated.

There is a short and finite period of time for socializing your puppy. The socialization period begins at six weeks of age and is largely finished by the time your puppy is four to six months old. What your puppy learns during this period will affect your dog for the rest of his life. Proper socialization will produce happy, confident, well adjusted and easy to manage dogs. Improperly socialized dogs are likely to be anxious, nervous, fearful and difficult to manage. Very early training is absolutely essential to avoid life-long problems. Bonds can be established much more easily with dogs that were properly socialized as puppies.

The importance of socialization and how it is accomplished will be discussed later in Chapter 11. It is only mentioned here because of how it relates to bonding.

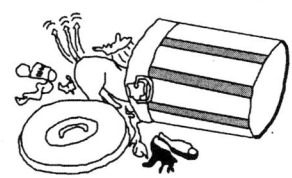

The Canine Connection

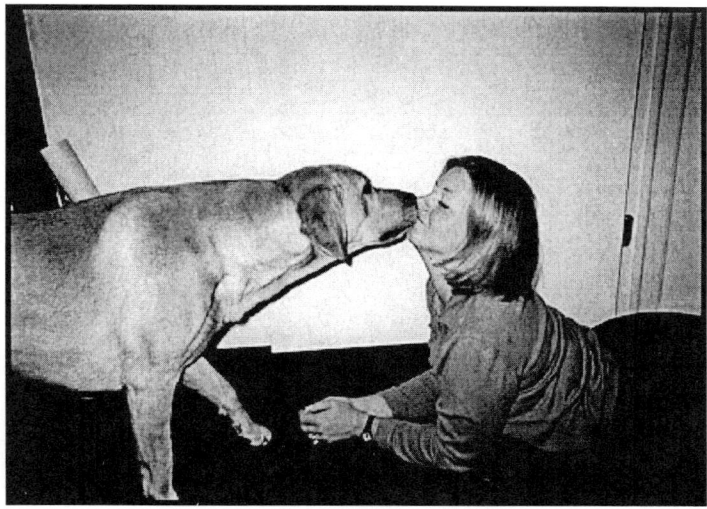

Left: Bonding need not be as intimate as this! Petting (or kissing) is not a prerequisite for bonding with your dog and has more to do with our needs than those of the dog. However, dogs are highly social and *need* to bond with their owners. Developing a strong bond with your dog is mutually beneficial on many different levels. A bond based on trust is an essential training tool. Trust comes from fair treatment and is reinforced by reward-based training.

Right: There is no better time to bond with your dog than when it is a puppy. Bonding can take place at any age but the initial socialization period will set the stage for all future interactions with the owner and other people. A strong bond with a puppy should always be forged through reward-based training. Punishment will always prove harmful to young dogs.

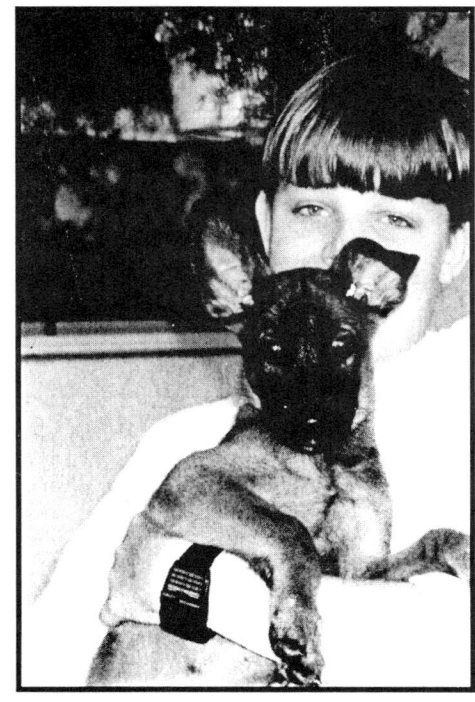

Chapter 7
The Canine Resume

In order to further our understanding of dogs, it is helpful to take a brief look at both their historical and current relationship with human beings. The association between dogs and human goes back to time immemorial. The exact origins of the dog and mechanism of its subsequent domestication is a subject of some debate in certain scientific circles. While a total consensus has not been reached the most widely held theory is that the domesticated dog descended from the wolf. Pre-historic cave paintings depict an association between man and dog that goes back to a time tens of thousands of years ago. The precise ancestry of the dog is blurred not only by time but the likely possibility that it was derived from more than one variety of Eurasiatic wolf. Even after domestication it may have been further crossed with both wild and domesticated dogs from other areas.

Regardless of the exact beginnings, we do know that dogs became domesticated thousands of years ago. At first they may have been simply hunting companions of early men. There is evidence to suggest that dogs or their early ancestors participated in the hunting of big game along with humans. It is possible that the relationship was a mutually beneficial alliance where the wolf/dogs would provide speed and cunning necessary for initially capturing and slowing the prey while human hunters would inflict final fatal wounds using spears and knives. The kill would then (perhaps reluctantly) be shared.

The most widely accepted theory suggests that the first dogs actually domesticated themselves. That is, they became less fearful and learned to follow human tribes, living in close proximity and feeding on human refuse. The scavenging type wolves were probably not as predatory as their close cousins. Humans may have tolerated the dogs/wolves in close proximity if they did not pose any threat. They could have been considered useful for helping to clean camp areas of waste that would have attracted larger predators that in turn might have been potentially dangerous to the human tribe. It is even conceivable that the dogs alerted humans to possible danger from intruders by barking.

The dog/wolves probably become increasingly dependant on humans. Soon, great size was no longer necessary. A smaller size actually would be advantageous under those circumstances.[14] Smaller animals would be perceived less of a threat to human tribes, therefore allowed to stay in the area. Combined with a more social temperament these smaller dog/wolves could thrive. Even if they were smaller they could still prove beneficial to human hunters.

It is only speculation but in time some of the wolf/dogs, especially the young, may have become more and more tame and social toward their human allies. Humans may have started hand feeding them scraps to encourage them to come closer. It would not be difficult to believe that perhaps they learned to come when called. It could very well have

---

[14] A smaller size would presumably have some survival advantages over large animals under certain circumstances. Smaller wolves could not ordinarily survive well since it would have been difficult for them to bring down bigger prey on their own, therefore they might not be able to get enough to eat. With human assistance a smaller size animal could still bring down large prey. Smaller animals would not have to eat as much as larger ones. Survival would favor small animal in situations when food was scarce.

been the very first attempt to train a dog! I am personally gratified to think that those first steps may have been grounded in motivational or reinforcement style training.

Eventually, the exact time lost in pre-history, humans and dogs began to form a much more intimate relationship with each other. As dogs became more docile towards humans their social dependence would have allowed for fewer contacts with their wild counterparts. Therefore there would have been fewer opportunities for wild wolves to breed with domesticated females.

Undoubtedly, dogs that were more docile but still had good hunting skills were considered the most useful by human tribes. The dogs that were not considered useful may have been driven out of camps or very likely used as food. While this may be repugnant to most of us living in a modern western culture, had it not happened, we would not have the domestic dog that we know today. Unwittingly, our ancestors established a selective breeding program that eventually produced the fully domesticated dog.[15]

There is an important side bar here that may help us better understand the domesticated dog. In the 1950's Dmitry Belyaev, a Russian scientist, conducted an experiment to see if a more sociable, domesticated type of captive fox could be selectively bred for the fur trade business (keep in mind that the fox is a distant cousin of the wolf and dog). In a very short time Belyaev was able to produce an almost totally domesticated fox. However, for commercial purposes, the experiment was a failure.

The only criterion for selective breeding was that the fox would have to be less fearful of people. After only twenty generations the foxes became so tame that they would actually come right up to a person and lick their hands. Even though "less-fearful-behavior" was the only the factor being selected for breeding, the fox also began to change in unexpected ways. By the end of the experiment the fox was almost unrecognizable in both appearance and behavior. The ears of the fox became drooped, the coat turned black and white (making it completely useless for the fur trade), and they even began to make dog-like sounds as well as wagged their tail like a dog. Even if the experiment was a commercial failure, it strongly supports the theory of wolves becoming more dog-like as they became less fearful.

On the surface it would appear that domestication produces some very profound changes. But in fact, it may not be so much of a change as it is a difference in development. Many characteristics of the domestic dog are actually typical of juvenile canids (*canidae* is the scientific name for the family that includes dogs, wolves, coyotes, foxes, etc.). Wolf puppies are less fearful and more playful than adults. They are more vocal and tend to wag their tails more. Licking is a "soliciting" behavior that young wolf puppies use as a greeting and to ask for food. Drooped ears could also be considered a juvenile characteristic.

A biological phenomenon, known as neoteny, has been theorized to play a big part in the evolution of the domestic dog. Simply stated, neoteny is a process where an animal never develops adult characteristics but is still capable of reproduction.[16] The "neotenic

---

[15]Some of the earliest known breeds are the so-called "sight hounds." A few breeds that we still have today are known to have existed thousands of years ago, e.g. the Greyhound. Carvings depicting Greyhounds have been discovered in an ancient Egyptian tomb dating back four to five thousand years ago. Greyhounds were bred specifically to chase fast moving large game, such as antelope.

[16] The classic example of neoteny is the so-called "mud-puppy" or "water-dog" (genus *Necturus*) that is found in certain lakes and streams. These unusual looking animals are actually salamanders. Most

wolf" theory was first proposed early in the 1900's and has been expanded ever since. According to this theory dogs are actually neotenic versions of the wolf or whatever canid ancestor originally gave rise to them.

Exactly how the domestic dog came to be may never be known with certainty. We do know that most of the major breed types were established before the first century A.D. and a tremendous proliferation of breeds began to take place around the fifteenth or sixteenth century.

It is estimated that today we have more than four hundred different breeds or varieties of dogs (although the American Kennel Club officially recognizes less than 150) in existence worldwide. The reason so many different kinds of dogs can be developed in such a relatively short period is probably due to the fact that ancestral wolves had the potential for a great deal of variation in their genes. In the wild, extreme variations are kept in check by harsh demands in the environment. However, as dogs became increasingly dependent on their human caretakers to provide more and more of their basic needs, environmental factors had a reduced affect. The custodial human could compensate for physical limitations that would have proven detrimental in the wild.

In addition to the potential in gene variation, another side effect to domestication was the increase in the number of estrus cycles. Most female domestic dogs can produce two litters a year compared to the one litter maximum of wild canids. The faster an animal breeds the faster it can evolve new characteristics.

At first, breed development was strictly for some utilitarian purpose. However, breeds were later developed purely out of aesthetic considerations. Dogs have an impressively diverse resume. No other domesticated animal has such a broad range of talents (or physical variation). The following list is some of the most common services dogs perform for mankind.

- Hunting - This was probably one of the earliest uses of dogs. Many breeds were developed, each with their own hunting specialty. Specialized breeds demonstrate a variety of hunting skills that include scenting, tracking, pointing, flushing, chasing and retrieving prey.

- Guarding – The first dogs probably provided sentry duty, simply warning humans of intruders. Breeding later produced dogs that were more actively protective, driving off intruders. When humans domesticated cattle and sheep, certain dogs would serve as protectors against wild predators. Dogs were also used in wars to attack the enemy. Today, dogs are still used in the military and highly trained police service dogs are almost commonplace. In contrast, far too many untrained, so-called "guard dogs" are improperly kept in the yards of ordinary, but largely misinformed, citizens throughout the United States and other countries.

- Search and Rescue – Search and Rescue (SAR) dogs do everything from finding people lost in the woods to searching buildings for hiding criminals. With their acute sense of smell they can help find people trapped in the rubble of collapsed buildings or even drowning victims under the water. Dogs are used to sniff out drugs, bombs and even illegal fruits and vegetables hidden in suitcases at airports.

- Carting and pulling – Many dog breeds were originally used as beasts of burden. They would pull small carts or even taught to help pull in fishnets or boats.

---

salamanders have gills only in their larval (juvenile) stage. Typical salamanders develop lungs and live on land but mud-puppy salamanders retain gills throughout their entire life and are confined to living in water.

Except for sport, few dogs do this kind of work today. Sledding dogs are still utilized in some remote areas.

- Assistance dogs – A growing number of dogs are being used to help people with certain disabilities. Guide dogs for the blind have been around since the end of World War I, when Germans first trained dogs to assist blinded war veterans. This type of training soon spread to Great Britain and then the United States. Today, assistance dogs are trained to help people with a wide variety of disabilities such as the hearing impaired or those confined to wheelchairs. Some of the most amazing uses for assistance dogs are the ones trained to help epileptics. Dogs are trained to sound an alert before an impending seizure. The dogs learn to recognize extremely subtle signs or symptoms that indicate a seizure is imminent. These signs are so subtle that the victim is often not aware of them. When the dog alerts, the owner can take measures to help prevent injury during the seizure.

  Similarly trained dogs have been used for diabetics. Apparently, some dogs can tell by using their acute sense of smell that the body chemistry of their owner is changing. When alerted by their dog a diabetic can quickly take insulin to avoid going into diabetic shock.

- Herding – Only a few farmers still use dogs for herding sheep and cattle on a regular basis in the United States. By no means common, herding dogs are used more frequently in Europe, Great Britain and a few other countries.

- Entertainment – Trained circus dogs have been entertaining people for hundreds of years. Dogs in movies and television shows are always popular. The popularity and universal appeal is not lost on marketing people who use dogs in entertaining ways to sell products in commercials.

- Companionship – Companionship is the number one reason for most people to own a dog. Many working breeds have ended up being strictly companions but some breeds were developed solely for the purpose of companionship. Perhaps some of the most unusual companion dogs are the hairless breeds, like the Chinese Crested, which may have been developed to be a bed warmer!

- Sports – Many breeds lend themselves well to a variety of sports. Some of these sports are designed to simulate real working conditions in order to test the working or functional abilities of certain breeds. Other sports are purely competitive games that test the skill of dogs and their trainers. A partial list of sports is as follows:

  ➢ Lure coursing – Primarily for testing sight hounds, dogs chase a fast moving "lure" across a field. The lure, attached to a light cable on a pulley system powered by an electric motor, is kept just ahead of the dogs and is set up to make sudden quick turns. It is an awe-inspiring sight to see a group of Afghan Hounds or Irish Wolfhounds chasing a lure at full speed. Lure coursing is very different from track racing which is a sport that is not in good favor with many animal rights groups. Lure coursing is often more of an activity than it is a sport but either way it provides an excellent energy outlet for many dogs.

  ➢ Protection sports – A number of protection sport organizations exist. They are designed to test dogs for soundness, working ability and courage. The standards are extremely high, often taking years to achieve certification. All organizations test the dog in obedience and protection but some include various types of scent work as well. Some of the most well known organizations are Schutzhund, French Ring, KNPV (Royal Dutch Police Dog Association) Mondio (or World) Ring and in the United States, NAPD (National Association of Protection Dogs).

➢ Tracking – Tracking is a sport where dogs are tested on their ability to follow a human trail. There are various levels and certifications. Most organization will accept dogs of any breed. Tracking dogs are fascinating to watch and can follow a trail for miles.

➢ Herding – The sport of herding has become more popular in the United States in recent years. A few organizations have competitions and offer certifications. Herding animals are usually sheep.

➢ Agility – Agility is an exciting, fast paced dog sport. Dogs must maneuver through a course that includes a variety of jumps, tunnels, weave poles and other obstacles. Agility is a timed event that is performed by one dog at a time.

➢ Flyball – Flyball is another fast paced event where two dog teams race, relay style, against each other. The dogs must run out and jump over a series of hurdles, then step on a box that has a spring mechanism that tosses a ball in the air. The dog must then catch the ball and return over the jumps to the starting point where the next member of the relay team repeats the performance.

➢ Frisbee® dogs – Competitions are held for dogs that catch a Frisbee® thrown by its owner. High flying Frisbee® dogs are real crowd pleasers.

➢ Weight pulling – Contests are held to see how much weight a dog can pull for a prescribed distance. Carts are loaded with weights and a special harness is fitted to the dog. These are especially popular with Pit Bull owners.

➢ Sledding – Sledding contests take place every year in various northern States. The most famous is the Iditarod race that takes place every year in Alaska. It is a grueling and sometimes dangerous 1200-mile race from Anchorage to Nome. The Iditarod is considered the "super bowl" of the sledding competitions.

➢ Freestyle – One of the newest dog sports is Freestyle. Freestyle is a sport that requires a dog to "dance" to music with the handler. It is a very entertaining sport. Spectators enjoy watching handler / dog teams do their routine.

Dog owners who want to participate in a dog sport should investigate the possibilities carefully. Some dog sports may not be available in every location however dog sport activities are becoming more popular. As the popularity increases so do the opportunities. Participating in dog sport activities can be very rewarding. It is great exercise, both mentally and physically, for your dog. Dog sports can provide an important, natural physical outlet for your dog that contributes to your pet's physical and emotional well-being.

Dogs At Work (And Play)

Left: For the really serious dog sport enthusiast, protection sports offer an exciting but highly disciplined activity for dog breeds of proper temperament. The photograph at left shows a professional trainer (Dwight Higgins) working a dog in a bite suit. Properly trained protection dogs are not "mean" or "vicious." They are confident, stable and well-behaved dogs. Untrained, or poorly trained dogs are much more likely to bite in inappropriate situations than highly trained dogs such as the one in this photo. The dog (Stryker) is performing a KNPV style exercise.

Right: The author's dog, Pepper, practices the "weave poles." Weave poles are just one of several obstacles that dogs must negotiate when performing in the sport of agility. Agility is good exercise and a lot of fun for both the dog and owner.

Chapter 8
Choosing the Right Dog

It has been said that getting a dog is one of the few times that people are allowed to choose their own relative. I suggest that you choose wisely. When you get a puppy, it is a fifteen-year commitment. This kind of commitment deserves some thought.

In general, most dogs are simply companion animals. While I would agree that companionship should be first on the list of any dog owner, real appreciation and understanding of a breed's utilitarian function is a huge factor in choosing (and subsequently training) the right dog. One of the biggest mistakes people make is choosing a dog based on looks or worse, popularity.

Be aware that the natural tendencies of certain breeds can create problems for some dog owners even though the same tendencies can benefit others. Owners should research carefully the breed in which they are interested before getting a dog. Talk to professional breeders and owners and find out what behavior characteristics are unique to the breed. Be suspicious of anyone who says only positive things. They may be more interested in just selling a dog than finding the right home. Positive and negative characteristics of a breed are always relative to your own particular lifestyle, expectations or circumstances.

One of the advantages of choosing a pure bred puppy is that certain physical, and to some degree behavioral, characteristics are predictable when it reaches adulthood. That is not always the case with mixed breed dogs. However as pets, no one can say that a mixed breed or pure breed dog is better than the other. Every dog, whether it is pure or mixed, is a perfect dog. They all know how to behave exactly like a dog. But not all dogs are alike or make suitable pets for just any owner.

The process of choosing a dog can be simplified somewhat when getting a pure breed. Mixed breeds may pose more of a challenge when choosing. I will say more about how to pick a mixed breed later but for now, let us just say you want a pure bred dog.

The remarkable thing is that early man had no knowledge of the science of genetics and yet, hundreds of breeds were developed. Each breed was carefully and purposefully created to serve a particular role. It is an unfortunate fact that the utilitarian use of modern dogs is somewhat limited by comparison to those in earlier times. A common criticism of many modern day breeders is that they often ignore functional ability. Many dogs are bred simply for their appearance with little or no consideration for their original purpose[17]. As a result, some modern breeds have lost (or they are in the process of loosing) their functional utilitarian characteristics.[18] The very best breeders (of utility

---

[17] There are some instances where breeding a dog for its original purpose is no longer desirable. An example of this would be the "fighting dogs." These dogs were originally bred to fight other dogs, various animals or even people for the purpose of entertainment. Obviously, we would not want to encourage the breeding of dogs for such purposes today. Commendably, breed clubs have worked very hard to produce dogs with modified behavior characteristics. It is unfortunate that "backyard" breeders thwart their efforts by paying little or no attention to the temperament of a dog before breeding.

[18] Examples of utility loss can be found in the Irish Setter and German Shepard Dog (GSD) to name just two breeds. As a general rule the Irish Setter found in Ireland is an active hunting dog and has a relatively short and somewhat rougher coat than the Irish Setter found in the United States. The so-called "American Irish Setter," which is bred primarily for the show ring, has a rather long silky coat not suited for the hunting environment. The differences in looks and utility have prompted some dog fanciers to suggest that

breeds) prove their dogs not only in the breed ring but also through demonstrating working ability in an appropriate dog sport.

Even with well-bred dogs, not all the puppies will necessarily be of the same "quality." Professional breeders will screen their puppies and group them into two or three major categories; working quality (if it is one of the utility breeds), show quality and pet quality. If you purchase a dog from a breeder you should consider carefully which category you want.

Once again, all dogs make perfect dogs but not all will be perfect for you or your family. Pet quality dogs, of an appropriate breed, are suitable for the average pet owner. Pet quality dogs usually have some minor deviation from the accepted breed standard that would be considered a "fault" in the show ring. These deviations or faults are often so minor that only an expert would notice. They would be inconsequential to the average pet owner. Because these dogs do not conform close enough to breed standards they are sold at a reduced price.[19] In spite of a smaller price tag, the pet quality dog is inferior to no dog as a companion and can make an excellent buy for the average pet owner.

Only someone who is willing to put in the necessary time and training required to enter shows should purchase a show quality dog. Show quality dogs do make perfectly good pets so a dual purpose is entirely possible. Breeders of fine, show quality dogs will probably require new owners to sign a contract. The contract puts certain obligations and restrictions on the new owner concerning their dog. Unless one fully understands the responsibilities of owning a show dog and is willing to devote a substantial amount of money, time and effort that will be required, a pet quality dog would be a much better choice. This is especially good advice for first time dog owners.

Working quality dogs are those that exhibit strong, natural behavior characteristics of the breed. Examples would be a retriever puppy that demonstrates an exceptional desire to chase a ball or a guard dog type puppy that is especially bold and fearless when presented with new and novel situations. Working dogs may or may not be of show quality. If socialized and trained properly they can be (like all dogs) great companion or family dogs. However, working quality dogs are best left in the hands of experienced trainers. Working quality dogs are often not good candidates for first time or inexperienced owners. Their working "drive" is strong and must be expertly channeled in some way to avoid all sorts of potential behavior problems. Good working quality dogs will come with a contract similar to show quality dogs. They are expensive to buy, especially if they are both working and show quality.

---

they be considered two different breeds. The same has been suggested for the GSD. Those bred in their native land, Germany, are quite different than the "American German Shepard Dog." The differences are mostly in temperament (although some argue that there are structural differences as well). In Germany, the quality of a GSD is determined by testing the dog in Schutzhund trials. Schutzhund is a sport where dogs are subjected to a set of difficult and rigorous tests in tracking, obedience, agility and protection. Only the most sound, stable and courageous of dogs can pass this demanding test. Dogs that pass are given their "V" rating and are considered suitable for breeding. Although Schutzhund trails are held in the United States, most GSD's are not tested before breeding. According to the critics, this has lead to a decline in the working ability of the American bred GSD.

[19] Reputable breeders will often require new owners sign a contract with the purchase of a puppy. One of the key elements in the contract will obligate the owner of a pet quality dog to have their puppy spayed or neutered by six months of age. However, there should also be some guarantees concerning the health and temperament of the puppy to protect the new owner.

Pure breed dogs are somewhat easier to choose because of the predictability in their physical and behavioral characteristics. Of course not all dogs are pure breed. Mixed breed dogs are common and readily available. Mixed breed dogs make just as good a pet as a pure breed as long as they are placed with the right person or family.

If one knows just what breeds went into creating a mixed breed puppy, some educated guesses can be made as to what the physical and behavioral characteristics might be. If it is all ready an adult dog or even an older puppy, simple observation can often reveal everything you need to know.

Whether you are selecting a pure breed puppy or mixed breed, it is helpful if you can see and interact with both parents. You will get strong clues about how your puppy will be as an adult based on the parents. It is not always possible to see both parents but if you are getting your puppy from the breeder, the mother should be available at least.

Most professional breeders will not allow prospective owners to pick out their own puppy. They will generally pick one from the litter that they think will be suitable. This may seem disappointing for new owners but it is actually the best way. It is difficult for most people to choose puppies without having an emotional response. An emotional choice is not necessarily going to be the best one. Besides, good professional breeders know their own puppies very well. They probably even have written notes on them. An experienced breeder will ask the prospective owner a lot of questions about what they want in a dog and under what conditions it will be kept, e.g. access to fenced yard or how many and what ages are the children. Give a complete and honest description of yourself, family, lifestyle, living environment and expectations. An experienced breeder will use this information to choose a good puppy for you.

If you are getting a puppy from someone other than a professional breeder, then it is even more important to see the parents. You will have to make some decisions based on your own observations. Try to remain objective. You do not have to take the first puppy you see. Be mindful that your decision will be one that stays with you for ten to fifteen years.

Two cautionary notes will be discussed at this point. The first caution is that pet stores are generally one of the worst places to purchase a puppy (pet stores that help place only homeless dogs are praiseworthy exceptions). Pet shop puppies are usually from unknown origins even if it comes with "papers" (see the second cautionary note below). It is common for pet shops to acquire their puppies from "puppy mill" operations. Pet shop puppies frequently have hidden health problems and an increased mortality rate.

The second caution concerns dogs with "papers." The general public is very misinformed on the significance of "papers." "Papers" or certification by one of several canine organizations (the most well known in the United States is the American Kennel Club) is often considered a guarantee that a dog is of high quality. Sadly, this is not true. The AKC, which is a very fine organization, will readily inform you that their certification does not imply approval or any guarantee of quality. This simply is not their purpose. Lineages can be researched by using the AKC registry. A dog can have a great lineage or a very poor one but still be AKC registered. An AKC registry is a useful and important tool for researching the background of a dog but there is no guarantee as to the outcome of that research.

Initially, when choosing a breed suitable to your life style, family and living situation as well as expectations, research breed books and articles in dog magazines. These will help you with your decision. If you cannot decide on just one breed maybe a "top two or three choices" list could be made. You may be able to narrow the list depending on availability. Once you think you know what kind of dog you want, try to talk to owners of such dogs. Definitely talk to breeders (remember, it is best if you are buying from a professional breeder). Breeders are one of your best sources of reliable information but be sure to do your homework first so that you do not waste your time or that of the breeder. You can talk to knowledgeable owners and breeders if you attend dog shows in your area. Most dog owners love to talk about their dog or favorite breed so there is no need to be shy.

If you are not getting a pure bred dog you may want to consider adopting from your local animal shelter. Acquiring a dog from a shelter is not always the best way to get a dog but it is, without question, the most noble (incidentally, many pure breed dogs can be found in an animal shelter). I do not want to discourage people from adopting a dog from a shelter but there are some drawbacks. The majority of shelter dogs have been abandoned or surrendered or in some cases taken away from abusive owners. The most common reason dogs are surrendered to a shelter is because of behavioral problems. Nevertheless, the animals in shelters are there through no fault of their own.

The dilemma is that these dogs will often come with "ready-made" behavioral problems. Even though I would urge the *right* person to adopt, I would not encourage everyone to do so. I strongly believe that a person should be aware of this potential problem. It does no good to re-home the animal if it is just going to be returned for the same reason it was abandoned in the first place. Social instability (being passed from one home to another) will often make behavioral problems worse. The good news is that if placed with the right owner and environment these dogs can almost always be rehabilitated and make fine family pets.

Because re-homed animals often have special needs, well-run animal shelters make every attempt to match dogs to the new owners. They will have a personality profile on each dog based on their own observations. As a prospective owner you will need to be interviewed by one of the staff to determine which dog would be most suitable. The operators of animal shelters want to make good matches so that a permanent home can be found for the dog.

Whether you decide to get a pure breed, mixed breed, adopt or buy, there are still some other decisions that you may want to make. Do you want a male or female? Do you want a puppy? Do you want an older dog?

When deciding on a male or female, there is really very little difference in their behavior. There are some minor secondary characteristics that may be more pronounced in certain breeds. Males of some breeds tend to be a bit larger or have a more masculine look but these are generally very slight differences. Male dogs tend to mark more often but then some females mark with equal frequency. Marking behavior in males can often be curtailed if he is neutered at a young age. Marking behavior is usually a minor consideration.

I have often heard that males are more aggressive or "dominant" in dog/human relationships. I personally have not found this to be the case. I suspect that the "aggressive male" theory is more a result of some anthropomorphic gender bias than actual fact.

If you already own a dog and you wonder what would be the best sex for compatibility, the answer is more difficult. Male-to-male dog aggression is more common but compatibility usually depends more on things like the age, social training and how they are introduced to one another. Procedures for properly introducing a new dog to a resident dog are explained in chapter 11 under **The New Arrival**. The bottom line to choosing the sex of your new dog is more a matter of your own personal preference.

As to whether or not you want a puppy or an older dog, there is much more to consider. In my business I meet people all the time who are disillusioned about their puppy. They get this image in their mind (probably influenced by a commercial or movie) of a little puppy running happily along side their laughing five-year-old daughter licking her hands or face occasionally. What they end up with is a puppy that is running along side their little girl nipping her hands, grabbing and ripping her clothes, knocking her down and causing her to cry. Puppies can be great fun but we must not have illusions about them.

Puppies are cute and cuddly but they are also unruly and destructive. Few people raise a puppy without at least some minor losses of property and plenty of messes to clean up. If this is going to bother you, do not get a puppy. Puppies grow up very fast but when they are chewing up your furniture, biting your children, urinating on your carpet and destroying your leather shoes it may seem like an interminable period of time. Yes, puppies do "grow out" of many of these annoying behaviors but it is important to control and train them so that unacceptable behaviors are not carried into adulthood.

If you raise your own puppy you will have more responsibility for ensuring that it is properly socialized (how to socialize your puppy is covered in chapter 11). Early socialization will influence your dog's behavior for the rest of its life. Early socialization is just as important as vaccinations that prevent life threatening diseases. Poorly socialized dogs can die because they are much more likely to end up being surrendered to animal shelters where they have to be killed.

Aside from socialization there are a number of training exercises that must be taught and firmly installed in a young puppy. Procedures for all of these are discussed in following chapters and can be categorized into two areas; good manners and command behaviors.

Essentially, socialization is acclimating your puppy to people (men, women, children of all ages), other animals (other dogs, cats, parakeets, rabbits or any other household pet you may have), places (busy sidewalks, vet office, automobile, etc.), things (broom, vacuum cleaner, rolling desk chair, clothes on a clothesline, automatic doors, stairs, etc.) and noises (slamming doors, thunder, aircraft, loud motor vehicles, etc.). Good manners are behaviors that do not require a command and are mostly "non-behaviors" such as not jumping up on people, not stealing food, not chewing inappropriate objects, not pulling when on leash and not getting on the furniture (optional). Command behaviors are those things that we want our puppy or dog to do when we tell him. The most basic and common command behaviors that all dogs should know are sit, down, stay and come.

If you choose to get a puppy, make sure it is more than six weeks of age. Most puppies are weaned by six weeks but puppies benefit from an extended stay with their mother. Research reveals puppies that stay with the mother until ten weeks of age have better motor skills, agility and are less likely to suffer from separation anxiety.[20] However, it is essential that the puppies be socialized at the same time, particularly to people, during the six to ten week period.

For those who do not feel that they are quite prepared for raising a puppy an older dog could be an option. Older dogs must be chosen carefully however. If they were properly socialized and trained then few problems would be encountered. Obviously it is somewhat more difficult to find fully socialized and trained adult dogs directly from breeders or owners. Be aware however, that an older dog can be just as bad as a puppy or even worse if they did not receive proper training. To avoid problems find out as much as you can about their background (socialization, training, living environment) from the owner.

There are a lot of adult dogs available in local shelters. But as I mentioned they are more likely (but not always) to have behavioral problems. At the same time, I have to say that I know of many stories about some really great dogs that came out of animal shelters. Once again, I certainly encourage the adoption of homeless dogs. We have a serious overpopulation of dogs in the United States and adoption is one of the better solutions to alleviate the problem (along with spaying and neutering pets). However, I feel it is only a good idea if adoptive owners are fully prepared to accept the special responsibilities that sometimes come with their new dog. Fortunately, most dogs with problems can be rehabilitated with enough patience and care. The owner's of a "problem" dog will want to read chapter 14 on behavior modification. In some cases a professional behaviorist should be consulted.

Your choice of a dog will also depend on the kind of environment in which you and your dog will live. As I have already mentioned, the breed of dog that you choose should match your lifestyle but in particular it should also match the living environment. Make an objective evaluation of your living environment. An apartment in a big city is certainly going to be a different living environment than a farmhouse in a rural area and will a have great influence on the type of dog that you get.

Once you have made your choice of what kind of dog you want you can go out and get your puppy or dog, right? Well, not quite. There are still a few things that you will need to do before you bring your new dog home. By being fully prepared in advance you will help to ensure a smoother transition for both you and your new dog. The next chapter explains what you should do before bringing your new dog home.

---

[20] Separation anxiety is a relatively common and stressful behavior malady. Dogs suffering from separation anxiety usually bark or whine incessantly during the owner's absence. Frequently the dog will become destructive, chewing or scratching at the edges of a door for example. In severe cases the dog may even injure itself during frantic attempts to be with its owner.

Perfect Dogs

Left: This is a fine example of a beautiful, "show quality," purebred Doberman Pinscher. If you are not interested in showing your dog it is not necessary or even advisable to purchase a dog of this caliber. "Pet quality" dogs can make perfectly acceptable pets for most dog owners.

Right: Mongrels are often a good choice for many pet owners. They are equal to any dog in their ability to provide companionship. One of the advantages of a "mutt" or mixed breed dog is that they are readily available and inexpensive.

Chapter 9
Preparing For a New Dog or Puppy

There is usually a lot of excitement involved with bringing home a new puppy or dog. It is a great time but it is only the beginning of a long, and if done properly, happy relationship. It is best to start your new relationship in a positive way. To do that, some preparations are in order.

Assuming you have carefully researched the kind of dog that you want and your dog has been located, you will no doubt be anxious to bring him home. Resist the temptation of bringing your new dog home until you are completely ready.

First decide exactly where your dog is going to live. Basically the choices are inside, outside or a combination. I personally feel that most dogs should live primarily indoors. With some training it is the safest environment for your dog and is the best way to provide social needs. Some people do not like dogs to live inside with them. This is okay but more attention will be required to fulfill the social needs of the dog. It is almost too easy to put a dog in the backyard and when the novelty wears off, just ignore him. Many owners feel that dogs are too dirty to live inside. The irony is that dogs that live primarily inside usually require far less bathing than those that are outdoors all the time. Ultimately, the owner must decide what makes them the most comfortable.

Some of the small toy breeds can be "paper" trained and virtually never go outside. This is sometimes necessary for apartment dwellers in big cities. It is not a practical situation with larger dogs because of the larger volume of waste that is produced. Most dogs will need to go outside at least occasionally if only to relieve themselves, so outdoor containment is a primary consideration.

The responsible dog owner does not allow his dog to roam freely in an unsecured yard. A wide variety of potential health hazards face free roaming dogs. They are in danger of being injured or killed by moving vehicles. Free roaming dogs are more apt to pick up parasites or diseases and are vulnerable to many other environmental hazards such as toxins and poisons. They can even be injured or killed by other stray dogs. They also often represent a nuisance to other people in the neighborhood and most communities have strict laws prohibiting free roaming dogs.

A securely fenced yard is usually a minimum requirement for maintaining most dogs. However, exceptions can be made, e.g. homes without fences or apartment dwellers may choose to take their dog outside on leash only. Electronic "fences" can be effective but have some drawbacks that will be discussed later. Also, some owners have specially made kennel runs. This is fine, but these dogs will need extra exercise and care. Kennel dogs in particular will require plenty of social interaction outside the confines of their kennel.

Dogs should never be tied out on a line. Even the best-designed tie-out system can entangle a dog and cause serious injury or death. Dogs should only be tied-out when they can be carefully and constantly supervised. A tied-out dog should never be left alone.

If a fenced yard or area is going to be used the fence should be of a height, strength and fit that will not allow your dog to escape. A three-foot high fence may be adequate for a Pomeranian but totally inadequate for a German Shepard Dog. The bottoms of fences and gates must fit tightly to keep toy breeds from squeezing through small openings. In some cases dogs will dig or chew their way out of a fence. Many larger breeds of dog can easily chew through a wooden picket fence if they were so inclined. Certain dogs will dig under a fence, particularly the terrier breeds, if the fence is not buried deeply enough or does not have some other type of underground barrier.

Electronic containment systems can be used but require some training. Most of these systems work with an electronic shock collar that the dog wears at all times.[21] A wire is buried just under the ground and is marked with flags or other boundary markers that the dog can easily discern. The dog is introduced to the system slowly and is allowed to get shocked each time it approaches a certain boundary. They soon learn not to cross the boundaries and can be allowed to remain outside.

The electronic fence has some flaws. A dog must first be properly trained and conditioned to the system. If improperly trained, the dog may suddenly run past the barrier getting shocked but because of the momentum the dog could end up on the outside of the boundary. It can be trapped on the outside because it will get shocked when attempting to return to the area. I have also heard of some very sensitive dogs that refuse to even go outside again after receiving a shock that was too strong. Even if trained well, your pet will always be vulnerable to attacks from dogs or other animals that can now easily come into the yard.

If you decide that your dog is going to be kept outside all the time or even for long periods, you will need to provide shelter from the weather. A well-designed doghouse or enclosed porch can work just fine as long as it is comfortable. At a minimum it should be dry, warm in the winter and cool in the summer.

All areas, whether indoors or out, should be free of any hazards. Puppies are particularly vulnerable. If you will be keeping your puppy indoors then you will need a "safe area" where your puppy can stay unsupervised without getting into anything that is dangerous. Puppies are particularly fond of chewing on things. Electrical cords, toxic substances or items that could be ingested should be removed or placed high enough that it is inaccessible to the puppy. If a fence or barrier is going to be used to block off the safe area be sure a puppy cannot get their head caught in any openings. Most people will use either a bathroom or laundry-room. Tiled or linoleum floors are the easiest to clean. Carpeted floors should be avoided since they will get stained and very likely chewed.

You will also need a crate for your dog or puppy. Crates should be tall enough to allow your dog to stand fully upright. The length and width should allow your dog enough room to lay down with her legs outstretched. Slightly smaller crates can be used when transporting your dog on relatively short trips. I find the smaller crates more convenient to move in and out of a car. The crate is one of the most important pieces of equipment an owner will need, especially for a new dog or puppy. How to crate train your dog or puppy will be explained in chapter 11.

Other items that you will need are food and water bowls, bedding, chew toys, collar, leash, food and treats. Food and water bowls should be of a size appropriate to your dog. You may choose between plastic or stainless steel. A variety of bedding is available at pet

---

[21] Some electronic collars use a system that sprays citronella instead of delivering a shock. Citronella is a harmless but, to a dog, unpleasant substance. It is considered a more humane method of repelling a dog. However, humane considerations aside, the drawbacks to the citronella system are the same as the shock collar.

stores. Again the size will depend on your breed of dog. Chew toys, collars, leashes treats are all covered in the next chapter and food is discussed in chapter 15. Once you have all of these items and have prepared a suitable living environment for your dog or puppy, you are ready to bring her home.

Before ending this chapter I would like to add some final advice on the subject of preparing for a new dog or puppy. If you have read this chapter and the one on choosing the right dog you will realize by now that it is not an endeavor that should be undertaken without considerable forethought. Surprising your family with a dog is not a good idea. Everyone in the family should be in agreement on getting a dog. Everyone should be prepared for the responsibilities of owning a pet. The planning process and research that goes into finding just the right dog can actually be an enjoyable family undertaking when everyone participates.

Surprising children with a puppy on a holiday or birthday is generally a bad idea. As you are about to find out, puppies (and even new older dogs) require a great deal of attention when you first get them. Although children may love their puppy, there are usually too many distractions during big birthday celebrations or holidays. If you want to give a puppy as a gift, the best way is to make sure everyone in the family will welcome a new pet first, then make the selection and preparation process, that could be announced on the holiday, a part of the gift.

Proper containment is a prerequisite to owning a dog. Fences should be of a height and strength suitable to the breed or type of dog that you own. Dogs should never be allowed to roam.

Part II

The Theory

Chapter 10
Reinforcement Training

- Technique -

Before we get into the mechanics of training it is important to, at least briefly, discuss the general technique behind reinforcement training. We live, for better or worse, in a very punitive society, so a reward-based philosophy is sometimes difficult to completely accept. I say "completely" because clients frequently tell me that using rewards for training is all fine and good but they think that there are times when force or punishment simply must be used. I believe that force or punishment is just a result of frustration, when we cannot think of any other way of resolving a problem. I hope that this book will provide alternatives that will prevent frustrations.

I cannot deny that punishment gets results but why use it when reinforcement training will work? Punishment can also produce "false" results when dealing with certain behaviors. This is especially true when treating aggression problems. Dog aggression should never be treated with punishment.[22] It is extremely dangerous, often exacerbating the problem. Even if punishment methods make aggressive behavior seem to disappear the dog is like a ticking time bomb or loaded gun just waiting to go off at an unexpected moment.

Reinforcement training makes behavioral changes at a deep psychological level. It creates new and enduring behavioral patterns in a dog. Punishment methods often make only superficial and temporary behavior changes. Other drawbacks to aversive methods have already been mentioned such as, breaking down rather than building up your relationship with your dog and the need for exceptional timing and appropriate intensity in corrections.

The most common argument that I hear from people who resist the notion of reinforcement training is that the handler will have to use food treats. For some reason it bothers them when they have to reward their dog for good behavior but it does not bother them to use a leash and choke collar to punish unwanted behavior. I believe the answer is just a question of ethics.

The follow-up argument is that the owner does not want to have to carry a bunch of treats around everywhere they go or every time they want their dog to do something. This is a legitimate concern. Bear in mind that treats are merely tools for the appetitive trainer. Leashes and choke collars are tools for the aversive trainer. The ultimate goal of both appetitive and aversive trainers is to discontinue using tools. Just as you would need tools to build a house, it is necessary to use tools when training your dog. Once a house is built, tools are put away but may be brought out to do occasional repairs. Training tools are used in much the same way.

---

[22] Dog aggression almost always stems from a socialization problem. The best "cure" is prevention. If you are experiencing aggression problems with your dog check with your veterinarian first to rule out any physiological causes. If your dog does not have any physical causes for aggression then you should seek the help of a pet behavior specialist. Dog bites represent one of the leading health problems in the United States. Aggression problems should be taken seriously. A qualified professional can cure almost any dog of aggression problems using counter-conditioning and desensitization techniques.

You will not have to reward your dog every time you give her a command if you utilize reinforcement training properly. Numerous and generous rewards are given during the learning phase of training but are placed on a "variable schedule" with time (variable reward schedules will be discussed in more detail in a moment). Many people proclaim that reinforcement training is a form of bribery. They believe that a dog is only obeying because the handler is holding a treat. The same people often believe that a dog should perform because of its desire to please their "master." This is a very romantic notion but it is unlikely that any dog follows commands for altruistic reasons.

Dogs do things for themselves, to gain some advantage. No one should be offended by this fact. Dogs cannot be held morally accountable. Moral issues are a human concern. Basically all living creatures do things for themselves, including people. For example, most of us have to work for a living. Even those of us who truly enjoy our work probably would not continue to do it unless we were paid. We may have loyalties to our supervisors or company but we do not work simply to please our boss. We expect remuneration for our efforts.

Why should a dog be expected to perform tasks for his "master" without some form of remuneration? We also enjoy a pat on the back and verbal praise from the boss but we still expect to be rewarded in a more meaningful way at some point. We are really asking the dog to behave at a higher standard than what we ourselves are willing. Just as we are motivated to perform our work in exchange for certain rewards, usually in the form of a paycheck, we can motivate a dog using rewards. Most dogs would not find a paycheck very motivating but they will work for more direct rewards such as food, toys or other meaningful resources.

Dogs that are trained with positive reinforcement respond quickly and willingly because they hope to gain by their actions. A dog that is trained using punishment does things simply to avoid being hurt, not out of any loyalty towards its master. Of the two possibilities, clearly a willing response is the more desirable.

With so many good reasons to use appetitive training it is difficult to understand why anyone would resort to aversive training. Intellectually, it is an easy choice but many of us are emotionally preprogrammed to react in a punitive manner, especially when we become frustrated. Make a conscious effort to remain light-hearted and positive when you train your dog. The effects are two fold; one is that your training is more effective and the other is that you will actually make yourself feel good in the process.

- Variable Reward Schedule -

It is important to understand variable reward schedules. At first you will want to reward your dog **every time** she performs a particular behavior on command. As soon as a dog learns to respond to your command using a continuous reward schedule it is then possible to shift to a variable reward schedule.

A variable reward system is where you will no longer need to reward with a treat for each and every correct behavior.[23] The amazing thing about variable reward schedules is not only do they allow you to reduce the number of treats, but when done properly, actually increase the reliability of the behavior. The key is switching to a variable schedule only after a fixed pattern of continuous reward has been established.

---

[23] Verbal or physical (petting) praise should always be used when possible regardless of whether or not other rewards are given, such as a treat or toy.

In human terms, variable reward schedules are not difficult to understand. I could actually train you to perform simple tasks using a variable reward method. Let us say I have hired you for a job that entails pushing a button. Let us also say I speak a language that you do not understand and I am unable to tell you that I want you to push a button. When you come to work I simply put you in a room that has a box with a big red button on the side. To you, I am just making sounds but nothing that you can understand. At some point, maybe out of curiosity, you decide to push the button on the box. The first time you do it a twenty-dollar bill comes out of the box. You take the bill and I seem rather pleased with you. You would probably be tempted to push the button again. If you got another twenty dollars you would most likely continue to push the button over and over again until I finally take you out of the room.

The next day I take you back into the same room. Of course it would not take you long to start pushing the button again. You get twenty dollars the first time you push the button and I seem pleased. But the second time you push it you do not get anything except that I still seem pleased. Would you stop pushing the button after that? Not very likely. Chances are you would push the button again. Lets say on the third and fourth try you get your twenty dollars each time. The fifth try, nothing happens once again. You might be a little puzzled but you would push it again. You still get nothing. At this point maybe you would try a little harder, perhaps pushing on the button with more force. You get your twenty dollars. You also begin to notice that I am making a distinctive sound that you are able to recognize each time just as you are about to push the button.

The following day you go right to work pushing the button but you get no results. I had not said anything and I remain rather neutral. I then make the sound that you recognized from before. You decide to push the button and a twenty-dollar bill comes out. After numerous trials over the next few days you notice that you only get rewarded when I make the distinctive sound first. You learn it does you no good to push the button unless you hear me make that particular sound. You also notice that when you push the button softly you sometimes get a twenty and sometimes not. When you push it hard you always get two twenties. So now you do not push the button unless you hear me make the distinctive sound and then you always push it hard. Without much difficulty at all I have now trained you to press a button not only on my command but you tend to push it a certain way.

But your training is not yet complete. I continue to give the command to press the button but now you only get one twenty when you press hard but soft presses no longer result in any reward at all. You also find that you must press the button as soon as you hear the command. If you are too slow in responding there is no reward. You must pay close attention to me in order to hear the command and be able to act quickly enough to get any money. Just when you are consistently pushing the button hard and quickly the criterion shifts once again. Even though you pay close attention and upon hearing each command you always push the button hard and quickly but you do not always get a reward. Sometimes you get two twenties and sometimes only one. Other times you get nothing at all. You never really know because there is no way to predict the outcome in advance. Even though you are not getting rewarded for every single push of the button on command you get enough rewards to make it worth your while so you continue to show up for work each day. To ensure you get enough money you pay close attention to me, you quickly react to my command and you consistently push the button hard.

Now I have reliably trained you to press the button hard on the box each time you are given a command using reinforcement training. I do not have to pay you for every single push of the button but I am assured of your continued good performance by the use of a variable reward schedule. The above training method will work on anyone. It will also work on any animal. Monkeys, birds, fish, cats and of course dogs can all learn in similar fashion.

I may refer to the preceding scenario at different times in this book to illustrate other techniques that are involved in training such as "behavior shaping" and "lure training." However, at the risk of belaboring the point, I would like to make some quick analogies at this time.

In our little training analogy one only needs to make some substitutions to see how we can train a dog. Of course instead of me training you it will be you training your dog. Instead of a button to be pushed (although a dog can learn to push a button) you might want your dog to sit or lay down. Instead of giving your dog a twenty-dollar bill you could give her something more valuable like one of her favorite treats. If pushing a button represents a "sit" then pushing a button hard means a straight, precise sit. The rest of the story remains essentially the same.

One aspect of variable reward schedule training that may not be very obvious from the story is the element of surprise. When you are putting your dog on a variable reward schedule it is beneficial to surprise her with the reward. In other words, she should be unable to anticipate whether or not you have a reward to offer. One of the easiest ways to do this is to store treats in various strategic locations around your house where your dog cannot get to them. We do this to make dogs think that we can produce a treat at anytime.

- Canine Cash -

Most reinforcement training will require food treats (canine cash). Generally food treats are the easiest way to provide high value rewards to your dog, especially a puppy. Toys can be used, a ball, squeak toy or tug are good items for dogs that are not very food motivated. Frankly, I have not yet found a dog that cannot be trained with food. Sometimes, if a dog is overfed, it may require skipping a meal to get the dog motivated. I am not implying that anyone should starve a dog. That is entirely unnecessary. Skipping a meal or even two is not going to "starve" an otherwise healthy or overfed dog.

Toys can be very effective in training if your dog has enough interest in them. However, they are sometimes not as easy to use and can become a distraction when teaching new behaviors. Early stages of teaching often require repetitive sequences. A reward is given after each repetition. A toy reward can take too much time and will distract the dog. Learning will occur more rapidly when repetitive sequences are performed with less interruption. However, once the dog has learned a behavior, quick repetitions are no longer necessary; toys can then be used very effectively as reinforcement to ensure that the behavior will continue.

Of course praise, both verbal and physical (petting) is almost always appropriate but it should usually be linked with a treat or toy. Dogs may work for praise alone but it is far more meaningful and effective if it is linked with more substantial rewards, like treats. This does not mean that treats must be given every time as you will see when we discuss "reward-marks" later in this chapter.

Verbal praise may inspire your dog for a while but if it is never linked to some other more meaningful reward, like a treat or toy, it will eventually lose much of its inspirational value. Verbal praise should be used almost all the time but frequently followed by a higher value reward. However, during training the owner should refrain from chatter. Restrict yourself to only one or two praise words or short phrases so that your dog can easily recognize them.

Petting is good for dogs that learn to like it, and most do. I even use a good "belly rub" as a special reward for a particularly fine performance if the dog enjoys that kind of petting. But, it is not always appropriate to pet your dog. Petting can sometimes be too distracting during training so I like to reserve it for the end of a session. I also like to use petting as a calming technique. During training sessions you need your dog to be enthusiastic so petting during this time should be restricted to no more than a pat under the chin.

Also, dogs that learn to like petting can become a nuisance in the home when they always solicit the owner or guests to be petted. If your dog comes to you and wants to be petted, you should not do so. Ignore the behavior. Once your dog goes away, if you want to pet her, call her back to you and pet her for coming. In other words make her do something for it first. Do not let your dog train **you**. You should always be in control and doing the training, not your dog.

For most training it is usually better to start teaching with food treats. Later, use toys as a reward when your dog becomes more proficient in the behavior. Food rewards should be of a size and texture that allows the dog to swallow it quickly. This will ensure that there will be more time spent on the behavior and less on the reward, speeding up the learning process.

It is important to experiment with a variety of treats to find out what your dog likes the most. Commercial dog treats are not necessarily the best. A manufacturer of a commercial dog treat must design a product that first appeals to the person who is going to buy the product. Its appeal to the dog, although important, is a somewhat secondary factor. Commercial treats are fine but just make sure that they really do appeal to your pet and not just to you.

Make sure your treat is easy to handle. Cheese, for example, is a great food treat for training under most circumstances but if it is in the middle of the summer and you live in Florida, you may want to reconsider. In the hot sun your cheese treats are going to melt. Raw chicken livers might be very appealing to your dog but would be difficult (and unhealthy to you) to transport and handle while training at your local park; although, as a quick reward in the kitchen for some good behavior, raw chicken liver would be fine.

A final, but by no means the least important, factor in choosing a reward for your dog is safety. Fresh, raw chicken, as mentioned earlier, is not harmful to your dog, contrary to popular belief. Dogs are immune to certain diseases that we are not. However, a **cooked** chicken **bone** is not safe, whereas cooked chicken meat is fine.[24] Also, some dogs may have allergies or other negative reactions to certain foods. Obviously you should avoid any treat that may be harmful to your dog. If you are uncertain then ask your veterinarian.

---

[24] Cooked bones, particularly chicken, are brittle and will splinter. They can puncture a dog's intestines or become lodged in the colon. Never give your dog cooked bones of any kind. On the other hand, any kind of raw bones are very good for your dog (see chapter 15, **Food For Thought**)

To review, when choosing treats for your dog consider palatability (to your dog, not you), ease of ingestion, ease of handling and safety. Keep in mind that dogs are natural scavengers and, when given the opportunity, will usually eat a wide variety of things. Scientific experiments have shown that when puppies are exposed to a variety of foods at an early age they never become fussy eaters. Puppies that are fed on mono-specific diets frequently do become fussy eaters. Allow your dog the opportunity to sample a wide variety of food treats. Keep track of and try to rank each food item in the order in which your dog likes them. You should be able to identify at least four to six different treats that your dog likes.

The treats that your dog likes the most are high value rewards. The ones she likes the least are low value. Knowing the relative "reward value" will assist you in training as you will see later. If you are having difficulty coming up with ideas for treats the following is a list of some suggestions:

> Cheese cut into small cubes or slices of string cheese
> Hotdogs* cut into thin slices (or smaller for toy breeds)
> Turkey-dogs with cheese
> Summer sausage* cut into small cubes
> Cooked chicken (nuggets or pieces)
> Cooked liver cut into small pieces (some dogs like liver seasoned with garlic)
> Dried fruit (raisins, cut up dried apples, etc.)
> Well-cooked steak cut into small cubes
> Tortellini (cheese or beef)
> Dry cereal
> Commercial treats (must be soft and easily cut into small pieces, such as jerky)
> Dry dog food kibble

*These items can be cooked for a short time in a microwave oven to dry them out a little for easier handling. However, the process may reduce its reward value to your dog.

Make a list of treats that your dog likes and try to rate them in order of your dog's preference. Keep in mind that some dogs will change their preference from time to time. Just as we might get tired of a favorite food after a while, dogs seem to do the same thing and enjoy a change. This is one trick for "revving" up a training routine. If you have been working hard on training and your dog seems to start loosing interest, one of the things you can do is switch to a different reward. This will often get the dog motivated again.

Another motivational trick is to "jackpot" your dog. A jackpot is an especially tasty treat that you reserve for only the best behaviors. A jackpot can also be an unusually large reward. Generally, if your dog is performing a behavior but it is not exactly what you want, you give an ordinary reward. But, if your dog suddenly does a behavior perfectly, or makes some significant improvement, you could give her a "jackpot" to emphasize the correct behavior.

The size of the treat will depend on the size of your dog. Your dog should be able to swallow the treat without chewing. It should also be large enough that your dog considers it worth the effort. If the rewards are too small your dog will lose interest.

You can keep your rewards in your hand, in your pocket or in a "bait bag" tied to your waist. Bait bags are sold commercially or you can use a small "fanny" pack. As mentioned previously you can also place treats in various locations around the house, such as bookshelves, tops of picture frames, window frames or anyplace readily accessible to you but not your dog.

If you are doing a lot of training you may worry about overfeeding your dog. This is a legitimate concern. Obesity is one of the most serious health problems facing dogs in the United States. If you are giving a lot of treats then cut down on the amount of food you are feeding at meals. In fact some trainers do not use a food bowl to feed their dog. Instead, a daily ration is measured out and the dog is fed by hand the entire amount throughout the day one handful at a time in return for obeying commands. By the end of the day the dog has received its full ration of food along with plenty of training.

- Training Equipment -

You will need very little training equipment for pet dog training. There are a number of optional items that one could have but essentially all you need is a collar and leash.

The collar should be a flat collar made of either leather or nylon. It should be of sturdy construction. The collar needs to be of a size where it fits securely but not tightly around your dog's neck. A standard rule for determining how tight the collar should be is to have just enough slack that you can fit two to three fingers (width-wise) between the collar and the dog.

If you have the sort of dog that likes to slip out of the collar you could use a partial or limited choke collar. This is a flat collar that is loose when there is no tension on the leash but tightens snuggly around the neck when pulled by the dog or handler. The collar is adjusted so that it never chokes but cannot slip over the dog's head.

A standard leash made of either nylon or leather approximately six feet long is the best general-purpose leash. Long lines can be useful for certain kinds of training. Long lines are usually between fifteen and thirty feet long. They are made of nylon, leather or cotton. Long lines are used for "distance training" or tracking. It takes some practice and some special handling to keep them from getting tangled. Leather is very expensive but easy on the hands. Cotton is better on the hands than nylon but not quite as strong. Short, so-called "traffic" leads are not very useful for pet dog training. To the best of my knowledge the very short "pull tabs" (leashes about six inches long that are left on the collar that can be grabbed quickly) only have uses in aversive training.

Other optional training equipment that you may want to consider is a bait bag, target stick (for toy breeds), a retractable lead and a clicker. Bait bags are a convenient way to carry your treats for your dog. They can be obtained through a number of on-line, mail order, pet supply businesses. The owners of toy breeds may want to consider the use of a target stick. A target stick and "target training" will be described with Lure Training and Behavior Shaping at the end of this chapter. The retractable lead can be both useful and counterproductive, depending on how it is used. Its use will be discussed when we talk about recalls (calling your dog to you). A Clicker and its possible use will be described next.

- The Reward-mark -

When you finally start training your dog a useful technique is to "reward-mark." Timing is very important in dog training. Your dog can learn faster if she knows the moment she has done something right. For example if you tell your dog to sit and she does then you fumble around getting out your treat to give her she may stand up again to take the treat. She will think that standing up is how she gets her treat. To avoid this problem you simply reward-mark.

A reward-mark is usually a distinctive sound that can be used as a precise indicator that your dog has just done something right. Some trainers use "clickers" to reward-mark. Clickers are made with a small, thin piece of spring steel that gives a distinctive click sound when pressed with your finger. It is easily carried in the pocket or in the palm of your hand. Each time a dog does something right the handler will "click" their dog and then give a treat. The click comes at the precise moment the dog does the right thing, therefore "marks" the behavior. The dog learns to associate the sound with two things; first that it has done the right thing, which helps speed up learning, and secondly the dog knows that, as a result of doing the right thing, a reward is going to follow (actually rewards are put on a variable schedule once the dog has learned to associate the click with a treat).

Clickers are great tools for training. They can be very effective. Many people object to them because it is one more training tool that you need to keep track of and carry with you. They are probably not that troublesome once you get used to them but I have the same objection. Once someone gets hooked on the clicker system they seem to become "born again trainers" fervently preaching the virtues of the clicker. I sometimes use clicker training but prefer just to use my voice as a reward-mark. Perhaps someday I too will become converted but for now I am the most comfortable with vocal reward-marks. Vocal reward-marks are not quite as distinctive as a clicker but dogs learn to recognize them well enough.

Vocal reward-marks should be a distinctive short phrase, word or just a sound. I know of some trainers who just click their tongue. I like to use an enthusiastic "YES!" whenever a dog does something I want but you can use "right" or "good dog" or any number of words or phrases. Pick something that is quick and natural for you to say. It should be a word or phrase that is distinct enough that your dog will have no difficulty recognizing it.

You can pre-condition your dog to a reward-mark if you want. Clicker trainers often do this. Pre-conditioning is accomplished by making your reward-mark sound at random times which is always followed by a food reward. Your dog will soon learn that each time she hears the reward-mark that a treat will be offered.[25] This generally takes only a few trials. It has been scientifically proven that once the association has been firmly established the reward-mark is just as valuable as the reward itself (as long as it is reinforced occasionally). When your dog becomes conditioned to the reward-mark you would begin your training.

---

[25] Famous scientist Ivan P. Pavlov was the first to recognize the "conditioned response" of an animal to a particular sound. His experiments showed how a dog could be conditioned to anticipate food each time it heard a bell ring. To condition the dog all he had to do was ring a bell and then present food. Before long the dog would begin to salivate just at the sound of the bell even though the dog could not see food. This type of learned involuntary behavior in response to a stimulus (in this case a bell ringing) became known as a "Pavlovian response" or "classical conditioning."

It is not entirely necessary to train the reward-mark first. When I go to see clients the first time they are usually anxious to see results right away so I generally do not bother teaching the reward-mark separate. However, it is important to use a reward-mark right from the beginning of your training. Although this may sound strange, you will see later that commands for the behavior are not that important and are usually taught later but reward-marks are used right away. Your dog can learn a reward-mark and a behavior simultaneously.

It is essential that the instant your dog offers the correct behavior that she is given a reward-mark. If you always reward-mark the instant your dog performs the right behavior she will learn more quickly. Poorly timed reward-marks will slow the learning process because your dog has to figure out exactly which behavior was correct. It is no better than a slow reward. The idea is to make a reward-mark something much easier and faster than pulling a treat out of your pocket.

A precisely timed reward-mark makes the association between a particular behavior and a reward much simpler for your dog. Even if you are a little slow in getting out a reward your dog will still learn. Better still, you do not have to reward each time once a reward-mark has been established. As I have already mentioned the reward-mark itself is just as valuable as the reward. Only if the reward-mark never or rarely resulted in a real reward would it lose its value.

Think of a reward-mark as a compliment that might later be translated into some reward. If your boss compliments you it would make you feel good, especially if you were rewarded later, maybe with a raise or bonus or perhaps a Caribbean cruise. You would continue to be encouraged by compliments by your boss as long as they eventually lead to tangible rewards. If your boss always gave you compliments but never followed up with a reward then the compliments would not mean very much. Keep reward-marks meaningful by rewarding frequently.

- Lure Training and Behavior Shaping –

Two very important appetitive training techniques are lure training and behavior shaping. Lure training is a method where the dog is lead, usually by a treat in front of the nose, to a particular position. Behavior shaping is where we get our dog to perform an approximation of the desired behavior first and then gradually raise the criteria for earning a reward until we get exactly the behavior that we want.

These techniques have a couple of advantages over more conventional manipulation training, where the trainer actually physically places the dog in position. In luring and shaping the dog learns to manipulate his own body during training so stress levels are very low and the dog takes responsibility for getting into proper position.

When you lure a dog into position the dog must do all the work and he is more aware of how he must position his body to be rewarded. The trainer simply holds or moves the treat in such a way that the dog is obligated to move his body into a desired position in order to get the treat. He can learn much more rapidly this way.

Behavior shaping can best be explained by reviewing our hypothetical training scenario described earlier in this chapter. Remember I trained you to push the button for a reward but I also taught you to push the button hard. This was behavior shaping. I first got an approximation of the behavior I wanted by getting you to push the button in any old way. But later I "shaped" the behavior by rewarding you only when you pushed it hard.

The strengths of lure and shaping correspond directly to the weaknesses of physically manipulating your dog. At first a dog will automatically resist physical manipulation (called the "opposition reflex"). Instead of concentrating on what he needs to do to get rewarded your dog is distracted by your handling. Depending on what is being done, the dog can become anxious and distressed by the handling. This is not the optimum mental state for learning.

Luring and shaping takes some patience on the part of the trainer but they are powerful training techniques. Reward-marks are used to facilitate both techniques. Dogs that are taught using these methods rapidly become "thinking" dogs. This is how dogs learn to learn. If you use these techniques regularly, your dog will begin to recognize when you are trying to teach him something new. Because he knows that he can benefit from doing what you want, i.e. gets a reward, he will begin offering all sorts of behaviors.

At first the behavior will not be what you want. Your dog will probably do all the behaviors that you have rewarded for in the past. This is called "rehearsal" behavior. You can either try to lure your dog into the right position or be very passive and just wait until your dog "accidentally" gets into position, at which point you give a well-timed reward-mark followed by a treat. After a couple of "accidents" your dog will realize what earns the reward and will offer the behavior more readily as time goes on.

A dog that has absolutely no interest in retrieving can be taught to fetch a newspaper using a rather long series of very passive shaping techniques. The procedures for teaching this behavior go beyond the scope of this book but are mentioned to underscore the effectiveness of the technique. Shaping and luring techniques will be explained more thoroughly in the next part of this book entitled *The Mechanics*.

A special form of luring, called "targeting," will also be explained when I cover walking your dog on a leash. Although, it can have many other uses. Targeting is where you teach your dog to touch his nose to something, e.g. the palm of your hand or the end of a stick, and follow the target wherever it goes. Target training can help you manipulate your dog into a desired position without actually using a treat. This becomes especially useful when dealing with small or toy breed dogs because a target stick can be used to eliminate the need to bend over.

- Basic Rules –

The basic rules for appetitive training are really very simple: If a behavior is rewarded then that behavior is more likely to occur again. If a behavior is not rewarded then that behavior is less likely to occur again. In other words, all we have to do is reward those behaviors that we like and ignore the ones that we do not. The only trick is that we have to make sure an undesirable behavior is not self-rewarding. For example, if your dog gets into the trash you cannot just completely ignore the problem and expect it to go away. The solution is still simple however. The easiest solution is to simply put the garbage in a place where your dog cannot get at it. In that way you have removed the reward.

Tools Of The Trade

Toys can be used to motivate your dog but for most training food treats are best. Food treats should be relatively small and soft for easy swallowing. The plate in this photo shows a variety of suitable treats, cut up hot dogs, cooked chicken, cheese, raisons, breakfast cereal and "jerky" sticks. The secret is to find out what your dog likes the most and then make him work to get it. Always be generous with your rewards and later, when your dog has learned the behavior, be unpredictable.

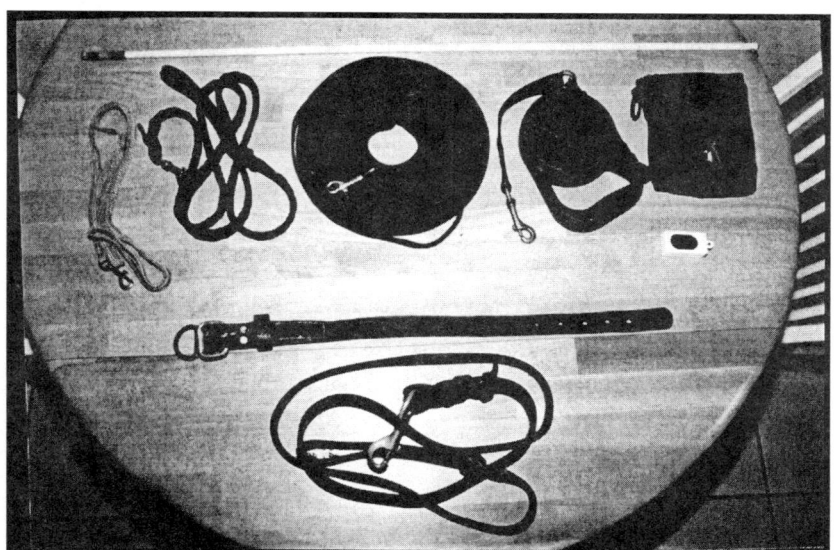

The only equipment needed for most training is a flat collar and six-foot leash. These items can be made of leather, as shown at the bottom of the above picture, or made of nylon. Standard walking leashes should be approximately six feet long and of a thickness appropriate for your size dog. For example, in the upper part of the picture, starting from the left, is a ¼-inch wide nylon leash for small dogs. The next leash is a 5/8-inch leash for medium size dogs. The center leash is a thirty-foot long line, which is good for practicing recalls. To the right of that is a retractable lead, generally not recommended for obedience work. On the right is a bait bag, which clips to a belt and is a convenient way to hold treats while training. A clicker is shown just below the bait bag. At the top is a target stick. Target sticks are particularly useful for small dogs.

Part III

The Mechanics

Chapter 11
Social Conduct

Before we discuss the training of specific behaviors this chapter will cover a more general area of social conduct. Correct social conduct is an absolute prerequisite for dogs to be successfully integrated into human society. Social conduct behaviors do not have commands. They are simply behaviors that we expect from a dog. But this does not mean that we do not have to teach the rules. Most of these rules can be taught easily. They are best taught when a dog is a puppy but it is never too late to learn.

Liberal use of bold face type in this section is for drawing the reader's attention to key points. Although you are now into the mechanics of training, training a dog is anything but mechanical. Be patient and be sure to proceed at your dog's pace, not your own.

- The New Arrival -

You have been planning and preparing for your dog for weeks. The big day has finally arrived and you are ready to pick up your newest family member. Be sure to bring a crate. Crates should always be used while driving with a dog. It is the safest way to transport your dog in a car. Sudden stops or sharp turns could cause injury to the dog or other passengers. Also, it is not uncommon for dogs or puppies to get "car-sick" the first couple of times they are in an automobile.[26] A crate will at least minimize the clean up once you reach home.

Once you arrive home with your new dog or puppy be sure to give them an opportunity to relieve themselves before going inside. It is better to error on the side of caution. Taking your puppy out to relieve himself too often causes no harm and is much better than not going out enough. Allow your new dog or puppy to sniff around and familiarize himself with the area.

Once your dog or puppy has relieved himself or you are reasonably convinced that he has no need you can take your puppy or dog inside (if you plan to keep your dog outdoors at all times then you should stay out with him until he is comfortably acclimated). Once again allow your dog or puppy to explore and investigate his new home. It is usually best, especially for puppies, to have the dog restricted to a single room right at first.

As your new dog or puppy explores, remain calm and observe his behavior carefully. If something in your house frightens your dog you should say nothing. Just let your dog adjust to the new surroundings on his own. Forcing your dog to accept new or novel things will be counterproductive. Also, trying to reassure or comfort your dog by petting him when he is afraid will only reinforce the fear. It is best to let your dog deal with the environment on his own at first. Later, once your dog has learned to trust you, you can use some positive encouragement techniques to teach him to be more confident should that be necessary.

---

[26] Carsickness can cause a dog to dislike automobile rides. Dogs that dislike riding in the car can usually be "converted" with little trouble. Using some very simple techniques most dogs learn to love going for rides in a relatively short time. If your dog or puppy develops a dislike for car rides see the chapter 14 under *Miscellaneous Problems*.

Your puppy or new dog should be under constant supervision. You need to be alert for the first signs of needing to relieve himself (housetraining procedures will be discussed in the next section). This is also a good time to see if you forgot to remove any potential hazards from the room. If there are any hazards, your puppy will find them.

If you have not consulted a veterinarian you should do so immediately. Make arrangements to bring your new dog or puppy in for examination and possible vaccinations. Your veterinarian can advise you on all of your puppy's health requirements. See the chapter 15, **Food For Thought** for advice on feeding your dog.

Contrary to popular opinion, you may start training your puppy right away. Early puppy training is not only possible but beneficial as well. The reason some trainers do not recommend any "serious" training until the dog is six months or older is because they employ aversive techniques, which can indeed cause problems in young puppies. Appetitive methods can be used at virtually any age without harm. You need only allow your puppy (or new dog) enough time to familiarize himself with his new home. Depending on the dog this is usually a matter of a few minutes or hours at the most.

Early training has a number of benefits but one of the most important is leadership formation. My clients frequently comment on how their dog behaves so much better when I am around. They seem very impressed and seem to think that I must really be a talented trainer. I wish that I could confirm their estimation of my abilities but in all honesty I have to admit that I have an advantage. When I am around their dog I am something novel and interesting. I already have the dog's attention. Training becomes rather easy when I have a dog's attention because I become the leader at that point.

You can establish your leadership with your dog at anytime but there is no easier time than when you are still new and novel to your dog or puppy. Using lots of praise is fine but most dogs will get rather bored with that in time. You should use the opportunity to impress your dog as to how really interesting you are by producing unexpected treats, toys and games. You should always mix plenty of play in with your training (specific training will be discussed in the next chapter). When done properly your puppy or new dog will be unable to distinguish between training and play. It should all be fun (for both you and your dog) and should all be rewarding.

Always remember that you are competing with the environment. Dogs, and puppies in particular, are naturally curious about their surroundings. They are going to be attracted to the most interesting thing around. If you want a responsive, obedient dog, and everyone does, then you must compete with the environment and be the most interesting thing there.

Being interesting is not always easy, but during early training you can use your advantage of being novel to your dog for establishing a reputation for being interesting. If your dog knows that you are always full of surprises and a lot of "high value" fun, then he is more likely to pay attention to you even when the environment is quite stimulating. Boring, or worse yet punitive, owners will surely be ignored in a stimulating environment. To be a leader you must be interesting to your dog.

Once the day has come to an end and you have had a fun filled day with your new dog or puppy it is time to get your dog ready for bed. Take your new dog or puppy outside to relieve himself first. It is best to discontinue feeding or watering two or three hours before bedtime. You can put your dog in whatever safe and comfortable place you have chosen but I recommend keeping them in a crate next to your bed for at least the first two or three nights. If you do not have a crate, then tying them to the bedpost with a six-foot leash is okay. You do not want them to be able to wander around without your supervision while you are asleep. Keeping your dog close to you during the night makes the transition to his new environment easier and also helps with bonding.

Young puppies (ten weeks or more) should be able to wait at least six hours before needing to relieve themselves as long as the have been resting. Refer to the housetraining and crate training techniques later in this chapter for details. Puppies and dogs should be given the opportunity to go outside immediately upon being let out of the crate to avoid any "accidents." The idea is to use an "errorless learning" method. You should do everything you can to control the situation so that your dog never gets a chance to make a mistake, therefore developing good habits. Rarely does everything go according to plan however. If "accidents" happen or your puppy chews up something that is not allowed just try to make sure it does not happen again. With some patience and practice your new dog or puppy will grow into a well-adjusted companion animal that will bring you happiness for many years.

If you already own a dog and are bringing new dog home, some precautions may be needed.[27] It really depends on the personality of both dogs but the resident dog in particular could object to the newcomer. Each situation needs to be addressed individually so there is no way to give a step-by-step procedure. Instead, I will offer you a few hints that may prove useful to you.

I occasionally "dog-sit" for some of my friends. I like to bring their dog to my house where I already have two dogs of my own. I have found the easiest way to introduce the dogs is to have them meet in some neutral location, say in a park just down the block. My friend brings her dog and meets me with my two dogs at the park. They are allowed to sniff each other and get friendly with each other. We then walk home together. The new arrival is accepted right away because he has been "invited" into the territory.

Another method is to keep the dogs completely separated from each other for a while but alternate them to the same room or area. That way each dog will get a chance to smell the other dog. Be sure to keep them separated by a solid door or gate so that they cannot see each other.

Most likely if there is going to be a challenge it will come from the resident dog. To help prevent the resident dog from viewing the other dog as a threat, each time you notice your dog sniffing an area where the other one has been (or even on your own clothes or hands) become very happy, praise and give your dog a treat. Eventually you will change the association of the scent of the other dog from a threat to something positive.

With someone's assistance, arrange to meet in a neutral location, say just down the street. It is important never to seem anxious during the encounter. In fact it is helpful if you and your assistant act very happy, even to the point of appearing silly. This will put the dogs in a good mood (dogs love it when their owners act silly!) and will help diffuse any apprehension in the dogs. Then it is just a matter of walking home together as described earlier.

---

[27] I often get clients who have gotten a second dog in the misguided belief that the second dog would provide a diversion to alleviate problems they were having with the resident dog. This almost never works. If you have problems with your first dog, do not expect another dog to correct it. You are the only one who can correct the problems (seek the help of a professional behaviorist if necessary). Adding another dog to the situation is more likely to cause what I like to call "double trouble."

If you are not sure that an encounter will go well between two dogs, particularly larger breeds, it might be advisable to muzzle one or both dogs for their first encounter. This is purely a safety precaution and should only be used for initial contact between two potentially aggressive dogs. If a fight did break out, properly muzzled dogs are prevented from causing damage to each other and a handler can safely separate them.

If you decide to use a muzzle, make sure it fits well. Do not leave muzzled dogs unsupervised and if a fight breaks out do not allow it to continue. Distract dogs from fighting by becoming very playful and happy (fake it if you have to) and try to maintain a light hearted and exciting atmosphere. If the dogs seem determined to fight you will need to back up in your training, letting the dogs get used to each other gradually.

Never allow dogs to continue fighting with muzzles in the hope that they will give up. It will actually do more harm than good. Under these circumstances muzzled dogs become increasingly agitated and even fearful due to their inability to defend themselves. When the muzzle is finally removed a very serious fight may ensue.

Muzzles should be removed as soon as it seems safe to do so. The owner must then allow the two dogs to work out their own relationship. It is important that the owner does not interfere with the process and remain completely neutral. A dominance hierarchy must be established and it is entirely up to the dogs to work it out. The owner should not try to influence the outcome. There may be some pushing, staring, mounting, growling, minor nipping and many other behaviors that the owner may not like but it is important to say and do nothing unless the situation really looks like it is going to escalate into a full fight.

If you believe that the situation is intensifying you want to stop it before it reaches a flash point by using a "parting behavior" technique. Parting behavior is where a third dog within the pack acts as peacemaker by walking between two potential combatants when tensions are running high. This often has the effect of diffusing the confrontation. It is best not to pull dogs apart; this can often precipitate an attack the instant one dog is pulled away. The owner can simulate parting behavior by calmly walking between the two dogs without saying anything (this must be done **before** a fight starts!).

With a little time the dogs should be able to establish a peaceful relationship on their own. But whatever the outcome, the owner must support the hierarchy that is established by the dogs. For example, be sure to give the dominant dog his or her food first when serving meals or giving treats or allow the dominant dog to be petted more, etc. Any attempt on the part of the owner to change the relationship will most likely result in fighting.

There are about as many ways to introduce two dogs together as there are households with dogs so it is impossible to cover every method here. Some of the most important keys are to never let either dog feel the need to be defensive or suddenly surprised by the appearance of the other dog. Make sure any apprehension that you may be feeling is well masked. Act happy and relaxed, even if you are not. Use plenty of treats to reward any and all good behavior on the part of each dog. One final note is that you should put away any chew toys, bedding or other coveted items at first if you have a very possessive type resident dog. This will help avoid any accidental intrusions by the newcomer and getting the relationship off to a bad start. The items can be brought back out slowly at a later time if all is going well. It is usually best to allow the dogs to work out any possession rights on their own at this point. The resident dog will generally establish the rules with minimal aggression.

- How To Housetrain Your Puppy -

Housetraining is no doubt first on the list of things that you will want to teach your new dog or young puppy. Many people have difficulty with this training. But difficulties are rarely due to the dog. It is simply something that requires great vigilance on the part of the owner. Owners with busy schedules and limited time are going to have the most difficulty. **Housetraining requires constant supervision** by the owner of their new puppy or dog. How long the process will take will depend on many factors and it is a question that cannot really be answered definitively. However, **the fewer mistakes that are made, the faster your puppy or dog will learn. Preventing mistakes is entirely the responsibility of the owner.**

This system was written for puppy training but will work for an older dog too. There are basically six simple rules.

Rule #1 – While housetraining your puppy, **never** leave him unsupervised. Watch your puppy carefully for signs that he needs to eliminate. Usually, he will begin to sniff the floor and walk in circles. With a little practice, you will be able to "sense" when your puppy needs to go outside. Remember it is better to err on the side of caution. Take your puppy out frequently.

Rule #2 – **Every time** your puppy eliminates outside, be sure to reward-mark.[28] You can follow up your reward-mark by giving your puppy a small food treat once he has finished his business.

Rule #3 – If the inevitable happens and you see your puppy starting to urinate or defecate while in the house, say "NO!" in a stern, but not too loud voice (a frightened puppy cannot learn, so don't over react) and take your puppy outside immediately without scolding any further. Once outside, your puppy should finish eliminating. Make sure you reward-mark the correct behavior. Reward when he is finished.

Rule #4 – It is important that you never scold or try to correct your puppy <u>after</u> an accident has occurred. You **must** catch your puppy in the act. If it is even one second after an accident, it is too late. Say nothing to your puppy. Taking your puppy back to the "scene of the crime" will not work. Puppies live in the *here and now* and cannot make a connection between your reprimand and any past event. Your puppy will only be confused if you punish it after the fact. The old so-called remedy of rubbing your puppy's nose in an accident is nothing short of animal cruelty and does nothing but teach your puppy to distrust you.

Rule #5 – **Do not** become angry at your puppy because it had an accident in the house. Anger has no place in any kind of puppy (or dog) training. Remember, if your puppy has an accident, it is your fault for not supervising closely enough. **Getting**

---

[28] It may be advantages for some owners to teach their dog to eliminate on command. This is especially useful to people who must take their dog out on leash each time. There is nothing worse than having to stand outside in inclement weather while your dog, completely oblivious to your discomfort, is distractedly sniffing and exploring instead of doing his business. If you say a particular word **every time** your dog eliminates and then reward him afterwards your dog will soon learn to eliminate on command. Use whatever word you want, "go" or "potty" are commonly used. When your dog learns to associate elimination with your command word you can use it to speed up the process when you are in a hurry.

angry over an accident will just teach your puppy to go off and hide from you when it wants to eliminate, making it harder for you to train.

Rule 6 – If you intend to keep your puppy in the house (recommended) then it should be crate trained. There are many advantages to crate-training your puppy (see *How (And Why) You Should Crate Train Your Puppy*). Utilizing a crate is the **fastest** and **simplest** way to housetrain your puppy. When introduced properly, dogs will perceive a crate as a safe, comfortable den. Crates are not only a convenience for owners, but also a humane and safe way to restrain you puppy as well as being useful throughout your dogs life.

Here are some helpful hints that will make your housetraining easier:

- Puppies will eliminate on a fairly predictable schedule; after vigorous play; after eating or drinking; after waking up from a nap; after being let out of a crate. If you keep this in mind and anticipate when your puppy needs to go outside you will have fewer mistakes in the house. The fewer mistakes you have (error free training), the quicker your puppy will be house-trained.

- Younger puppies need to eliminate more often than older puppies (ask you veterinarian for advice). This is an especially important fact to remember if you are using a crate. Generally, puppies from six to twelve weeks will have only enough control to wait two to a maximum of four hours in a crate. Gradually, with practice, by the time puppies are six months old they can wait as long as seven or eight hours in a crate. After about ten months to a year, a normal, healthy dog can wait at least ten to twelve hours or more before needing to eliminate (provided it has not recently eaten) but should not be in the confines of a crate for such long periods of time.

- Put your puppy on a regular schedule for feeding and watering (ask your veterinarian what is appropriate at your puppy's age). If you stick to the schedule, it becomes very easy to predict when your puppy needs to go outside to eliminate. However, it is prudent to **err on the side of caution; it is better to take your dog outside too often than not often enough.** If you take your dog or puppy out to eliminate often, fewer mistakes will occur and he will learn more rapidly.

- How (And Why) You Should Crate Train Your Puppy -

Why?

A crate-trained dog actually enjoys being in a crate and will often, when given the choice, choose on its own to be in a crate at certain times. Dogs have a very different view of the world than people. Dogs are "den" animals. The fact is, **dogs often feel more secure in a small place when they are resting or become stressed**. Where does a dog go when it is frightened? Usually under a table, a couch or a bed. People frequently consider a crate to be a small jail cell, but dogs (when properly introduced) see it as a den, a safe and comfortable place to rest. For the dog, it is like having his own private room.

Here are just a few practical reasons to crate-train your puppy (Note: Older dogs may be crate-trained as well):

1. If your dog must be kept quiet due to illness or injury.
2. You have visitors (especially small children) who are uncomfortable around dogs.
3. It is the easiest way to house-train your puppy (see *How to Housetrain Your Puppy*).
4. It is the safest way to transport your dog whether it is just around town or on long trips.
5. It provides a safe place to keep a puppy when you cannot directly supervise him, e.g. while you are sleeping at night.
6. It provides your dog with his own private place to "get away from it all."

How?

You must first get a crate appropriate in size and strength for your breed of dog. It can be made of metal or plastic. A dog should be able to fully stand up or lie flat on its side, legs extended, in a properly sized crate.[29] If you are getting a crate for your puppy, you can save money by buying a crate that will be large enough for him as an adult. However, if you are house-training your puppy, you will need to block off part of the crate until your puppy is trained. Make the space just big enough for him to sleep.

Introduce your puppy to his crate in a slow and casual manner. Encourage him to investigate the crate by keeping the door open and placing treats or toys inside. **Never** force your puppy inside the crate. Praise and reward your puppy for any attempt he makes to go inside. At feeding time, you can put the puppy's food bowl inside the crate and have him eat there without closing the door.

Once your puppy is comfortable about going into the crate on his own, lure him in with a treat and close the door for just a few seconds then let your puppy back out and praise. **Slowly** increase the amount of time the puppy stays inside the crate. Begin giving a simultaneous command like "kennel" each time you lure him into his crate. Eventually, you will be able to reduce the number of treats and simply give the command.

You can gradually increase the amount of time the puppy can stay in the crate but do not proceed too quickly. You must be patient. At first, watch your puppy closely. Try to let your puppy out of the crate **before** he reacts to being isolated. Put interesting chew

---

[29] If you have a larger dog then a slightly smaller crate is acceptable for short duration confinement such as traveling across town in a car. Smaller crates are easier to handle and will fit into an automobile more easily. However, a larger crate will be needed for home use or long distance travel.

toys and treats in the crate to keep his attention. Eventually, your puppy should become quite comfortable in the crate and you can then attempt to leave him for an hour or so. It is better if you remain nearby but remain fairly quiet. For example, watch television or read a book.

If your puppy refuses to go into the crate for rewards just place them in front of the crate at whatever distance your puppy is willing to take them. Continue to reward close to the crate but gradually put rewards closer each time. If necessary, decrease the distance one inch at a time. Proceed at your puppy's pace. If he refuses to take food at a critical point, back up your training and feed from a slightly further distance for a while before attempting to go closer. Eventually your puppy will lose his fear of the crate and go in readily for treats. You can then begin closing the door briefly as described above.

Once your puppy is staying in the crate for short lengths of time there are three rules that must be followed:

Rule #1 – Never leave a recently fed or watered puppy in a crate. Most puppies will need to eliminate within a half hour of drinking or eating. Before putting your puppy away in a crate for any length of time make sure he has been allowed to eliminate first.

Rule #2 – When locking your puppy in a crate, never exceed the amount of time appropriate for your puppy's age (check with your veterinarian or refer to *How To Housetrain Your Puppy*).

Rule #3 – Unless it is a real emergency, **never** take your puppy out of the crate when it is whining or barking. If you do, he will learn to whine and bark incessantly while in the crate. **Do not** scold or say anything to your puppy while it is whining or barking in the crate, just ignore him. This may take an iron will on your part, but remember that dogs are often better at training humans than the other way around. If you remain resolute, the whining and barking behavior will extinguish itself in time. **When your puppy stops whining or barking, be sure to wait at least one full minute before taking him out of the crate.** This is to leave sufficient time for him to associate quiet behavior with being let out of the crate.

During the first few weeks I suggest keeping a crate near by at all times and place treats in it without your dog knowing. Allow him to find the treats on his own. If you follow all the above procedures and rules, before long your puppy will be going into the crate voluntarily to take naps or on command whenever you decide.

If you keep your dog or puppy in a crate for long periods of time, it is vital that the crate be very roomy to allow your pet to move around. This is especially important for growing puppies whose bones and muscles are still forming. I do not believe that a dog should spend any more time in a crate than is necessary. Overnight confinement is fine but if you are away for long periods of time during the day as well you need to provide a better place for your pet to stay. Dogs do sleep most of the time that you are not around but they get up to change position or location occasionally. Dogs are indeed den animals but that does not mean that they spend all their time there.

- How To Stop Your Puppy From Chewing -

Good News, Bad News

First the bad news; actually you can't stop your puppy from chewing. Now the good news: chewing *can* be redirected to appropriate objects. Chewing is a natural behavior for puppies that help them develop strong jaws and teeth. Puppies investigate the world with their mouth. Chewing can also be an important energy outlet for your puppy. Trying to stop your puppy from chewing is not advisable or possible. The best approach is to provide your puppy with chew toys and teach him to chew only on these objects.

To your puppy, the whole house is full of perfectly good chewing objects, such as furniture, carpets, shoes, houseplants, lamp cords or your dirty laundry! If you leave your puppy unattended then you should expect him to chew on things. You cannot get angry with him because you have not taught him what objects he can chew. Also, some things are dangerous for your puppy to chew. Puppies can easily chew through lamp cords and be electrocuted. Other objects may be toxic. Early on, it is strongly advised that you confine your puppy to a "puppy proofed" room. Do not allow him to roam the entire house. When you are unable to watch your puppy he must be in a safe place like a crate.

What To Do

- Crate-train your puppy. It is almost impossible to watch your puppy constantly. You need a safe place for him when you are unable to directly supervise his play. If you do not want to crate-train, then you must provide your puppy with a secure, escape proof areas where he can be safely left alone.
- Have on hand several chew toys, e.g. hard rubber toys, Nylabone™, **raw** beef bones (**important: never cooked!**), etc.[30]
- When you catch your puppy chewing on something inappropriate, firmly say "no" and immediately take him away from the object. Then present your puppy with one of the chew toys. As soon as he begins chewing on the toy, praise him with petting and soothing words.
- Always supervise your puppy closely. You must be vigilant and catch him in the act of chewing inappropriate objects. It does no good to scold a puppy after he has chewed something up and already abandoned the item. **You must catch him in the act.**
- Never leave tempting items around for your puppy to chew on. Keep small objects out of reach.
- Be consistent and persistent and your puppy will soon learn which items he is allowed to chew.

Some Helpful Hints

When your puppy begins to lose his puppy teeth for adult teeth, his gums will be sore. Take some old washcloths, wet them, and put them in the freezer. After freezing, give

---

[30] Make sure chew toys are safe. Some items may be safe for your young puppy to chew but not an older puppy with adult teeth. Ask your vet to be certain. I strongly suggest raw beef bones but some veterinarians may not agree. Never give your dog a cooked bone of any kind. Cooked bones become hard and brittle. Older dogs can break or chip teeth these hard bones and they can cause severe damage to the intestinal tract. Most raw bones are softer and will not present any problems. Relatively thin rib bones are better than large leg or "knuckle" bones. (For more on feeding bones see chapter 15, **Food For Thought**).

them to your puppy from time to time to chew on. The cold cloth will help relieve some of the discomfort. Supervise this activity however. As soon as the washcloth has thawed out, take it away from your puppy so he does not continue to chew and accidentally ingest some of the cloth.

Rawhide "bones" and pig ears may or may not be as safe for young puppies as some other chew toys. There is some controversy about giving these to your dog. I believe supervised chewing of these items is okay for puppies but suggest that you check with your veterinarian for advice before giving these items to your adult dog.

Important! Practice taking your puppy's chew toy away on different occasions, then give it back after a few seconds or better yet replace it with another special treat. Why? Many dogs will become aggressively possessive of their toys (or food). These dogs are dangerous and may bite anyone, especially small children, who may innocently reach for the toy. Sometimes, just touching a dog while he has a toy is enough to trigger the bite reflex. This is one of the leading causes of dog bites.

This kind of aggression (often called possession aggression) is common. It can occur in any size or breed of dog. It is best to prevent this kind of aggression by training early, showing your puppy that there is no threat when a human takes away his toy (because he always gets it back or a better treat instead), then he will not learn to guard objects. The exercise is relatively safe with a small puppy but only an adult should initiate this kind of training.

Above: A puppy chewing on a toy. Chewing is an important energy outlet for young dogs and puppies. It is an essential activity that contributes to their proper physical and psychological development. Owners should not, and cannot, stop their puppy from chewing. Instead, owners must provide and then direct their dog to appropriate items for chewing. Ask your veterinarian for advice on appropriate chewing items.

- How To Stop Your Puppy From Biting -

Biting or nipping behavior of puppies is normal. The frequency of the habit will diminish as the puppy gets older but some bad habits may extend into adulthood if proper steps are not taken. Puppies need to learn "bite inhibition." This is a natural process that all puppies learn in a normal social setting.

Puppies must learn to reduce the amount of pressure that they apply with their jaws. This is a surprisingly easy thing for dogs to learn. A mother dog has jaws powerful enough to chew through a bone and yet she can be gentle enough to pick up and carry a fragile puppy without harm. When dogs play together they frequently bite one another and yet do not pierce the skin.

Most puppies first learn bite inhibition while they are still with their littermates. It is inevitable that play will escalate and become rough at some point. One puppy will get overly excited and bite its littermate too hard. Its littermate will yelp and squeal loudly. It is quite startling. The bitten littermate will stop playing and move away. The offending puppy is surprised by the sound of its littermate and finds itself without a playmate. A lesson has been learned; do not bite hard while playing.

Bite inhibition is a survival instinct inherited from the wolf ancestor. When the pack is playing together no one wants to suffer an inadvertent life threatening injury. Well-socialized adult dogs rarely bite one another too hard during play but the same pressure that can be safely applied to another dog will cause considerable pain for a human.

We must teach our dogs that human skin is quite sensitive. It is an easy process when your dog is still a puppy. Mouthy (not aggressive), older dogs can also be taught to have a "softer mouth" but it may prove to be a somewhat more painful process for the trainer.

To teach bite inhibition we must simulate the natural process. When a puppy bites you should instantly yell "ouch!" preferably in a very loud, startling and high-pitched voice. Immediately move away from your puppy and ignore him. After a few seconds you can resume play but be prepared to repeat the exercise at any moment.

You do not have to wait for your puppy to bite on his own. You can initiate the exercise by intentionally putting your hand in the puppy's mouth. The instant you feel any pressure yell "ouch!" and pull your hand away. Make a special point of ignoring your puppy for a few seconds. Being a good actor is a plus during this exercise. Pretend that you really got hurt even if there was barely any pressure. You want your puppy to think that his teeth should never even come in contact with your skin.

Some puppies like to grab hold of your pant leg or shirtsleeve. When this happens do not get into a tug of war with your puppy because he will find that very rewarding. Instead, yell "ouch!" as if you were bitten or if you prefer "no!" and grab your puppy by the collar. If he does not immediately let go of your clothing, carefully and calmly extract his teeth from the cloth and quickly put him in an isolated safe area. A playpen or safe room is perfect but a crate will do if that is all you have. **Do not continue to scold your puppy. Just react swiftly and firmly.**

It is important that your puppy not consider being put in the crate or safe area as a punishment. There should be plenty of access to distractions in the area such as chew toys that will help your puppy redirect his energies. Let your puppy back out after a couple of minutes of isolation if he is being quiet. (Never let your puppy out if he is barking or whining.) Be prepared to repeat the exercise as many times as necessary.[31]

It is important to **always** react in the manner just described to a play bite from your puppy. It is also important that everyone in your family react in the same way. Small children in the family must be taught how to react but only an adult should put the puppy in isolation (adults should always be supervising puppies and small children anyway). Older children may be less inclined to bother with bite inhibition training. They often simply put up with the biting as part of the fun. Even if the bite does not really hurt, they must pretend that it does. Parents should explain carefully how important the training is so that their dog does not grow up to nip people when it is an adult, which can be very painful.

---

[31] Many owners become discouraged when their puppy goes right back to biting as soon as he is released again. Do not be discouraged. It is simply an opportunity to train through repetition. Repetitious training will ultimately be the most effective.

- How To Stop Your Puppy From Jumping Up -
Things To Consider

Actually, many owners do not mind their puppies jumping up on them. They find it cute! At least it is cute until the puppy grows up and some of the novelty wears off. Jumping up on you may be fine when you have on old clothes. But when you are in good clothes, do not expect your puppy to know the difference or be able to realize her feet are muddy after she has just been running around on a wet lawn. Puppies often grow up to be large dogs that can cause others to fall, especially children and older persons. The time to teach your dog not to jump up is while it is still a puppy. A dog at any age can be taught not to jump up, but it is much easier to do while it is still a puppy.

For those owners who would like to allow their dog to jump up, I would advise them to reconsider. If your dog jumps up on you it may not be a problem but what about other people. Friends or relatives may not be quite so enamored with your dog. Large dogs can easily knock people down. Some people are terrified of dogs and even friendly jumping will send them into a panic.

It is best to teach a dog not to jump up. Later, when the dog is more mature, you can teach a command that allows your dog to put her paws on you. This is simple to do but you must have patience and wait until your dog fully understands not to jump up first.

Jumping up is a natural greeting behavior for your dog. If you watch puppies greet their mother or even another familiar adult dog, they will jump up and try to lick the mouth. Wolf puppies will lick the mouth of their mother and other wolves to get them to regurgitate food for them.[32] Licking the face becomes a standard greeting and this instinctual behavior is well preserved in dogs.

Because we are so much taller than dogs, they will jump up to try to get to our face. This is just normal behavior for your puppy. You must teach your dog a different greeting. This greeting involves keeping all four feet on the ground.

There are many ways to train your puppy not to jump up. There are both aversive methods and reward-based methods. While aversive methods can get results, an inexperienced owner could inadvertently injure their dog, especially a puppy. Because this is perfectly natural behavior for your dog, aversive training is more likely to seriously undermine your relationship with your dog. She may learn to distrust you, which makes future training much more difficult.

When a dog is greeting you it wants reassurance. Most people mistakenly believe that the tail wagging is a sign of happiness. Happiness may be involved but a wagging tail during a greeting is actually a sign of some insecurity. Owners need not feel guilty about this. A dog is naturally insecure during reunions or when they are trying to get some response from you. Jumping up, licking and tail wagging is a dog's way of asking you to reassure her that everything is all right. When we punish our dogs for jumping up we are confusing them. With reinforcement training though, you can show your dog how to get the reassurance by simply altering the greeting ritual.

---

[32] Licking the face to solicit food has a significant biosocial importance. This behavior marks the beginning of the weaning process. It re-directs the attention of the puppy from the mother's teats to the face. Wolves and dogs use numerous facial expressions to communicate with one another. Young puppies soliciting for food learn to focus on the face and begin to learn facial language. Attention exercises will be discussed later in this book but the idea of attention work is to get your dog to focus on your face.

What To Do

Never pet your puppy when it jumps up on you. Even pushing her away will only serve to encourage her to jump more. That is just a form of rough play. Instead, **always** turn your back and either stand still or walk away. **Do not** say anything. Simply pretend to ignore her. If your puppy has been in the habit of jumping up for a while, then she may not give up easily. Just be patient and do not even look directly at your puppy. Eventually, she will stop jumping. The instant she does stop, praise and pet her. Give her a small treat if you have one. If she starts to jump up again, stop all praise and petting immediately and ignore her once again.

The usual pattern is that your dog will jump on you then you ignore her. She stops jumping so you bend down to pet her. The instant you start to pet her she begins to jump again. You should go back to ignoring her immediately. You may have to repeat this sequence several times before you actually get to pet her. That is okay. She is learning to control herself.

Some Training Hints

Warning! Dogs are notoriously adept at training their owners! Your dog enjoys jumping on you, so you must be the trainer, not the trainee. Because jumping is a greeting and soliciting behavior they want you to pet them. You must show them that the only way for them to get what they want (petted or maybe an occasional treat) is by greeting you without jumping up.

Everyone in your family must train your puppy not to jump up by following the same procedure as described above. Dogs do not generalize well. Just because your puppy has learned not to jump up on you does not mean she will not jump up on others. How many times have you seen a dog that will not jump up on Dad, but Mom and the kids are fair game? Your dog must be taught that jumping up on people is never allowed and is a universal rule. By practicing with several different people your dog will eventually learn that jumping up is never a good option.

Be **persistent** and **consistent**. Do not make the mistake of petting your puppy "just this one time" while she is jumping up. This will only confuse your puppy and prolong the problem.

It is a good idea to teach your puppy an alternate behavior. For example, teach your puppy to sit as a greeting instead of jumping up. It sounds too simple, but it works. When your puppy comes to greet you wait until she sits then pet and praise her (reinforcing the behavior with an occasional treat is also a good idea). The instant she gets up, stop petting her. If she sits down again pet her. Soon your puppy will offer the behavior on her own without being told each time she greets you.

The same procedures will work on adult dogs however it may take longer to eliminate the behavior. Adult dogs that are jumping up have probably been doing it for a very long time and like all habits can be very difficult to change. If the owner perseveres the jumping up will slowly be extinguished.

- When To Say No -

The word "no" can be used as a negative reward-mark to let a dog know that its behavior is counterproductive. In other words, if I say "no" to my dog she will realize that she is <u>not</u> going to receive a reward. Aversive trainers will couple the word "no" with a punishment. I have already made clear my reservations about aversive training so I will not belabor the point at this time.

I strongly recommend that the word "no" be used **sparingly**. It should be reserved for special circumstances. The use of "no" should be entirely eliminated in training except for a few rare exceptions, e.g., housetraining or nipping clothes. Most owners over use the word "no" resulting in what is known as "learned irrelevance." Essentially, learned irrelevance is when your dog hears a word over and over so much that it no longer has significant meaning.

Generally when we are training a dog we want to focus on the positive aspects of their behavior and not the negative. Rewarding good behavior and ignoring bad is the standard rule. However, certain behaviors will not be extinguished by ignoring them. For example, when a dog urinates on the carpet or decides to jump up on the bed. Ignoring these behaviors will not make them go away.

Under these circumstances the word "no" is appropriate but it should **always be followed** up by appropriate corrective action. In the case of a dog urinating on the carpet a command of "no" can be given but the dog must immediately be taken to an appropriate location to urinate. A dog that jumps on the bed can be told "no" but must immediately be lead off the bed and back to the floor or perhaps to its own mat. (Keep in mind that it is always a good idea to reinforce the proper behavior with a reward even if you did most of the work.)

Conversely, you should never say "no" if you ask your dog to lie down and it sits instead. As you will see later you should say and do nothing, just wait for the proper behavior before rewarding. Saying "no" when training a new behavior is especially damaging. It can totally confuse and frustrate your dog. Learning should be fun. The word "no" generally means that the fun is over. We do not want our dog to think that the fun is over during training.

- House Rules -

Every home will have its own special rules. There may be places or furniture where your dog is not allowed. Perhaps your dog is only allowed to be in a certain room or cannot freely go outside without your permission. This is fine. Mostly these are all a form of "boundary training" where dogs learn certain limits and restrictions.

Because every house can have its own set of rules it would be impossible to give specific instructions on how to teach every rule. A few examples of the most common rules will be provided here. Owners with other rules will have to develop their own training exercises based on what they have learned from these examples and other information in this book. Most house rules can be taught by controlling the environment to promote errorless learning. For example, if you do not want your dog to learn to chew on your shoes, never leave your shoes out. After a year or so your dog will probably never even think of chewing on a shoe, even if you accidentally leave them out one day.

I have only one rule for dog owners. **Keep your expectations realistic.** Some owners expect too much from their dog. While dogs can be trained to do many things, there are limits to their abilities. Make sure your demands do not exceed those limits. Some owners put so many restrictions on their dog that I often wonder why they have a dog in the first place. Keep your rules reasonable and let your dog be a dog, not a prisoner.

Door-Manners

One of the most useful rules is door-manners if your dog likes to rush the door as soon as it is opened. A well-mannered dog should wait until invited to go through a door.[33] If you loose control of your dog when she goes out the door it may be wise to put a leash on for safety when you first teach this exercise. **Do not use the leash to control your dog**, only to keep her from getting away should she get outside. You can have a second person hold the leash if you would prefer but no tension should be on the leash during the training.

Go to the door and put your hand on the handle as if you were going to leave. If your dog is like most, she will rush to the door in anticipation of going out. As soon as that happens take your hand away from the handle. Wait for your dog to settle or back away from the door (as long as it takes). Put your hand back on the handle. Be prepared to repeat the exercise until your dog no longer responds to your hand on the door handle.

The next step is to actually turn the handle. If your dog rushes the door release the handle once again and start over. When you are able to turn the handle with no reaction from your dog then open the door only slightly, half and inch or less if necessary. As soon as your dog rushes the door close it once again. Repeat the exercise until you get no reaction from your dog. Then try opening the door a little wider, perhaps one or two inches, closing it immediately if your dog rushes to the opening. (Be quick but careful not to close the door on your dog) Continue the progression until you can open the door wide enough for you to pass through without your dog reacting.

At this point you are ready for the next step, literally. Try stepping through the door opening. If your dog rushes, you must either close the door completely again or close it partially and block the opening with your body to prevent your dog from escaping. Eventually, you will be able to step out the door, turn around and come back in without your dog moving. You can usually reach this point in training the very first session but practice it several more times that day or over the next two or three successive days.

Notice that you have not been instructed to say anything to your dog. There is no need for a command. If you are going out a door your dog should learn to simply wait for you to go through first. While training avoid saying anything, especially using the word

---

[33] Some trainers train this behavior as part of "rank reduction" therapy. The idea is that if you have a "dominant" dog, one of the ways to reduce his dominance is to reduce his rank in the "pack." Teaching him to wait for you to go out the door first is considered one way of achieving rank reduction. I believe this may be a classic case of anthropomorphic thinking. In human society we allow a person to go through a door first to show respect. Dogs are not likely to grasp this concept. Consider that wolves allow subordinate members of the pack to take the lead when hunting. This probably has biosocial significance. Lead members on a hunt are in the most vulnerable position should prey animals decide to fight. Since subordinate wolves do not breed, they are the most expendable in terms of genetic survival. Perhaps in wolf society subordinate wolves take the lead out of "respect" for dominant members. Dogs are more likely to have a wolf's view of the world than a human view. Perhaps going out the door first is really a self-sacrificing gesture of deference to a dog. Should this be the case, teaching door manners, as a form of "rank reduction," would be counterproductive. I teach this behavior primarily for convenience and safety reasons but if rank reduction were the goal, I would suggest teaching the dog to wait while the door is opened. The owner could then allow their dog to go through first but only on command.

"no." Remember, you want to reserve the "no" command for special occasions. There simply is no reason to use the command during this exercise.

Once your dog is willingly waiting at the door as you pass through, it is time to allow your dog to follow you. Once you are outside, call your dog to you or give a "free" command (see recalls and stays). Add some unpredictability to your routine. Instead of going out the door and calling your dog right away, you should close the door behind you, then open it again and call. Or, walk through, wait for a few seconds, then call your dog. Make a special point of being unpredictable not only during training this exercise but throughout your dog's life. If any problems develop do not hesitate to back up in your training steps.

Table Manners

As I have mentioned before, dogs are great trainers. And as I have also mentioned, food treats are a great motivator for dogs. Combine the two and you have some real trouble on your hands. Most owners do not want their dog to beg for food at the table. It is actually a very easy behavior to control, especially with puppies.

Like most social conduct, controlling resources is the key. Simply **never** feed your dog while you are eating. Do not let your dog train you by coming over and giving you his best "sad dog" look. The moment you reward this behavior he has actually trained you. He will come back again and again to give you his signal to feed him, which is the "sad dog" look.

If you have small children a problem sometimes occurs when food is dropped on the floor. Your dog will be there in an instant to snap up the treat. You may not mind your dog doing this after dinner is finished but during the meal it is unacceptable. You will have to teach him to stay away while you eat. A "stay" or "place" command will be discussed in Chapter 12. These commands will help you control this particular behavior. Alternatively, you can put your dog in his crate during meals.

Whether you teach the place, stay or put your dog in a crate, I recommend that you allow your dog to see you while you eat. This may seem cruel to our human sensibilities but there is actually nothing wrong with making your dog wait while you eat. In fact it may even help to affirm your dog's social bond to you and your family. Subordinate wolves always allow dominant members to eat first. This does not mean I am suddenly favoring pack theory training. I only mean that I believe that dogs come genetically pre-programmed to wait for their meal while others eat and that it does not harm our relationship with them in anyway. I like to feed my dogs soon after I have eaten as a sort of reward for them being well mannered during my own meal.

In essence, the best way to teach your dog not to beg is to never allow him to get anything to eat while you are eating. He will easily accept this rule if you always enforce it. Watch out for accidental reinforcement of begging, like dropped or worse stolen food when your back is turned. You must be vigilant and convince your dog that you are always aware of what he is doing.

Once again this is a form of errorless learning. Prevention is the best approach but if you already have a begging dog, the same rules apply. It may take him a while to accept that he is not going to be fed but eventually he will give up. You simply must be more determined than he is and never give in to his begging behavior.

Boundary Restrictions

Some owners want to restrict their dog to one or two rooms or perhaps have certain rooms be off-limits. Once again, controlling the environment is the best way to do this. Just keep doors shut or put up gates to prevent the dog from entering restricted areas. After enough time has passed with errorless learning the gates and doors can be opened.

The chances are very good that your dog will not go into the rooms that have been blocked for a long time. However, you will need to be vigilant. If she goes into the room, then you must use your "no" command and quickly bring your dog out of the restricted area. It is really as simple as that. Most dogs will learn this easily.

The amount of time it will take can vary depending on the individual dog and environment. Young puppies are keen on exploring their world. It may be advisable to maintain barriers for two or three months. A mature, laid-back kind of dog may learn in a couple of weeks. However, if your dog has had access to an area in the past and you suddenly want to impose a restriction, this could take a very long time but it will eventually work.

Be sure to supervise your dog carefully when you first open doors or gates to ensure that you can correct any trespassing immediately. When you cannot supervise it is advisable to keep doors and gates closed until you are certain your dog will not go into the restricted areas. If you are not sure when to open the gates you can experiment occasionally just to see how your dog reacts to the open doors and gates. (Caution: You want to stand nearby right at first to avoid any errors. If you open doors and gates prematurely and do not watch your dog carefully, each error will set you back in your training.) If she is showing any interest at all in going into restricted areas, then keep doors and gates closed for a few weeks more before trying again.

If you cannot put up a gate or close a door to restricted areas then you will have a somewhat more difficult task. You will need to supervise your dog closely and constantly. Give the "no" command each time your dog enters a restricted area and bring her back out. If you ever see her voluntarily stop at a boundary be sure to praise and give her a jackpot reward.

The drawback to this method is that you can never leave your dog unsupervised until the training is complete. This may take from a few weeks to several months depending on the dog and the environment. Puppies may take longer to boundary train because they are often much more curious than older dogs. The training period may have to be extended if the environment in the restricted area is highly attractive to the dog.

This may all seem like a lot of trouble. You will need to decide which is more problematic for you, having restricted areas or unlimited access. If unlimited access is going to be too much of a problem then the few weeks or even months of training will pay off in the long haul. Remember your dog will be with you for ten to fifteen years or more. A few weeks of inconvenience while you train is a small price to pay for fifteen years of good behavior.

With patience and consistency most any dog can be boundary trained. It is probably an inherited trait from their wolf relatives who have and maintain home territories. The key for training is to keep errors to a minimum. What you are doing is establishing good habits. Dogs are strongly habitual animals, thus making them easy to train.

Furniture Manners

Once again, individual house rules vary. Some owners allow their dog on the furniture and others do not. Some allow their dog on only certain pieces of furniture. Generally, toy breeds are more likely to be allowed on furniture than larger breeds. Whatever you decide is fine but I would strongly recommend that you train your dog carefully to comply with the rules.

The best approach, regardless of what rules you will have in the future, is to train your dog *not* to get on the furniture first. Once this habit is solidly established the owner can then invite his or her dog onto the couch, bed or other furniture on special occasions. By controlling access to the furniture you will avoid a sometimes serious behavioral problem, a form of possession aggression, where dogs actually chase owners from their own chair.

Early training is essential. You should begin as soon as you get your dog or puppy. Do not allow a problem to develop first. **Prevention is the best solution**. The method is really the same as boundary training. Supervise your dog closely and do not allow her to get on the furniture. If she does, say, "off," and lead her back to the floor.

Do not use the word "down" to mean get off the furniture. "Down" is the command that we will use to teach our dogs to lie down. If you teach your dog a down and then say, "down," to her when she is on the couch your dog is likely to comply by lying *down* on the couch! Use the word "off" to avoid any confusion.

It is helpful if you have comfortable bedding for your dog in each room that you are going to be training in, at least initially. Every time you correct your dog for being on the furniture you should **take her to her own bed. This is especially effective if you give her a treat** that may take a little longer to chew, like a raw bone or a hard dog biscuit. The idea is that you want her to associate her bed with something pleasurable.

Never get angry at your dog if she gets on the furniture. Simply give her a firm "off" command and lead her (do not drag her in anger) off the couch.[34] Each time you see her lying on the floor near the couch or in her own bed, be sure to praise and give her an occasional treat. If you allow yourself to get angry or handle your dog roughly during corrections, she is more likely to learn how to avoid you by sneaking on the furniture only when you are not around.

Bear in mind that you will not be able to allow your dog free roam of the house until you are confident that she is fully trained. Close supervision is essential in order to achieve errorless training. Later, if you decide that you want to allow your dog on the furniture you can coax her up while you are in the room. You should be able to ask your dog to get off the furniture at anytime. Practice by giving a treat each time you ask her to "off." If you do not want your dog to get on the furniture when you are not around, then it is best not to allow them on it at all. However, always provide a comfortable alternative.

---

[34] If you have a "stubborn" dog that refuses to move when you try to lead them, you may do one of two things. If your dog is small enough, go ahead and lift your dog off the furniture if she does not comply with your command. If your dog is larger, or shows any sign of aggression (**never attempt to correct aggression with force, it will only exacerbate the problem**), lure her off with a special treat. Give the "off" command at the same time you offer the treat and lure her to the floor.

House Manners

Left: Smaller dogs are often allowed on the furniture in many homes whereas larger dogs are not. The decision is entirely up to the individual owner but they must be consistent. The dog cannot know that he is not allowed on furniture when his feet are dirty when other times it is okay. Whatever the rules are, the dog must be trained to obey them.

Above: The author's two dogs, Jack and Pepper, wait at an open door for permission to go out. This is one of the more important house manners that all dogs should be taught. Fortunately, it is very easy to train. Eliminating escape behavior is not just a convenience, it could save your dog's life.

- How and Why You Should Socialize Your Puppy -
What?

What does it mean to socialize your puppy? Socializing means exposing your puppy to as many different kinds of people (tall, short, children, babies, adults, males, females, white, black, loud, quiet, etc.) and different environments (outdoors, indoors, steps, ramps, tile floors, elevators, loud noises, whistles, bells, crowded cities, veterinarian's office, examination tables, bicycles, motorcycles, trucks, cars both inside and out, etc.) and other dogs as is possible.

Why?

Dog owners should not underestimate the importance of socialization. Properly socialized puppies grow up to be well-adjusted, stable dogs. Dogs that are not socialized are fearful, nervous and can be difficult to train. Properly socialized dogs can be trusted around children and other people. They are comfortable in any setting or situation. It is especially important for owners of protection dog breeds to socialize their puppies. Many good protection dogs are ruined by not having them properly socialized. These dogs may become dangerous, unpredictable fear biters instead of reliable, confident family guardians.

When?

The critical period for socialization begins when the puppy is about four weeks old. They are most easily socialized from then until around twelve weeks age. The puppy's ability to be socialized begins to slow down at this point. By the time the puppy is about eight to ten months old, the window of *easy* socialization has all but closed. After around ten months of age it becomes much more difficult to socialize a dog to new situations. **It is important to begin socializing your puppy from a very early age.** Time is your enemy. **Note:** While exposure to the environment is very good for a young puppy mentally, it does come with some risk. Until your puppy has been fully immunized it is susceptible to certain diseases that can be transmitted to them, either directly or indirectly, by other dogs. It is best to ask your veterinarian for advice on exposure restrictions at your puppy's particular age and immunization level. Keep in mind that you must weigh the risks with the benefits.

How?

By the time you understand "what, why" and "when" you will pretty much know how. Just expose your puppy to as many new situations as your imagination and time allow. You cannot do too much socializing assuming you observe adequate health and safety precautions. Some precautionary measures may be having children and other people wash their hands before handling young puppies to prevent the spread of disease. **Always** supervise children closely. If you are exposing your puppy to other puppies, be sure that they are all adequately immunized (check with your vet for recommendations). If you are exposing your puppy to an adult dog, be sure it **has had all** its shots and is dog friendly.

Never force your puppy to do anything. If your puppy is unsure of something try to entice him with a toy or treat. If you see him overcome his apprehension of something, praise him for his bravery and give him a treat. If you see him startle or avoid something,

do nothing! If you try to reassure your puppy when he is afraid, he will think that his behavior is appropriate. **Ignore timid or frightened behavior, but reward bravery.** Remember; use enticement techniques to help your puppy overcome unwarranted fears.

Be sure to socialize your puppy to common "real world" experiences. In particular, visits to the vet and groomer. Practice these events, i.e., play "doctor" using lots of treats and encouragement. While petting your dog frequently open your puppy's mouth to examine the teeth. Handle and look inside your dog's ears. Touch and handle your dog's paws, legs and tail. All of these things can become part of a normal petting routine. Your dog will actually enjoy the attention as much as the petting itself.

If your dog is sensitive to anything, proceed slowly and be patient. Get your puppy used to the idea in stages. For example, if your puppy does not like you to look into his ears (and your vet has ruled out an ear infection) begin by just lightly touching the ears and rewarding. Over several days gradually touch the ears more and more, rewarding each time. Eventually your puppy will look forward to you touching his ears. You can gradually "shape" the behavior until you are able to examine the ears thoroughly.

Have other people examine your puppy as well. Ask friends or neighbors to "play doctor" while you stand by. Give your puppy plenty of treats and praise. Your puppy will soon be completely comfortable and relaxed while being examined by anyone, including the veterinarian.

Most good breeders will already have your puppy well socialized to standard types of handling; brushing, nail trimming and baths in particular. You should continue to reinforce these routine events by making them very pleasant for your puppy each time. But, if you find that your puppy does not like to be brushed or have his nails trimmed or take a bath, you will need to work on these things slowly.

Always start at a point where your dog is comfortable and slowly "shape" the behavior. For example if your dog does not like a bath you could perhaps start off by feeding your dog next to the bathtub each day for a while. Then, try feeding your dog in the tub without water for a while. Eventually, you could put just a little water in the tub and feed your dog there. Over several days keep increasing the amount of water in the tub. Eventually, you could start to pour a small amount of water from the tub on his leg, then back.

Alternatively, you can use a toy. Play games with a toy near an empty tub. Eventually get your dog to go in the tub to play with the toy. Then follow the same procedure as above.

Each situation is going to be different and require an individualized training program but the idea is to start at a point where your dog does not feel threatened and then keep increasing the criteria gradually. You must proceed at your dog's pace. Be prepared to back up in the training at any time you get a negative reaction. Patience and lots of rewards will soon change your dog's view of the situation (it is called counter-conditioning and desensitization). This kind of appetitive approach can take your dog from disliking a particular situation to actually being enthusiastically in favor of it in a successful training program (see *The Fearful Dog* in the following section).

It is unfortunate that our society is rather polarized when it comes to feelings about dogs. While many are ambivalent, studies show that the majority of people in the United States either love or hate dogs. The "dog lovers" are on the rise but the anti-dog portion of our population is much more vociferous. As a result more and more restrictive laws, ordinances and regulations have been imposed on dogs and their owners.[35] This has actually made it more difficult to socialize dogs properly and thoroughly.

The more places you can go and the more things that you can do with your dog the better. While socialization has an initial critical period during the early years, you need to expose your dog to as many social situations as possible throughout his life. If you are lucky enough to be able to take your dog to work with you then I strongly recommend doing so. Your dog can, and should, learn how to function in everyday society. Many work situations are perfect settings.

Before you take your dog to work, parks or any other public areas, come prepared. While your dog needs to function in socially acceptable ways, so do owners. Do not allow your dog to soil private lawns or public areas or become any kind of nuisance. Bring disposable clean up bags and other items that will help you clean up messes. Of course you should maintain control of your dog at all times. Besides having common sense good manners it will be your civic duty to know and abide by any local laws, ordinances and regulations.

If there were more well-mannered dogs out in the public view, perhaps the voice of "dog lovers" would be heard and fewer restrictions would be imposed. But to do this, owners will need to take full responsibility by properly training and controlling their dog's behavior.

The Fearful Dog

I would like to take a little time to write about fearful dogs because it is a misunderstood and often overlooked facet of dog behavior. It is a subject that is near and dear to my heart because one of my personal dogs is a "rescue" that came to me as a severely fearful dog. The fearful dog is really quite common, more common than many people think. Dog owners often do not even recognize that their own dog is actually fearful. The problem stems from the fact that many dogs mask their fear, at least to a lot of human observers, with aggressive behavior.

Perhaps it may seem somewhat counter-intuitive but fearful dogs represent more of a serious risk than fearless dogs. Early socialization during the critical stage as a puppy is the best way to prevent the development of a fearful dog but many of us get older puppies or dogs that are already fearful. The vast majority of these dogs can still be socialized but the training will be more focused and specialized.

The "fight or flight" reflex in dogs is strong. Many dogs choose "fight" when dealing with fear but most people think that the dog is just mean or vicious, when in fact the dog is really afraid and dealing with the situation the only way he knows how. Many of the so-called "aggressive" dogs are essentially fearful. Also, most fearful dogs are indecisive about whether they should run away or stand and fight.

Some dogs do prefer flight over fight and simply run away from a stressful situation. A few dogs, when severely frightened may completely shut down and go completely rigid when alarmed. Fear is easily recognized in these two types of dogs.

---

[35] The irony of more restrictions is that owners of dogs are forced to keep their pets more isolated, which makes dogs even less capable of proper social behavior. Anti-dog legislation has even gone so far as to include legal bans on certain breeds. People who really do not know very much about dogs are perhaps the ones who are making up the laws. It is kind of like having a person making up rules for driving on the road but they have never driven a car.

A dog that barks aggressively at strangers is most likely being fearful, especially if the dog also has raised hackles and is growling. I have had the opportunity to work with several dogs that were superbly trained in "protection" work. This kind of training is a subject not suited for this book but there are some important lessons that can be learned from protection training. I was always struck with the fact that the best protection dogs never barked at me unless they were told to do so. (They also never bit me until told to do so. Of course, I had protective equipment on at the time.)

Many more times than I should, I come across people with dogs that they believe are good "guard" dogs because they bark, growl and raise their hackles whenever a stranger comes near. These owners do not want their dog to actually bite a person under normal circumstances but just scare them. However, most seem to think that their dog would actually protect them if they were attacked.

The fact is, dogs that are barking at virtually every stranger or slight sounds near the house are afraid. The barking is a way of relieving stress, alerting the owners (so they can come and help chase away the intruder) and a show of bravado that is choreographed to frighten off the stranger without any real contact.

While it is hard for owners to believe, the romantic notion of their dog coming to their rescue in time of real need is highly unlikely with these dogs. Most dogs would not come to the owners rescue if a stranger attacked them. The dog might stay around and bark from a safe distance but few would actually attack, especially with any degree of effectiveness. True protection dogs must be trained to bite. It takes many months and sometimes years of intense training to properly teach a protection dog to bite effectively.

I know most of you right now are thinking, "He doesn't know my dog" and firmly believe that your dog would rise to the occasion should anyone really threaten or attack you. Well, perhaps, but I would still caution you that the odds are not in your favor. The reason it is unlikely is because of what separates the well-trained protection dog from the typical "junkyard" dog (No offense, I am not calling your dog a "junkyard" dog, I am merely using the term as an example). The biggest difference can be summed up in one word, **confidence**.

Fearful dogs that do bite almost always bite while a person is in retreat or if they feel cornered and have no avenue of escape. Children are bitten more often than adults. The fearful dog will assess each perceived threat and decide whether to run or fight. It feels more confident attacking a smaller threat, so children are more vulnerable. Few untrained dogs would intentionally confront an adult head on. "Fear biters" are by far the most common culprits in attacks on human beings.

When training protection dogs, a large portion of the training (actually in a good program it permeates nearly all the training) involves building confidence. A dog that is not confident will not bite or will bite poorly and is difficult to control. The irony is that dogs that are not trained are far more likely to bite in an inappropriate situation than dogs that are trained to bite. This is another one of those facts that is often lost on those with antipathy for dogs and wants to ban breeds or impose other restrictions. I am not suggesting that all dogs be trained in protection, which is not practical or possible, but all dogs should be trained to be **confident**.

Confident dogs are far less likely to bite. A confident dog has no reason to rush out to the fence and "chase off" a person walking or riding by on a bicycle. Confident dogs do not overreact to novel situations, objects or people. Socialization is all about developing confidence in your dog. A young puppy between four and twelve weeks is easily socialized. If you have an older puppy or dog that did not receive socialization it is not necessarily too late. However, depending on exactly what is lacking in the socialization process and how old your dog is, the process will be more challenging than socializing a young puppy.

With an older puppy or dog, the owner will need to isolate and work on each sensitivity or fear elicitor separately rather than a general socialization program as with a young puppy. For example, if your dog is afraid of the vacuum sweeper you will need to set up a program to desensitize your dog to that one thing. Although a fear of vacuum sweepers may seem like a minor problem **the principles for resolving the problem can serve as a generalized formulae for eliminating virtually any fear.**

Where you start will depend on just how sensitive your dog is to the fear elicitor. Always start at the point just beyond where your dog begins to show fear towards the elicitor. The proper starting point is often a certain physical distance or it could simply be a function of intensity, for example certain sounds.

By way of example, let me briefly outline a plan for eliminating a fear of vacuum sweepers (this scenario merely illustrates how the technique works). Start by rewarding your dog for coming anywhere near the vacuum when it is not on. If your dog is not afraid of a non-functioning vacuum you can skip to the next step. Otherwise, you will need to find out what distance your dog is willing to approach the vacuum without showing any signs of fear. Reward you dog at this point using food treats and or toys with exuberant play. Gradually entice your dog closer to the vacuum using favorite treats, toys and play.

Do this slowly and not necessarily all in one session. Depending on just how fearful your dog is, you may have to stretch this exercise out over several sessions that may take days. It is better to go too slow than to go too fast. Your dog must be completely comfortable near the vacuum sweeper before going to the next step. Do not rush. Proceed at your dogs pace.

If your dog does not react to the vacuum while it is not on you can go to the next phase. Turn the vacuum on when your dog is a long way from it, maybe even in another room with the door closed. This will help avoid startling your dog. Reward your dog for having little or no reaction to the sound. If your dog reacts nervously, you are too close, increase your distance.

If you have started in another room, open the door after a few trials if all is going well. Continue the reward system, treats or play with a favorite toy. If your dog is comfortable, get a helper to bring the vacuum a little closer but not enough to make your dog nervous. After a few sessions, leave the vacuum on but no one should move it. Call your dog to the doorway so that he can see the vacuum and reward generously if your dog is still not afraid.

If your dog shows any sign of fear back up to any point where your dog is once again comfortable. Encourage your dog closer in very small increments using your rewards. Continue in this way until you can get your dog all the way up to the vacuum without any apprehension. This process will take numerous sessions and, as always, should be done very slowly.

The last step is to actually be able to move the vacuum around without stressing your dog. Start by increasing the distance again even though your dog does not mind being close to the motionless vacuum. Movement that is close by will be much more startling than from a distance. Have a helper move the vacuum sweeper slowly while you continue to reward your dog. Just as with the preceding steps, start out slow and do not advance too quickly. Eventually you should be able to vacuum all around your dog without any signs of worry. The whole process may take days, weeks or months, depending on the dog and the severity of the fear.

This may seem like a lot of work (and it is!) so it may not be worth the effort just to get your dog over his fear of a vacuum sweeper. It may be easier just to manage the problem by putting your dog in the backyard whenever you clean the house. Only you can decide what is best for your situation. Each fear that your dog has must be evaluated and either managed or changed through a behavior modification program that would be similar to the one outlined for the vacuum sweeper.

However, when it comes to "fear aggression" a very proactive behavior modification program is always the best option. Dogs that display fear aggression, especially towards people, need to undergo behavior modification. Management is risky because mistakes can occur. The fear aggressive dog is a liability to you and a menace to others.

Dogs that show fear aggression towards other dogs or people (even just certain people, e.g. only men or people wearing hats or small children) can be desensitized in a fashion similar to the method used with the vacuum sweeper. You will need some cooperation from friends to set up training scenarios. Also, you should take all the necessary safety precautions to avoid accidental injury to your helpers by your dog.

If your dog has severe fear aggression or you are not certain how you should set up a behavior modification program, you would be well advised to seek a professional behaviorist for assistance.[36] The cost of such a service may seem expensive but when you consider how long you will have your dog, the liability issues and the peace of mind factor, the real value can be appreciated.

Ultimately, what you want to accomplish with any behavior modification program is to completely change the association that your dog has with what was once frightening for your dog. For example, by the time you finished the program outlined for the vacuum sweeper, your dog would not only be unafraid of it he might even get excited when he sees the vacuum because he thinks you are going to reward him with a treat or play.

Such a program will also produce a happier dog. Imagine being afraid of things all the time, like vacuum sweepers. It is difficult to enjoy life when you are afraid. By changing the association from fear to pleasure, you help your dog enjoy life. Dogs that are afraid are very difficult to train. A fearful dog is not a thinking dog.

Not all programs are going to be 100% effective. Some dogs have too many fears. But, you can make significant changes. As I mentioned, one of my dogs, Jack, is a rescue and was quite fearful of almost everything that moved or made a sound. I have worked with him for many years and he is still sometimes "spooky," especially in strange surroundings, but can tolerate far more than when I first got him. To the best of my knowledge he spent the first ten months of his life in a commercial kennel and was not socialized.

[36] See your veterinarian for a referral to a qualified behaviorist. Professional dog trainers are not necessarily qualified to do this type of behavior modification. If you cannot get a referral, try to choose someone who can produce evidence of his or her qualifications. Ask a lot of questions and if the behaviorist suggests using any type of aversive measures (choke chains, pinch collars, shock collars, etc.), find someone else.

Strange people, sounds, new surroundings, movement (e.g. even curtains slightly moving in the breeze) would send Jack into a panic when I first got him at nearly one year of age. I had to work with him on numerous fears. I am very proud of him for earning his Companion Dog certificate in an obedience trial just a little over a year after I got him. He even got "high in trial" (highest number of points scored), although it was not a major dog show, it was still quite an accomplishment for him. People who knew him when I first got him could hardly believe he was the same dog.

The point is that if you put enough effort into it, you can change the way your dog feels about the world and make great improvements in the quality of your dog's life. Jack went from being frightened almost all the time to a really terrific family dog that is happy and comfortable in an everyday environment. It takes time, commitment and patience but the benefits are well worth the trouble for both you and your dog.

It simply is not possible to write out a protocol for an effective treatment of every possible fear that a dog might develop. Most owners can develop and successfully execute their own program for most minor fears using the technique described previously. More severe or socially dysfunctional fears (especially those that involve aggression) can be treated in the same way but a professional behaviorist may be needed to help owners outline an appropriate treatment program.

Chapter 12
Foundation Training

In this chapter you will learn how to train some of the most basic behaviors, which will include simple primary stationary commands (like sit, down, stay, etc.), action commands, which is the recall (coming when called) and loose leash walking (not pulling on leash) and secondary stationary commands (attention). The learned behaviors in this chapter will form the foundation for all future training. The techniques described in this chapter will help owners develop better training skills and prepare for more advanced work.

- Name Game -

The "name game" is a simple but important part of your foundation work. In spite of its simplicity its value should not be underestimated. Whether you are building a house or a training program for your dog the foundation must be strong enough to support everything. The "name game" is a training exercise that will help support all future training.

The name game can be described as teaching your dog her name. More accurately, it is teaching your dog to pay attention to you whenever you say her name. A dog that is not paying attention to you is going to be very difficult to teach much of anything. Eventually, what you want to be able to do is to call your dog's name, she will look at you, and then you will give a command. For example, to call your dog you would say, "Princess, come here!" Every command should be preceded by your dog's name.

The name game is really the beginning of attention work. Attention work will be discussed later in the next chapter (see **Secondary Stationary Commands**). To teach the name game make sure you have some treats on hand. The training should be done very informally and randomly throughout the day. Anytime your dog is not looking at you, but you are nearby, call her name. If she looks at you, reward-mark and give her a treat. Wait until she is not looking and repeat. Do this exercise over and over until she looks at you every time she hears her name. If your dog does not look at you, **do not repeat her name**. Wait for at least a minute and try it again.

When your dog is responding reliably to her name, it is time to go to the next level. Start adding time before you reward-mark the behavior. Call your dog's name and when she looks at you delay your reward-mark for two seconds. If your dog maintains eye contact with you reward-mark and repeat the exercise at random times throughout the day. The next day practice reward-marking for immediate responses one or two times first then go back to doing a two second delay. If these are successful try adding two more seconds.

Each day, increase the delay by an additional two seconds until you get reliable eye contact for up to ten seconds. As you increase the time delay always do some short delays or immediate reward-marks as a "warm up." This will help keep your dog interested and successful. If eye contact is lost at anytime during a session be sure to back up in your training. You have probably proceeded to fast. You must always proceed at your dog's pace, not yours.

At first it is best to train the name game in a quiet location where your dog is not too distracted, inside your home for example. When your dog seems reliable in a quiet location try working on the name game in different locations. Increase the level of distractions slowly. Remember, you always want your dog to succeed so do not increase distractions too rapidly. For example, do not go from doing the name game in your living room then immediately to a children's playground full of kids in one step. Be inventive and work up to it gradually. The proper way to go from the living room to the playground would be to work outdoors first in a quiet location. Then approach a playground but stay far enough away that your dog is not too distracted. As your dog shows reliability slowly get closer and closer to the playground. Always be patient and back up in your training if your dog fails at any step.

Because the name game is so simple many people do not bother teaching it to their dog. Do not make that mistake. **Do not let the simplicity of the exercise deceive you.** You should continue to work on the name game even after you have begun other training exercises.

Training hint: It is important that you do not over use your dog's name. I often hear owners saying their dog's name over and over again. You should say your dog's name **once** and if she does not respond do not repeat it. If you train the name game properly, it will only be necessary to say it once.

When I remind my clients of this before class sessions they will sometimes respond that they are not training their dog at that moment. I have to remind them that **all interactions** between you and your dog is training. Training is not always a formal session. Dogs must learn to behave under all circumstances.

With time, it will no longer be necessary to give a food reward to your dog for looking at you. However, your dog's name should always be followed by either a command or pleasant consequences. Simple verbal praise or a scratch under the chin is adequate praise in most circumstances. You do not want to say your dog's name and then follow up by punishing her. I never recommend physical punishment but many owners will say their dog's name and give a verbal reprimand like "no." From the dog's point of view she is being punished for looking at you. If you are going to use a reprimand, do not use your dog's name.

- Primary Stationary Commands -

The commands "sit," "stand" and "down" are some of the most basic. Every dog should be taught to reliably respond to each of these simple commands. The commands are easy to teach and very useful throughout the life of your dog. It is also a good starting point for you, as an owner, to develop your training skills and begin establishing a leadership role with your dog. Even if your dog already knows how to sit on command I would encourage owners to teach their dog again using the methods outlined in this section. There are important principles that will have carry-over value for both you and your dog.

You are going to use a technique called "lure training" for teaching these commands. Lure training is where you "lure" a dog into a desired position rather than physically placing them. With a little practice, lure training is the easiest and most effective way to get your dog into a desired position.

The classic aversive method for teaching a sit is to pull up and back on the leash (while using a choke collar) and simultaneously pushing down on your dog's hips with your free hand. This aversive method can be stressful (puppies or young dogs not used to a choke collar may even panic) but has been used with success for many years. The choke collar tightening around the neck creates some of the stress but also pushing on the dog will add to the situation. Pushing a dog in position normally results in what is called the "opposition reflex." The opposition reflex is a natural and automatic reaction of a dog to counter being physically pushed or pulled.

We also have an opposition reflex although it may not be quite as well developed as that of a dog. For example, if I walked up and tried to push you, you would most likely resist, at least enough to keep me from knocking you over. A dog is doing much the same thing; it is simply automatically reacting to being pushed or pulled. A dog cannot know why you are pushing on them so they naturally resist and this causes anywhere from a little to a lot of stress.

A dog that is resisting being choked around the neck and pushed from behind is not going to be thinking clearly. He is more likely to be attempting to get out of the situation in any way he can. Eventually the dog may learn that the way out of the situation is to sit. That is the basis of aversive training.

Lure training removes nearly all the stress, except the mild stress that the dog feels about how he is going to get his treat. Low stress also allows the dog to figure out how to best get the treat on his own. With lure training the dog has to move his own body. He has to figure out in what position his body needs to be in order to get a reward. This is a thinking dog, not a panicked one.

The Sit Command

The first things you need are suitable treats for your dog. With this kind of training you will want to start with high value treats, i.e. something your dog really likes. Hold the treat in your hand between your thumb and fingers, with your palm up. Put the treat right at your dog's nose to get her interested in the treat. Slowly bring your hand up and slightly behind your dog at the same time. Your dog's nose should follow the treat causing the head to come up and tilt back. This action will almost always result in your dog sitting. If it does not, be patient and try again.

As soon as your dog is in a sitting position be sure to reward-mark immediately and then give her the treat (if your dog is snapping at the treat see *The Gentle Command* at the end of this section). Repeat this exercise several times. Soon, your dog will be sitting with almost no effort at all. Notice that we have not had to give the verbal command "sit" yet. Do not worry about the command at first. At this point the reward-mark is the most important. Your dog will learn what to do simply by your hand position. As you will see, the hand position will become a signal later on (remember it is much easier for your dog to recognize body language).

Once your dog is sitting without hesitation using a treat as a lure, try doing it without a treat in your lure hand but have one ready nearby or in your other hand. Be sure to use the exact same hand motion as before. If your dog does not respond then you should continue to use a treat for a while longer. If, and when, you get a correct response, reward-mark and give your dog a treat.

It is best to do only a few repetitions at a time of this exercise, especially with puppies. Conducting several quick sessions spread out over the day or evening is better than one long session. If you have progressed to doing sits without a lure (treat) in your hand and your dog "forgets" how to sit at any time, say nothing. Wait for a minute or so and try again using a lure a few times to reinforce the behavior. Never be afraid to back up in your training when a problem occurs. Remember, you are still not using a verbal command.

In only a few short sessions most dogs will be sitting readily on cue. It is now time to add your command. We did not use a verbal command before because your dog will not be able to concentrate on what you were saying at first. She would be too busy trying to figure out how to get the treat from your hand and the word would be meaningless to your dog anyway. Also, most dog owners develop a bad habit of repeating a command when their dog does not respond right away. Your dog should require only one command.

To teach the verbal command, **say your dog's name**, then use your hand signal for sit (by now the luring gesture will be a clear hand signal to your dog). At the same time say "sit" **once**. If your dog responds correctly, reward-mark and give a treat. **It is important that you only give the command once.** Before long she will associate both the hand signal and the verbal command with the behavior.

It is important to note that if your dog ever fails to respond you should not repeat the command. You can say something like "too bad" and simply walk away from your dog and ignore her for ten or fifteen seconds then try the command again. If you are continuing to have problems then you need to back up in your training steps. You want to teach your dog to respond to your commands the first time you give them. Do not fall into the trap of having to say sit, sit, **sit, SIT!** Your dog will quickly learn not to pay attention to you until you get to the fourth and very loud **SIT** before obeying. This "one command" rule is always applied.

At this point in your training, you can phase out the hand signal if you want. I recommend that you maintain it but begin to change it somewhat. Once your dog is reliable to the command, start giving your verbal command but do not put your hand quite as close to your dog's nose. Keep it an inch or two away. Gradually give the signal from a little further away during each practice session. Eventually, you can teach your dog to sit from several feet away by keeping your hand next to your side palm facing your dog and just lift your four fingers.

Hints:

➢ Practice giving your dog hand signals without a verbal command. If your dog does not respond correctly you will need to back up in your training. Go back to the stage where your dog understands.

➢ Make sure your dog is looking at you. If you are using hand signals only, you must have your dog's attention. If your dog is not looking at you, say her name then give the signal. If your dog *is* looking at you, then you will not have to say her name first.

➢ Begin to put rewards on a variable schedule once your dog is responding reliably with continuous rewards.

➢ You will need to change the context of your training often. If you always train the sit at home in your kitchen the chances are your dog will not respond so well outside in the yard or at the park. Train your sit in a variety of places and situations until your dog realizes that sit means sit no matter where you are.

➢ Slowly add distractions to your training. A dog may sit on command with no difficulty when it is quiet and there are no distractions in the area but if a small child or another dog is running around near-by she may not respond to your command. Teach your dog in a quiet area at first but later take her to places where there are more distractions. Add distractions gradually. Do not teach a sit in a quiet home and then immediately go to the middle of a crowded playground. Work up to it slowly by adding just one or two distractions at a time.

The Stand Command (or "four on the floor")

Teaching your dog to stand on all four feet can be a convenient behavior to have on command. It can, and should, be taught at the same time as a "sit" and "down" command. Your dog should learn to sit, stand or down from any alternate position. Many people "pattern" train their dog. The pattern trained dog is one that can only move from one position to another by going through a specific sequence. For example a pattern trained dog may not be able to do a down unless it is in a sit position first or a sit without being in a standing position, etc.

There is not necessarily anything wrong with pattern training but your dog can, and I believe should (see Dynamic Training, chapter 16), learn to go into any position from any other position. Since you have just taught the "sit," you can temporarily use that as your starting position.

Command your dog to sit. Now put a treat between your thumb and the base of your index finger. Stand in front of your dog but to one side. Put the treat at your dog's nose with your palm facing down and fingers extended parallel to the ground. Lure your dog forward. Your dog should follow your hand. Stop as soon as she is standing up, reward-mark, and give her the treat. Be sure to stop luring and give your reward-mark the instant your dog is up. You do not want her to take a step. You only want her hindquarters to come off the ground.

Your dog should learn the stand rather quickly. If desired, you can begin adding the voice command "stand" with your luring (which will become a hand signal before long) nearly right away. **Remember to say your dog's name before the command.** Use a constant reward schedule for a while, however. This is because you are going to change the sequence shortly and want to avoid any confusion.

As soon as your dog is doing the stand without hesitation, it is time to change the sequence. First you will need to teach your dog the down position (see The Down Command), if she does not already know it, and then return to teaching the stand. With your dog in a down use the same procedure to lure the dog to a stand as you did out of the sit. Again, be sure to stop luring and give your reward-mark the instant your dog raises her body to a full stand but before taking a step.

When your dog is standing from either a sit or a down consistently you can begin holding your hand slightly further from the nose. Gradually work up to where you can give the hand signal while standing normally in front of your dog.

The Down Command

The sit, stand and down commands are all interrelated. It is difficult for the dog to do one without being in one of the other two positions. Of the three exercises, the down is the most difficult to teach to many dogs. Some will catch on right away but others will not. Be patient and do not try to force your dog to down. A down is a subordinate position and some dogs simply do not want to assume that position. Remember, we are not trying to dominate our dog. We want an enthusiastic, low stress, response not a high stress, fearful one.

Start your dog from either a sit or a stand. Mix up the starting position if you want to avoid pattern training. Stand directly in front of your dog and hold a treat between your thumb and fingers, palm down. Put your hand close to your dogs nose and **slowly** lower your hand. Keep your hand close to your dog's chest to make her look down with her head. Your dog should be following your hand with her nose. When your hand reaches the floor flatten your hand out and trap the food under your fingers. Ideally, your dog will follow your hand down and end up in a sphinx position on the floor. If, by some miracle, this happens reward-mark immediately and move your hand to expose the treat. If your dog remains in the down keep her there for a few seconds by continuing to put treats between the legs. Be sure to use the same hand position, palm down and hand flat on the floor, each time (this will later become a hand signal).

Some dogs will perform a down right away but the majority will not. If your dog does not follow your hand all the way down, do not be concerned. When your hand reaches the floor, it should be between your dog's feet, just wait for your dog to begin sniffing your hand to get at the treat. If your dog does not sniff at your hand or is distracted, put your treat near her nose again and repeat the exercise.

Once you have your dog's attention, she should be sniffing and licking at your hand while it is on the floor in an attempt to get at the treat but may not be in a down position yet. Do and say nothing at this point. Be sure to hold your ground and do not let your dog get the treat. Frustration may set in at this point and your dog may start whining, barking and pawing at your hand. Ignore all of this behavior and remain motionless. If your dog turns away, lure her back again using the same hand motion as before. Keep her attention on your hand.

Eventually your dog will lie down, often out of frustration. As soon as your dog lies down, reward-mark and let her have the treat. If your dog stays in the down, continue to place several treats between her front legs with your hand in a palm down position.

You must be patient with this exercise. It may take several tries and even several minutes before your dog will go to a down position. Repeat the exercise several times. Even if your dog is going down simply out of frustration or by chance she still will eventually figure out that the way to get a treat is to lie down.

You can begin to add your verbal command "down" once your dog consistently lies down with your hand signal. **Make sure you say your dogs name before the command**. You can also begin reducing the dependence on luring by making your hand signal less precise just as you did with the sit and stand exercises. Start by holding the treat near but not right on your dog's nose and instead of putting your hand flat on the floor, try keeping it just a couple of inches off the floor. Keep in mind that if at any point your dog seems confused about your command make sure you back up in your training to a point where she responds correctly. You need to proceed at your dog's pace, not yours.

Most dogs will eventually get the down if the owner is patient but for those who are not so patient or truly feel their dog is never going to lie down (how does she sleep?) there is another way to speed up the process. I call it the "tunnel method." Depending on the size of your dog, you can use a chair, coffee table or your legs to get her to lie down.

To use your legs you will need to sit on the floor with your dog. Pull your knees towards your chest to form a tunnel. You may need to be a bit of a contortionist but try to get your dog's attention and lure her under your legs with a treat in your hand. Use the hand position described above. You will need to pass your hand through your legs from the opposite side then slowly pull your hand back while your dog tries to squeeze under your legs to get at the treat.

Keep your hand low to the ground while luring. As soon as your dog lies down in the "tunnel" reward-mark and give her the treat. If your dog is big then a chair or coffee table may be more appropriate than your legs. Once your dog is easily going into the tunnel to lie down you can add your verbal command. I then suggest that you try to get your dog to down without using a tunnel as soon as possible.

If your dog will almost do a down but the hindquarters are still up try gently pushing them down with your free hand. If your dog reacts by looking at your hand, resists or is distracted in anyway **do not continue**. Often a *gentle* push will get your dog in the right position without adding stress. However, if your dog reacts negatively to your touch then you must do one of two things. One is that you must not touch her again and just wait until she goes all the way down no matter how long it takes. Alternatively, you can go ahead and reward-mark and treat for a partial success. Later, wait for a better response. This is the "shaping" method similar to pushing hard on the button in the hypothetical training scenario in chapter 10.

The Release

Something that is often overlooked in basic dog training is the release. This oversight often results in sloppy training. To get more reliable results and to make commands more clear-cut to your dog a release is important. The release basically tells your dog when he can stop a certain behavior that you have commanded.

For example, if you command your dog to "sit," when is your dog's obligation to remain in the sit over? If your dog performed an instant sit when commanded but immediately got up and walked away he would have done just as you asked. However, it may be that you want your dog to remain in a sit for several seconds or more. To accomplish that many trainers teach a second command of either "stay" or "wait" (to be discussed in chapter 13). This is fine but not really necessary.

If you ask your dog to sit he should sit and then remain in that position until he is told to do something else. You should always encourage your dog to remain in a commanded position until you say otherwise, which would be another command or a word that tells your dog that he can do whatever he wants. You can think of it like a traffic light. When you approach a red light you have been trained to come to a stop. You remain at a stop until the light turns green. Then you can go wherever you want. If the light never turned green the red light would lose its significance to you after a while. You might stop and then go whenever it suited you.

When you ask your dog to do something you must let him know when it is okay to do something else. If you never make that distinction your dog will naturally decide for himself. Every stationary command must be followed by one of two things, either another command or a "release." Always give your dog a clear signal, called the release, when it is okay to stop the behavior that you have requested. I like to use the word "free" as a release but you may use any word you want.

I strongly urge you to use the release after giving any stationary command whether you want the behavior to last only a second or several minutes. It must become a habit to you. If you forget to use a release after every command your dog will start deciding when to discontinue the behavior just as you would at a faulty traffic light.

For right now, as a preliminary step to teaching your dog to remain in a commanded position just make sure you release your dog right away after every command. This is primarily to help you develop the habit. Using the sit as an example, command "sit" then when your dog complies, reward-mark. Give your dog a reward and then release your dog (or you can give another command such as stand or down but you must release your dog from these positions as well). Eventually, the release word can be delayed for a longer and longer period as your training progresses. The procedure for this will become clear later when I explain how to teach the stay or wait commands outlined in the next chapter.

Polishing The Stationary Commands

Think back to the training allegory where I wanted to train you not just to push a button on command but do it in a certain way. It is now time to improve the performance level criteria for the sit, down and stand. Now we are going to train our dog to react quickly and respond to more subtle and convenient commands.

Be very generous with your rewards at first and mix up the sequences of sit, down and stand. Practice getting your dog to sit from a down position or down from a stand and all sorts of other combinations. I like to avoid pattern training because I believe that it makes your dog think and pay more attention to you. If your dog can never anticipate what command you will give next she will have no choice but to concentrate on you in order to get rewards. When you finally give a command she will have to think about what you are asking to make the right choice.

Recall that dogs can pick up on, and respond more easily to, body language than verbal. However if you want to, you can begin to eliminate the hand signals altogether once your dog is reliably responding to simultaneous verbal and hand signal commands. Your dog may be confused at first. If you give a command without a hand signal and your dog does not respond, go ahead and give the hand signal as a hint. Repeat the same exercise several times and your dog will soon learn to respond solely on a verbal command. Once again you will need to go through all the different possible combinations to ensure your dog understands how to get from one position to another.

I personally prefer to continue with hand signals. They are actually very convenient under certain circumstances. For example, I may be talking to someone and see my dog doing something I don't want him to do. I can give a hand signal to sit without shouting or interrupting my conversation with the other person.

The reason I was very specific about hand position when teaching stationary commands is because first they are distinctive and second we take those signals and "economize" them into some very convenient motions. This is called "fading" the signal. You may use any hand signal that you like but I am going to suggest the following for two reasons; they are similar to the lure motions that we used in the initial training, and they are very unambiguous. If you use other signals, just remember that they must be very clear. Generally, small gestures are better than large ones just for this reason.

Stand in front of your dog. Say your dog's name and give the verbal command to sit. At the same time turn your palm facing forward and raise your hand up slightly just as you have always done but try keeping it a few inches from your dog's nose. A treat can be held in your signal hand or not, depending how much luring your dog still requires. It is the same lure motion used to teach the sit but farther from your dog. If your dog does not respond, exaggerate the movement by bending your arm more at the elbow. Reward-mark your dog for sitting and be generous with treats for a while. Your dog will quickly learn to associate the new hand signal with the voice command "sit."

Teach the other two hand signals in a similar way. Start with your hand just an inch or two away but gradually increase the distance as your dog learns to respond correctly to the signal. Fading the signal to a fully economized version may take several days, weeks or months, depending on how often you practice. The point is, as always, be patient and progress at your dog's pace.

Eventually, you can give the signal for a sit by holding your hand at your side, palm facing forward, lift your hand at the wrist. The hand signal for the stand is to turn the back of your hand forward, lift your hand 90 degrees forward from the wrist then rotate your wrist 180 degrees. The signal for down starts the same way but instead of rotating the wrist, tip your hand down slightly. Keep your hand movements crisp. All of these signals are economized versions of the original lure motions. If you want to, it is possible to continue this training to the point where you need only use a single finger to signal your dog.

During this training give your dog verbal commands with simultaneous hand signals (reinforce with plenty of treats) for several days of training each time you fade the signal slightly. To test whether your dog is really responding to the hand signal try giving just a hand signal occasionally without the verbal command. Be sure to say your dogs name first to get her attention. Jackpot reward your dog for a good response. If she does not respond, give the verbal command then continue to work on simultaneous commands for a while longer. It should not take long before you can use either verbal or hand signals.

One final note, if your dog is looking at you then a hand signal can be given without saying your dog's name. If your dog is not looking at you then it is important to say her name first. Just as a matter of habit, the name should always be used before a verbal command regardless of whether or not the dog is looking at you.

The Gentle Command

Some dogs will snap at a treat in your hand. You need to teach your dog to take the treat gently. This is easiest with puppies but older dogs can learn too. Some dogs are so excited about the treat that you may have to sacrifice a little skin on your hand at first or, if you are sensitive about such things, wear a glove in some cases. The idea is to make your dog take treats in a way that is not painful.

If your dog is in the habit of snatching a treat from your hand without regard for your fingers quickly pull the treat away and say "gentle" or "easy." Offer the treat again, but if your dog lunges for it pull the treat away again. Repeat the exercise as many times as necessary until your dog figures out that she must move towards the treat slowly or not at all.

Once she approaches the treat slowly she must also take it without nipping your fingers. If your dog is nipping do not let her take the treat. Close it in your hand. Tell her "gentle" then offer the treat again. Repeat the exercise as many times as needed. **She only gets the treat when it is taken carefully from your fingers.**

This is not a difficult exercise to teach. Most dogs figure out how to take treats gently in a short time. You may have to endure a little bit of nipping when first training this exercise to very determined dogs. Once dogs have learned to take treats gently be sure to insist that they always do so. If your dog gets too aggressive about taking treats then do a refresher training session.

Lure Training

Lure to a sit. The treat is held between the thumb and fingers with the palm up. With the dog in a standing position the treat is held directly in front of the dog's nose. The treat is then brought up and slightly back causing the dog's head to tilt back. Most dogs will follow the lure and naturally sit to get into position. As soon as the dog sits, reward-mark and treat.

Lure to a stand. Standing slightly to the side of the dog hold the treat between the thumb and the base of your first finger, palm down, fingers parallel to the floor. Position your hand at your dog's nose and lure forward from either a sit or down. Reward-mark as soon as the dog is standing on all four feet then give the treat.

Lure Training

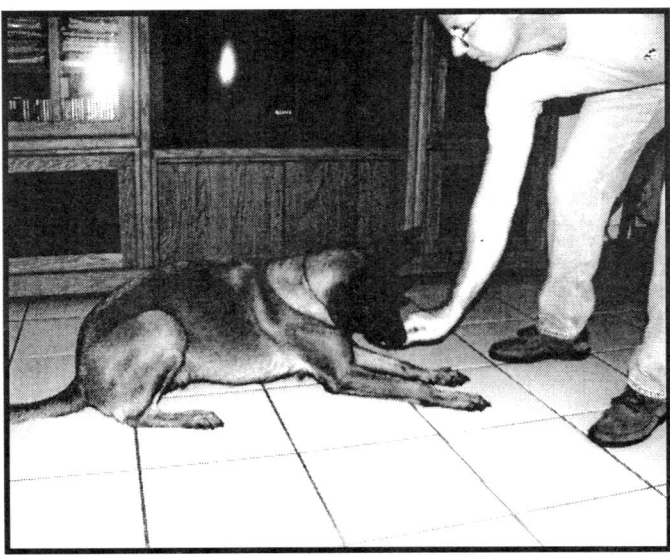

Lure to a down. Hold a treat between your thumb and fingers, palm down. Position the treat at the dog's nose and lower your hand to the floor staying close to the dog's chest. If the dog follows the treat it should end up in a down. Reward-mark immediately and expose the treat under your hand. Be patient with this exercise. It may require some time to work.

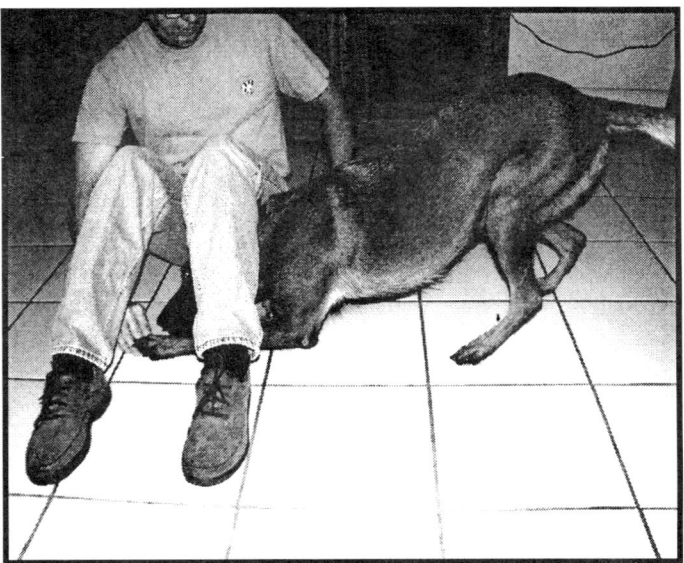

Alternative lure to a down. For impatient owners a dog can be encouraged to down by luring them under a low table or your legs as shown in this picture. As your dog crawls under your legs to get at the treat it must go to a down position. Reward-mark as soon as the dog is in the correct position then treat. After a few successes try it without using your legs or a low table.

Fading The Lure

Fading the sit signal. Use the same hand motion as was used to teach the sit but start fading the signal by holding your hand a few inches away from the dog's nose.

Fading the stand signal. The procedure for fading the stand hand signal is similar to that of fading the sit. Lure the dog forward with the same hand gesture used to teach the original stand but keep your hand a few inches away.

Fading the signal for down. Once again the mechanics are the same as the original exercise except the hand is kept a few inches away from the dog. Also, do not put your hand all the way to the floor, only as far as needed to get your dog to down.

Hand Jive

Hand positions during lure training can eventually lead to simple hand signals. Below, lure signals are compared to suggested hand signals. Hand signals are achieved in a gradual process called "fading the signal."

<u>Lure Signals</u>   <u>Hand Signals</u>

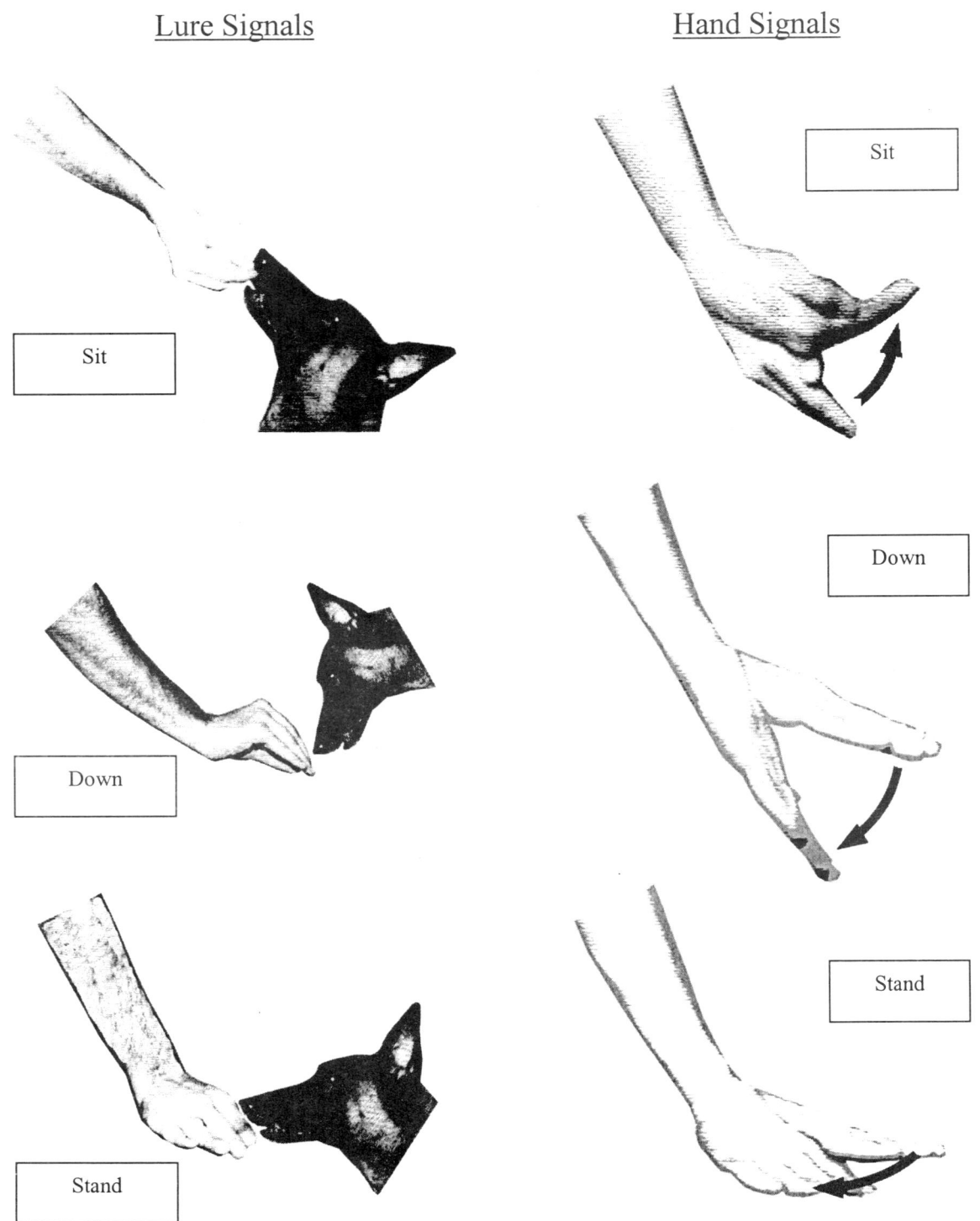

Sit

Sit

Down

Down

Stand

Stand

- Action Commands -
Recall

A poor recall, or coming when called, is one of the three most common yet simple obedience problems that owners have with their dog (the other two are jumping up and pulling on the leash). Teaching the recall to your dog is not really very difficult if the owner thinks about the problem from the dog's point of view.

Learned behavior of dogs (and all animals) is dependant on consequences. Your dog will be more likely to repeat any behavior that has resulted in pleasant consequences in the past. If consequences were unpleasant the behavior is more likely to disappear.

When you call your dog to you the consequences of his actions, whatever they might be, will have an affect on how likely he will repeat or discontinue the behavior next time. In other words, if you call your dog and reward him in some way that is very pleasant he is more likely to come to you again the next time you call. The more frequently this occurs the more reliable the recall. Conversely, the more times consequences are unpleasant the less likely the behavior will occur.

To illustrate the point, let us take a hypothetical example. Two owners have met at the dog park with their dogs. They stay there for twenty minutes while their dogs play with each other. Owner number one calls her dog and gives him a tasty treat and then lets her dog go back to playing. She repeats this sequence three times during the stay. It is finally time to go home. Both owners call their dogs and the dogs return. Owner number one rewards her dog with a treat once again but puts a leash on afterwards. Owner number two simply puts a leash on her dog and they leave the park agreeing to meet again tomorrow.

The next day the owners allow their dogs to play in the park once again. After twenty minutes they decide to leave again. Both owners call their dogs. Owner number one's dog comes quickly. He is rewarded with a treat and his leash is attached. The dog belonging to owner number two has not returned. He is still busy exploring the park.

Previous consequences have influenced the behavior of each dog in this hypothetical story. It is easy to see why dog owner number one would be more successful than dog owner number two when recalling their dogs. It is important for dog owners to always reinforce a recall with pleasant consequences. But consequences are not the only factor to influence the recall. Owners must also compete with the environment.

Competing with the environment is often the most difficult part of teaching a reliable recall. Rewarding a recall is easy but getting your dog to come to you in the first place is often frustrating to many people. The degree to which a dog will be interested in its environment will vary. Factors influencing interest can depend on the particular surroundings as well as the individual dog. The irony is that well socialized, confident dogs tend to be more interested in the environment, therefore more difficult to get a reliable recall than the more timid and insecure dog.

One of the reasons so many people have difficulty with recalls is that it is a behavior that must be built. It is not a behavior that can necessarily be taught in one stage, like a sit or down. A reliable recall is built step by step. Each step is more challenging for you and your dog.

Before any steps are taken, you will first need a foundation. The foundation should already be in place. The bond that you have with your dog is of primary importance. If you have been working and playing with your dog, building up trust, the bond should already be quite strong. **Your dog should want to be with you.** If your dog does not want to be with you then you need to ask yourself, "Why not?" Bear in mind that if you have been using only positive reinforcement with your dog, he **will** want to be with you.

Assuming you have a good relationship with your dog, the name game, described earlier in this chapter is the first training step towards a reliable recall. Your dog should be looking at you each time you call his name. If you have not taught your dog the name game, you should do so before going any further. Recalls will be more reliable if you proceed one step at a time. Skipping steps will only reduce the reliability.

If you have taught your dog the name game you can begin calling your dog to you. Choose a command such as "come" or "here." Be prepared ahead of time by having some high value food rewards on hand. The best location to start teaching a recall is in your home or enclosed yard; a place where your dog is comfortable and will not be overly distracted because of a novel environment and cannot escape. Be sure to have a collar on your dog but not a leash.

Start off by calling your dog when he is a very short distance away at random times. Call only when your dog does not seem too distracted and you are pretty certain that he will respond to your command. If you have the kind of dog that seems to be distracted most of the time you will just have to work a little harder. You are now beginning to compete directly with the environment. You must become more interesting than the immediate surroundings.

The best way to become interesting to your dog, at least initially, is to start talking in an excited, high-pitched voice. This will be the one of the few times that you can break the "one command" rule. For a while you can repeat your command to come to you just to get and keep your dog's attention. You can gradually stop this practice with time.

For the really difficult dog, it may be necessary to stand only an arms length away and lure him to you with a treat. Walking away backwards is also a good way to get your dog moving towards you when you call. The point is, do whatever it takes to get your dog to come to you short of physically compelling him. It is often helpful to bend or kneel down while calling your dog. Open your arms wide in a welcoming gesture. Continue to practice in low distraction situations and make your recalls at random times. The idea is to surprise your dog and turn it into a fun game.

Every time your dog comes to you be sure to reward with a high value treat and give a lot of praise. Make your approval very clear. A reward-mark is not necessary since this is a motion exercise. You can gradually increase the distance of the recall if your dog is responding well to your command. **Try to make sure every recall ends with success.** If you are not sure your dog will respond, do not try a recall. You want "errorless" learning at this point. You are installing a good habit in your dog.

It is also important for you as the dog owner to develop a good habit at this point in training. **Each time your dog comes to you, reach out and grab the collar**. Only after you have grabbed the collar should you give the reward. If you do not do this many dogs learn to "flinch" away when called to avoid being put on a leash or restrained. If your dog learns that you always touch the collar before he gets his reward the leash will never be associated with the action.

To increase your dog's desire to come to you when called get another family member or friend to hold your dog by the collar as you call him. Let him get worked up by calling him while your helper continues to hold him back. This is a good time to back away from your dog and add a little distance. After just a few seconds have your helper let the dog go. You can build on this game by running away and hiding in another room or behind a tree. Anything you can do to increase the excitement level of the recall will benefit your training.

Do not over practice the recall. Too much repetition will diminish the excitement value to your dog. You always want recalls to be a very exciting event. Do a recall one or two at a time and go for at least five minutes or so before doing another. Three or four practice sessions in a day will be quite enough.

If your dog is responding well it is time to "raise the bar" on his performance. Try doing a recall while he is mildly distracted. Perhaps a helper can be playing with your dog while you do a recall. Whatever game your helper is playing with your dog it should stop immediately when you call. If your dog responds quickly to your command give him extra treats and be especially exuberant in your praise. Make sure that you allow your dog to go back to playing after the recall. You do not want your dog to think that every time he comes to you the fun ends.

If at any point in your training you find your dog's response to be slow you should back up in your training by decreasing the amount of distraction for a while but if your training is going well, continue to slowly increase distractions. Take your dog to a new location. Make certain that it is a safe area, preferably fenced and not too large. An empty tennis court is often a good place to start. If you cannot find a fenced area then you should invest in a long-line (if your dog is not yet leash trained, read "Leash Manners," next section). A long-line is simply a very long leash (most are made from nylon or cotton, leather long-lines are very expensive) and can be purchased at most pet stores. Alternatively, a retractable lead can be used but they are not as good for this kind of training.[37] Retractable leads are popular because they automatically spool up and are less prone to getting tangled.

I prefer long-lines because usually you do not even have to hold on to them. As long as you are sure that your dog will not simply make a straight, all out run for it when you let him out, just let your dog wander around dragging the line behind him. I prefer a fifty-foot line but you can use one that is shorter or even longer. The idea is to let your dog have a sense of freedom but the long-line is for safety. In an emergency you can just step on the line to keep him from getting away.

Try not to hold on to the long-line. Your dog will soon be pulling on it and will lose his sense of freedom. If you need to hold on then practice calling your dog to you just before he gets to the end of the line. Do not wait until the line has gone tight. If the line does go tight just wait for it to go slack again. Do not say anything to your dog when the line is tight. Once the line is slack for a few seconds you can try calling your dog.

Now practice your recalls as you have been doing in or around your home. It is important to reward with high value treats and release your dog to go back to exploring right after you have touched his collar and rewarded. That way your dog will not associate being called with having to stop playing. Do three or four recalls in a twenty-

---

[37] I have found that dogs that are regularly walked on retractable leads develop what I call "bolting" behavior. Because the retractable lead allows a dog a fair amount of freedom they learn that they can run off at any time without restriction up to a certain point. Dogs accustomed to a retractable lead often catch an owner off-guard and suddenly bolt in one direction or another. The danger is that the lead can be pulled out of the owner's hand and the dog could run into traffic. I strongly urge dog owners to use a standard six-foot leash as a primary walking lead.

minute period. On the last one, reward as usual, give a lot of verbal and physical praise then exchange the long-line for a six-foot leash and discontinue the lesson.

Find other environments that will increase the distraction level for your dog and continue to practice your recall. As you can see this process takes a long time, weeks perhaps months. You must be patient and inventive to come up with new but safe scenarios to practice a recall. Remember to try for "errorless" learning but go back a step in your training if you do not get a good response. Continue to make recalls exciting for your dog.

If your dog loves to chase small animals, like rabbits, or play with other dogs, you will face your greatest challenge when confronted with these distractions. If you are lucky enough to live near a dog park, or if there is a dog daycare center in your area, you can use these facilities for some really advanced distraction work. However, you will need the cooperation of two or three of the other owners.

Get your dog to play with one or two other dogs with their owners standing nearby. Let them play for a short time but before they get tired, try calling your dog to you. If your dog comes, grab his collar and reward with some very high value treats and enthusiastic praise for only a couple of seconds, then immediately let your dog go back and play. You should use a release word such as "free" or "go play" (review The Release).

Just as you have been doing, repeat this procedure two or three times before actually ending the exercise to keep your dog from associating your recall with having to stop play. If your dog does not come to you when you call, and this should be an immediate response, the other owners should quickly grab their dogs and give them some rewards. Everyone should completely ignore your dog except you. Eventually your dog should be coming towards you since the fun has ended. If necessary, call your dog again to get him to come to you. When he finally arrives, grab his collar and reward with a quick treat then everyone should release their dog to go play again. Continue to repeat the exercise but if you ever get a recall without the other owners having to stop the play be sure to give extra treats or "jackpot" your dog.

To get the cooperation of other owners you can explain what you are trying to accomplish and if they are interested in improving their recalls, then you can all take turns calling their dog. If you are unable to get access to a dog park or dog daycare then invite friends to bring their own dogs to your house for a training session (note: make certain your dog is not territorial and all the dogs involved are friendly and well socialized).

If none of the preceding options are possible then you will have to use a slightly different approach. First, if these options are not possible, I might assume that there will be very little chance of you or your dog ever encountering a situation where you would need to call your dog from away from other dogs. Should that be the case then training of this type would simply be unnecessary. However, you can not be certain that an encounter with a strange dog will never occur in an off leash situation. In this non-social circumstance you may just want to call your dog back to you to avoid any contact between the two dogs.

Training recalls under these circumstances will be the same as preventing your dog from chasing a cat, rabbit or other small animal. Unless a dog has been strongly socialized to certain small animals there is often an instinctive drive (called prey drive) to chase them. Some dogs have stronger prey drives than others. Your recall must be able to override this instinctual reaction of your dog.

If your dog encounters another dog there are several possibilities for interaction. If your dog was socialized properly as a puppy she may want to go play or at least approach the other dog. If your dog has not been properly socialized she may decide to challenge or behave aggressively. You certainly do not want your dog to behave aggressively and it is entirely possible that you will have no idea if the other dog is friendly. You will want to call your dog to you to control the situation.

This kind of control will require three things: training, bonding and awareness. None of these things will be trained or accomplished the first day you get your dog. It will require constant training, conditioning and observing over weeks, months and, if your are vigilant, will continue to improve through the years as your dog gets older. Fortunately, it is still possible to train a very reliable recall into your dog without the cooperation of other dog owners.

You will need to take your dog to places where other people will likely be walking dogs on leash or where you might be able to encounter small animals, such as squirrels, ducks or rabbits. Use the long-line in the manner described earlier but if there are other animals in the area you will probably need to hold the end in your hand. At first, try to maintain a distance from other dogs and animals that is just far enough away that your dog does not react strongly to them. This can be from just a few feet to several hundred yards, depending on your dog.

You must be very aware of your dog's reactions. If you see other dogs or animals watch your dog closely for the earliest signs of interest. Your dog may notice them before you so be very alert to your dog's body language. Watching your dog carefully, approach the other dog or animal in a slow but casual way (you do not want to send inadvertent signals to your dog that might overly excite her). At the very first signs that your dog has taken notice of another animal try recalling your dog. Do not sound panicked or concerned in any way. Just give your usual cheerful and excited recall. Be generous with the rewards but do not give your dog the slightest hint that you may be apprehensive about the other animal. Keep your dog distracted with treats or a toy and try to move a short distance away. Repeat the procedure. After two or three recalls discontinue the exercise.

If you practice this procedure often you will notice that your dog will start to do two things. One is that each time there is another dog or small animal in the area she will look to you for instructions. The other is that you will be able to get closer and closer to other animals before she has any reaction. Of course this all takes a great deal of time. The amount of time will depend on the individual dog and on the number of chance practice encounters. The more you work with your dog the quicker she will learn.

Leash Manners

Teaching your dog to walk nicely (heel) on a leash often seems to be something of an arcane art form in dog training. It seems like every trainer has his or her own special method so it should be no surprise if I tell you that I have my own method too. Once you understand the concept I hope that my method will not seem so mysterious. My approach differs not so much in methodology as it is does in the standard order of training used by many professional dog trainers. Most often dog trainers will teach a dog to walk on a leash first and then "off leash" later. I prefer to do it the opposite way. I believe that if you teach a dog to walk with you without the leash first then teaching them to walk with the leash would be a snap, pun intended. If your dog walks nicely with you without a leash then all that is left is to "snap" on the leash and you are ready to go.

For those of you who do not care about off leash walking or prefer a less formal way of walking you may skip ahead to the section entitled "Loose Leash Walking." However, I recommend the following "lure" method of off leash walking first for best results. Even if you already own a dog that has poor leash manners the lure method will work.

If you are going to work without a leash then you must have a safe area to practice, i.e., indoor setting or a fenced outdoor area. If you do not have a safe place to practice off leash walking or you just feel more comfortable teaching with a leash, then it is perfectly okay. The idea though is to **use the leash only as a safety device, not a training aid.** In other words the leash will keep your dog from getting away from you but just remember not to use it hold your dog in position. **Make sure the leash is always slack** while you use the lure method.

Start off by standing directly in front of your dog and put a treat in front of his nose. Start **walking backwards** luring him with you. You can start using a command of "let's go" or anything that you want. Let your dog have the treat after a few steps at first but each time you repeat the exercise try to lure your dog a little further before ending. Once you can walk about fifteen or twenty feet with your dog following you like this you are ready for the next step.

Now we are going to change the picture slightly. As you start to lure your dog with you going backwards, turn sideways but continue on a straight line. Most dogs make this transition with no trouble. If your dog seems unsure, practice this step until your dog has no trouble with it. If there are no difficulties you can immediately move on to the next step. Most dogs get it right away.

Start once again facing your dog. Lure him towards you and as you move, smoothly turn your body a full 180 degrees (whether you go to the left or right is entirely your choice but be consistent) but continue to walk in the same direction as you end up at your dog's side. Continue to lure the dog forward with the treat. Let your dog have the treat after a few steps and start again. Always pair your command "let's go" with the start of the exercise. If your dog is having no difficulty with this step try starting off at your dog's side instead of in front and lure him forward with you.

The key to this exercise is to keep your movements smooth and the treat right at your dog's nose. **If you have a leash on your dog, do not use it to guide your dog.** Let your dog figure out for himself where he should be to get the reward. Depending on the size of your dog, this technique may require you to walk bent over during the initial training stages. If your dog is very small or you have a limited degree of flexibility and coordination you may find this difficult. One solution is to lure by using a target stick.[38]

---

[38] A target stick can essentially be used an extension of your hand. A little preliminary training will be required to use a target stick. Dogs can easily be trained to "target" by holding a dowel (virtually anything can be used as a target, including the palm of your hand, which is useful with larger dogs) close to their nose. Most dogs will automatically sniff a novel object that is presented to them. The moment your dog sniffs the dowel reward-mark and give your dog a treat.

Repeat this procedure numerous times in several short sessions. Put a contrasting colored tape or paint on the end of the dowel to make a distinct target. Start rewarding your dog only when he touches the target end of the dowel. Before long, you may start requiring the dog to touch the dowel from slightly farther

Your dog should now be walking along side you as you move forward with the lure at his nose. It is now time to start fading the lure. Lure by holding the treat a little higher, just out of your dog's reach when all four of his feet are on the ground. Move forward as before. Most dogs will try to jump up slightly while walking to get at the treat. Ignore these attempts but do not let him have the treat. When he finally takes a few steps without jumping, give him the treat and praise. The idea here is to reward him for walking normally by your side. You do not want to teach him to jump.

Over the next few sessions, continue to fade the lure until you can hold the treat at your belt buckle (higher if it is a very large breed).[39] When your dog seems competent at this exercise it is time to start adding distractions, e.g., go to a new location, have other dogs nearby, traffic noise (**caution: always use a leash for safety**), children playing, etc. For those of you using a target stick, fade the target in exactly the same way as the reward lure.

The last step in this process is to eliminate the lure altogether. If your dog is walking by your side with distractions it is time to give fewer food rewards. Space out your food rewards more and more until you can eliminate them altogether. The walk itself should be enough of a reward for most dogs but verbal praise and petting can be substituted for food rewards. Do not be in too big of a hurry to eliminate food rewards. There is nothing wrong with using them. It always amazes me that many dog owners think nothing of keeping a choke collar on a dog for the rest of its life for maintaining control but the thought of carrying food treats around for just a few weeks or maybe even months is disagreeable to them.

Training hint: To help keep your dog focused on the lure and away from distractions use a very high value reward. Every dog has something that he is "crazy" about. One of my dogs for example will do anything and ignore everything for a chance to get a small piece of chicken (without the bones!) made by a certain popular fast food restaurant. I always use these high value rewards for difficult distraction training and get excellent

---

away, just a few inches. Then hold the stick slightly to one side or the other so that your dog must turn his head to touch the stick. Continue to gradually demand greater distance until you can make your dog follow the stick in any direction where your dog must take several steps. A lot of repetition is the key here but it really takes very little time. In a few short minutes it is possible to do forty or fifty repetitions, which is often adequate training to get your dog to take several steps.

Notice I have not put a command to this exercise yet. Once your dog is consistently touching the target every time you present it you can add a command such as, "target" or "touch." Now you can attempt to lead your dog forward as you walk using the target stick to position the dog correctly at your side. Take only a couple of steps at first before rewarding but gradually you can take more and more steps between rewards. As your dog becomes better at following the target stick start using your "walk" command instead of "target" or "touch."

Teaching your dog to target is easy and usually does not require much time. It is especially useful for small dogs or for people with any restricted physical abilities (like bad backs). Once your dog is target trained use the target in exactly the same way as you would use a treat. Just be sure to reward frequently to reinforce the targeting behavior. Once your dog is consistently walking by your side the target stick can be faded exactly the same way as any lure is faded (see main text).

[39] If your are training for competition style "heeling" the lure method can be taken to a new level by actually putting the treats in your mouth and spitting them at your dog when he is in the perfect heel position. The idea is to keep your dog focused on your face. This might seem a little bizarre or extreme but it is actually a proven technique used with a high degree of success by many top competition dog trainers.

results. If your dog ever does get distracted and walks away, simply stop and lure him back into position. Reward only when he is back at your side.

It is outside the scope of this book but the above method can also be used to train competition style heeling. Competition style heeling is fun to watch but it is usually impractical for everyday use. The dog could not enjoy a long walk due to the high level of concentration required during competition heeling. A slightly lower level of attention and precision is recommended for practical walking.

Remember, if you are having difficulty keeping control of your dog while walking, back up in your training. You have probably gone from one step to another too rapidly. Add distractions gradually. Also, be patient and **consistent**. It has been said that the difference between a dog that walks on lead nicely and one that doesn't is about a thousand miles. However, if you do not mind an even less precise way of walking your dog, read the next section on loose leash walking.

Loose Leash Walking

"Loose leash walking" is an informal style of walking with your dog on leash that should not be confused with "heeling." The heeling style described above gives you good control of your dog but it is not always necessary. I find that the majority of dog owners are satisfied with the loose leash style of walking their dog. With loose leash walking the dog need not be in any special position but at the same time does not lag, or more importantly, does not pull on the leash. (Note: Dogs can learn multiple styles of walking.)

There can often be a bit of confusion about the best way to teach a dog to walk on a loose leash. Some of the problems contributing to the confusion are that dogs have different ways of behaving on leash. This means that **no one method can work for every dog**. Exactly how and where you start will depend on the individual dog. You will need to evaluate your dog to determine which category he is in; keeping in mind your dog may fall into more than one category.

> ➢ *The wanderer* – These are dogs that are everywhere. Generally they are really into the environment and seem to forget all about you as they go first in one direction and then in another. They act as if they cannot even hear you. Puppies and young dogs are often in this category.
> ➢ *The lagger* – Dogs that walk very slowly or reluctantly on leash. They often seem uncomfortable with the leash or rebel against it by backing up and trying to pull out of their collars.
> ➢ *The puller* – This is the most common type of dog. Pullers strain against the leash almost constantly dragging their owner behind them. It can be an exhausting experience to take one of these dogs on a walk.
> ➢ *The leash fighter* – Some dogs will fight the leash by taking it in their mouths and biting. Usually it is a play-fight and the dog wants to engage in a tug-of-war game with the owner. Puppies and young dogs commonly exhibit this behavior. Sometimes a dog may just be inexperienced with a leash and becomes frightened. They might react defensively and try to bite through the leash. A few dogs will exhibit displacement behavior. They are trying to bite someone or something but are restrained by the leash. They will turn and bite

the leash out of frustration. These are potentially very dangerous dogs. (See behavior modification, chapter 14)

If you recognize your dog in the descriptions above, you can skip ahead to that section. You may find more than one description fits your dog. Read anything that applies to your dog. If you have not yet tried putting a leash on your dog then I will first explain the best way to acclimate your dog to the leash.

The acclimation process is quite simple. Put a flat collar on your dog (make sure it is fitted properly) and attach a five or six foot leash. A lightweight leash is best. Allow your dog to walk around dragging the leash behind him. You must constantly supervise your dog during this time to ensure that the leash does not become entangled. Always remove the leash when you leave your dog unattended. After your dog has dragged the leash around for a while and does not seem bothered with it, you can pick up the end every so often and restrain him for a brief moment.

If your dog turns toward you when you restrain him, reward-mark and give him a treat. Let go of the leash afterwards and repeat the exercise a few seconds later. If he starts to struggle on the leash, just wait until he calms down and stops pulling. Reward-mark immediately and give him a treat. Repeat the exercise. If your dog is biting the leash when you restrain, read *The Leash Fighter*.

Practice this exercise until your dog always looks at you when the leash gets tight. At that point you are ready to take your dog for a short walk. Bring treats along on your walk so that you can reward him for good behavior and to lure him in the right direction when necessary. Do not expect to go very far the first time you take your dog for a walk but carefully observe his response to the leash and determine if he is a wanderer, lagger, puller or a fighter.

The Wanderer

Remember that you are competing directly with the environment. The environment is fascinating to the wanderer. You must become even more fascinating, which is not always easy. I often point out to my obedience class students that a sewer drain may very well be more interesting to their dog than they are. It is a somewhat humbling fact. The trick is to tip the odds in your favor by working first in familiar, low distraction areas, perhaps your yard or even inside your house.

Use a high value food treat and get your dog's attention. Holding on to his leash give the command "let's go" and start to walk luring your dog along side you with the treat. Keep the treat high so that his head is turned up. Each time he drops his head put the treat in front of his nose and draw his attention back up and to you. **Do not pull on the leash to get your dog in position**. Let your dog figure it out. Go ahead and give him the treat after three or four successful steps but have another ready quickly to keep him from looking away.

When your dog becomes more focused on the lure, gradually increase the amount of time between rewards. You can also fade the lure. To do this, put the treat to your dogs nose and begin to lure him forward but then stand completely upright holding the treat up higher just out of his reach. Take a few steps before rewarding, then repeat. **Note: Never reward your dog if he is jumping up.** If your dog tends to jump while being lured keep walking and reward only when your dog stops jumping for one or two steps. The jumping behavior will soon disappear if you are consistent. You should also do a lot of independent attention work with your dog (see Attention Exercises under **Secondary Stationary Commands** in chapter 13).

If your dog seems to be getting less distracted then you may allow him to forge ahead a little during walks. Be prepared to make a sudden stop just before he gets to the end of his leash. Without moving from your position or pulling the dog towards you lure him back into position, reward and continue the walk. Repeat the exercise as many times as it takes but always be generous with rewards for walking properly. As your dog matures and learns, treats can be gradually eliminated.

The Lagger

Some dogs seem to resent being on a leash and will refuse to move or move very slowly. Their recalcitrant behavior is often very frustrating and the owners frequently try to pull their dog along to encourage them to walk. Instead of being encouraged, the dog's opposition reflex automatically engages and there is no learning curve at all.

The solution to lagging is to lure the dog forward. Have some high value treats ready and just lure the dog forward without any tension on the leash at all. Once you get your dog moving simply follow the same procedure as described for a wandering dog. A target stick may also prove useful for this type of dog.

The Puller

Pulling is the most common leash behavior problem. If you have a young dog the problem can usually be resolved rather easily. If your dog is older and has been used to pulling for a while, it may be somewhat more difficult.

Consistency is key to training a dog not to pull on the leash. I will outline the method for eliminating the problem of pulling but the owner must **always** follow the rule or the problem will not get better. I cannot tell you how many times I have caught my clients allowing their dogs to pull them into the training yard for an obedience class. If your dog wants to go some place he has to learn that the only way to get there is to wait for you to lead the way. Your dog must "follow the leader."

A tight leash is an easy way for your dog to keep track of you. Your dog knows exactly where you are without looking at you as long as he can feel a tight leash. A tight leash means that the dog is the leader and you are following. You want to change this concept in your dog's mind. You want a tight leash to mean you are not going anywhere!

From the moment you put the leash on your dog, from the moment you step out the door or leave your car to go for a walk, you must be in charge. If your dog pulls on the leash you should stop immediately. Do not make a gradual stop. Make a sudden stop. To ensure the stop registers to your dog it is important that you **anticipate** when the leash is going to get tight. Make your stop **just before your dog gets to the end of the leash.** If the leash is already tight, it is too late (if this happens just stop and call your dog back to you, reward for the return and then start over). The stop that you make must be sudden enough to get a reaction from your dog.

You want your dog's attention here but you want it voluntarily. Pulling back hard enough to spin your dog around is not the goal. When you stop your dog should turn to look at you on his own. In the early stages, offer your dog a treat for looking at you. If your dog does not immediately look at you do not react. Stand completely still and just wait. Eventually your dog will look at you to see why you are not moving. Offer a treat then start moving again but be prepared to stop again as soon as the leash is going to go tight once again.

Be patient during this training. It can be frustrating at first because you may find that it could take you twenty minutes to just get a few feet. Do not worry about how far you get. Do not suspend the rest of the lesson so you can take your dog for the rest of his walk. Remember; once you start this training **you must always** stop when the leash is about to go tight.

For dogs that are particularly stubborn you can change directions. Instead of just stopping, turn 180 degrees and walk in the other direction. Stop suddenly but still do not spin your dog around. If you do not get his attention right away it is okay to pull him around gently as you start off in the opposite direction but not with sudden force. Walk a few steps in the other direction. As your dog comes up along side you reach down and give him a treat. He will most likely lunge ahead of you again going in the other direction. Change directions again just before the leash goes tight and repeat the exercise.

Your progress may be slow at first but your dog will eventually begin to pay more attention to you. He will also learn that the only way to get someplace is to wait for you. As your dog gets better at walking with you, begin to phase out the treats and substitute more verbal praise and a quick pat on the head. With enough practice and persistence your dog will eventually learn good leash manners and walk with you nicely.

When your dog starts to learn how to walk with you on the leash you can begin putting a command to the exercise. For informal walking you may want to use "let's go" or "walk." I personally reserve the word "heel" to indicate a more formal way of walking which is required in obedience competitions but pet dog owners can use any word that they want. Say your dog's name, then say, "let's go" and begin walking. If you have to make any corrections, repeat the command just before the correction.[40]

I am reasonably convinced that the previously described method can be used to teach virtually any dog good leash manners. However, some dogs have been pulling their owners around for so long that the habit is deeply rooted. Pulling for these dogs can become so well established that the behavior is practically "hard-wired." Although very difficult to alter, I believe it still can be done if the owner has enough patience.

If you have a determined puller, and tried the methods described here but are still experiencing difficulties, there is an alternative. I would urge you **not** to resort to a choke or prong collar because you are frustrated as many people have done. Instead, try a relatively new device that is on the market called a "head-halter." My experience with them is admittedly limited but so far favorable.

---

[40] Some people tell me that they simply cannot do this kind of training due to special circumstances. For example, a person residing in an apartment must take their dog out to relieve himself before going to work in the morning. They simply do not have time to do stop and go training. I suggest giving the dog a different command. Command, "pull" (as if it were your idea) and let the dog pull to where you have to go. Later, when there is more time, practice the "lets go" or "heel" command as outlined above. In this way the dog can learn when it is okay to pull and when it is not. It is important however to practice **not** pulling, that is the "lets go" or "walk" command, at least a little while during each walk. Unless you work seven days a week, there must be some mornings when you could work more on loose leash walking than pulling. Also, set aside some time to work on this more when your personal schedule permits. The idea is to phase out the "pull" command as you increase the "lets go" portion of your walk.

The head-halter is a non-aversive means of controlling your dog's behavior on leash. The device is fitted in such a way that you can, with practically no effort at all, turn your dog's head toward you as you walk. The principle is the same as the one that allows us to control a horse. Horses are much stronger than we are but with a halter we can easily turn the head and where the head goes the body must follow.

When dogs are first placed in a head-halter they may rebel against it and struggle to escape. With a little distraction and encouragement they can learn to settle down in a short time and your dog becomes comfortable with the new apparatus. At the same time your dog becomes totally controllable. The change can be almost miraculous because it is so quick.

My only reservations about head-halters are that they look like muzzles to the unenlightened, giving the wrong impression, and you can become dependant on them. I like to get voluntary attention from a dog. The head halter gives you the means of forcing your dog to look at you (but in a humane way) but he may never learn to do it voluntarily unless you practice. Admittedly, this may be a minor drawback for the average pet dog owner. If you have earnestly tried the other methods in this book but continue to have problems controlling your dog, then I would suggest you try a head halter. (Be sure to buy one that comes with complete instructions. The use of a head-halter is quite different from that of other more conventional collars.)

The Leash Fighter

If your dog likes to play tug-of-war with the leash do not encourage this behavior. The easiest way to stop your dog from playing tug with the leash is to immediately reach down, grab the collar and drop the leash. Just stand there restraining your dog without saying or doing anything else. Be as boring as you possibly can.

As soon as your dog lets go of the leash, pick it up again and release your grip on the collar. Continue your walk but be prepared to repeat the exercise the moment your dog bites the collar again. Dogs will not hang on to the leash for very long if you are not tugging back. It simply is not very much fun. Your dog will learn that you **never** play tug with the leash and the behavior will extinguish itself after a short time.

If leash biting is motivated by fear you should not use the method described above. You must eliminate the fear behavior using behavior modification methods. Some of these methods are described in chapter 14.

As mentioned, it is possible to teach your dog to walk in more than one style. You may also teach your dog to walk on the left, right, in front of you, behind you and more. Dogs can even learn to pull or not pull on command. It all depends on what you train. Train each position or style separately and give each one a different command. Later you can teach your dog to go from one position to another. I like, for example, to have my dogs go from the heel position to "center," which is walking between my legs. It is not practical but my dogs love doing it. Training just one way of walking can become boring so why not add a little excitement and teach something new? (See chapter 16, Dynamic Training, page 169) The following photographs illustrate just some of the possibilities.

Walking The Dog

Left: The author takes his dog, Jack, on a walk off lead. This style of walking provides good practical control of your dog. The dog is only required to walk at the author's side but not with a high level of attention. Heeling with attention is rarely required except in a competition ring.

Right: Jack walks between the legs of the author. This way of walking has no practical value at all except that Jack enjoys it as evidenced by the "happy" open mouth and high wagging tail. Using methods outlined in this book, owners can teach their dog to walk in a variety of ways if desired. Just attach a different command to each way and train separately.

Left: A high stepping Happy Jack shows off his competition style heeling. Jack maintains constant eye contact with the author as they walk. Jack remains in a perfect "heel position" even during turns. An impractical way to walk a dog outside of the competition ring but it does serve to demonstrate that a dog can be taught how to walk in nearly any position the owner wishes. It only takes a little patience and training.

Leash Manners

Right: The author demonstrates with Pepper how to lure a dog into position while walking. The lure is being held a bit high at this point to encourage Pepper to look up. The lure is gradually faded by holding it higher and higher and rewarding less often. A command is paired with the behavior so that eventually the dog will walk in this manner on command with no lure at all, on or off leash. All it takes is a thousand miles.

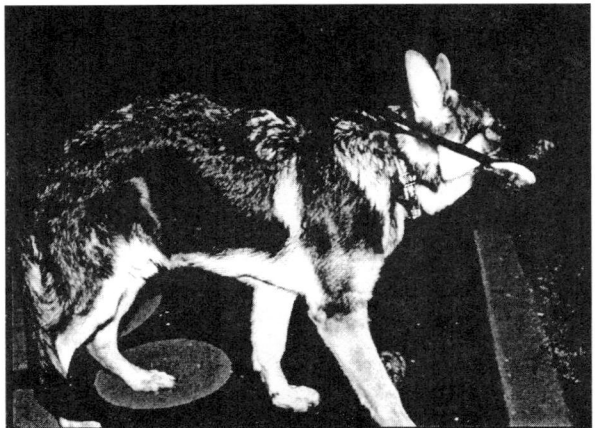

Left: This young German Shepherd Dog likes to bite at the leash, which is a common puppy behavior. To keep it from becoming a habit, always grab the collar and drop the leash. Hold the dog still but say or do nothing else. The puppy will find this game boring and let go of the leash. Repeating this exercise every time the dog bites the leash will soon eliminate the problem.

Right: Pepper demonstrates the "follow" command. Usually the author uses the "follow" while his dog is on a leash in crowds where it is easier to walk single file for short distances. However, the behavior is taught off-leash first then the leash is simply put on later. To teach, let the dog know you have treats and keep her attention on your hands as you drop a treat behind you. Say the word "follow" at each drop. Not surprisingly, dogs quickly learn to lag behind to pick up treats each time you say, "follow."

Chapter 13
Advanced Pet Dog Training

Some dog owners may consider the exercises in this chapter to be unnecessary. How much training you need for your dog is an individual choice. However, bear in mind that I have never had a complaint about an over-trained dog. Complaints always arise from under-trained dogs. There is no such thing as too much training. The training exercises in this chapter are useful and I strongly urge dog owners to train most, if not all of them.

Advanced pet dog training is not the same as advanced obedience training. Advanced obedience training calls for very precise and often stylized behaviors for your dog to perform. The behaviors are not always useful in everyday life. By contrast, advanced pet dog training is still based on practical needs.

Truly advanced training is not covered in this book. The term advanced is used to differentiate this training from the foundation training described in the previous chapter. In spite of the word "advanced" the exercises in this chapter are not very difficult to teach your dog. Advanced pet dog training is a natural extension of the foundation work in chapter 12. If you have done a good job with your foundation training the exercises in this chapter should not give you or your dog any difficulties.

- Secondary Stationary Commands -
Attention Exercises

Attention exercises are fun and easy to teach. They are also deceptively important. It is impossible to get your dog to respond to commands or learn them if he is not paying attention to you. Many owners complain that their dog ignores them and have behavior problems as a result. Attention exercises help solve many behavioral problems and makes training much easier.

The "name game" (described in **chapter 12**) was the first step in attention. We now want to go to a new level. The "wait" command is an integral part of attention exercises and we will begin with this command but attention is also trained in other ways. Basically, you want your dog to look to you for everything that she wants. For example, if she wants to go outside, she must look at you before you open the door. If she wants to eat her food, she must look at you and wait for your permission to eat. If she wants to go for a walk, she must look at you before you will put the leash on her collar.

This may seem like it will be a lot of trouble but it is not. Once you learn the basic principles behind teaching attention (which you will by teaching the wait), you will be able to do it with little effort. Your dog will learn attention quickly and all of your training will become much easier.

If the reader will indulge me for a moment, I would like to be very non-objective for a moment. Besides the practical aspects of attention training, there is something extraordinary that happens when a dog is taught how to pay attention. When your dog learns to look straight into your eyes you will begin to feel a connection with your dog that is almost mystical. It is a look that will always lift your spirit. It has been said that the eyes are the windows to the soul. When you look into your dog's eyes while her attention is riveted on yours, you will see intelligence, eagerness, humor and all the things that make up your dog's soul. Attention exercises are worth teaching on many different levels.[41]

Back to more practical matters, the "wait" command is similar to a "stay" (see next topic) but it is less formal. When given a command to "wait" your dog is expected to freeze in whatever position it happens to find herself the moment the command is given. The dog will look to you for further instructions because another command always follows a wait command. Waits are usually rather short in duration lasting not more than a minute.

Waits are used when you want your dog to simply remain in one place temporarily or to hold up until you want her to move again. I often use "wait" before crossing a road or while I am setting my dog up to do some other command, like a recall. In each case, when I use the "wait" command, my dog knows to freeze in position but keep her attention on me because I am going to tell her to do something else at any moment.

Begin your training in a quiet area where your dog is comfortable. You want your dog to concentrate on you so find a place where distractions will be at a minimum. To teach attention and eventually a wait, show your dog a treat in your hand but do not let her have it. Bring it close to her nose to get her attention but then hold it well above her head with your arm out stretched to the side. If she loses interest, bring it back to her nose and repeat. You want her to be looking at the treat or even trying to get it from your hand.

At first your dog will be confused and a little frustrated at not being able to get the treat. The most common response is for your dog to finally sit and turn their eyes towards you in confusion. Watch closely for the eye contact. The very moment she looks at you, reward-mark her and give her the treat. **Timing is critical** on this exercise because you are actually training the eye contact at this time. At first eye contact may only be a mere glance. Watch closely for it and be prepared to **reward-mark instantly.**

It may take some time for your dog to look at you. Be patient and wait even if it takes a long time for her to finally look at you. At this point in training you should not be giving any verbal commands to your dog. Again, just be ready to reward-mark and treat immediately for eye contact. If you repeat this exercise several times in a row you will notice that your dog is going to start looking at you more and more quickly every time you hold the food out in your hand.

Once your dog is only glancing at the food but looking to you immediately, it is time to go to the next level. Start saying your dog's name, just as you did in the name game. You should easily get to this next level with most dogs during the very first session. Remember, it helps if your dog is highly food motivated. I recommend training just before mealtime for best results.

If your dog is looking at you right away, start delaying your reward-mark. When your dog looks at you wait for one second (count to yourself one-thousand-one) before you

---

[41] If the attention exercises described in this chapter are taught properly the result will be a dog that likes to stare at its owner whenever it wants something. I have come across some behaviorists who do not think that it is wise to teach a dog to stare. They claim that staring to a dog is a challenge or threat and could result in problems. A stare from a dog can indeed be a challenge gesture or some dogs, not trained in attention work, could misinterpret a stare from its handler but dogs that are trained to watch their handler do not have any problems. A stare is considered a challenge among many animals, including human beings. However, we are all able to distinguish between the stare of two lovers on a park bench and the stare of two boxers in a ring about to do battle. Obviously, not all stares are alike and I believe that with only a little training that dogs can easily recognize the difference.

reward-mark. Make sure your dog looks at you the whole time. If she glances away, start the exercise again. If you get four or five successful one-second stares in a row try increasing the time to two seconds. When your dog will look at you immediately and maintain constant eye contact for two seconds, then go to three and so on. You should probably not go past four or five-second delays the first session. The next time you repeat a session start with a short delay before reward-marking and then you should be able to work back up to longer ones very quickly.

You can continue to add time, gradually adding up to as much as a minute or more if you want to over many training sessions. Build the time slowly. Do not proceed too fast. If your dog starts to look away or steal quick glances at the treat then you have gone too fast. Back up in your training. Another way to train your dog not to steal glances at your out stretched hand is to begin giving your dog a treat from the opposite hand at random times. In other words, put a treat in both hands and show your dog one of them and hold it out as usual, keeping the other behind your back. After your dog has maintained eye contact with you for a few seconds, reward-mark and give her the treat from the hand behind your back. This will keep her from anticipating which direction the treat will come.

When you have worked up to a reliable five-second delay start adding the command "wait" with a hand signal. For a hand signal, I recommend holding your hand out in front of you for just a second, like a policeman stopping traffic. If you have not already been doing so, make sure you "release" your dog after every exercise from this point on.

You should be ready to start phasing out showing your dog a treat prior to this exercise. Begin by saying your dog's name and then put your hand directly in front of your dog's face with your fingers spread out and say, "wait." Use this signal from now on with the simultaneous command "wait." Continue to hold a treat in your other hand with an out-stretched arm.

The next step is to eliminate any sign of the treat. Begin holding the treat out but with a bent arm. Continue to use your wait signal and command but gradually hold the treat closer and closer to your side until you are able to keep it behind your back. You should now have a reliable wait on command without showing your dog the treat first.

At this stage most dogs will freeze automatically in whatever position they are in when the command is given. If for some reason your dog is not freezing then you must teach them to remain in position. For example, if your dog is standing when you tell her to "wait" and she begins to sit, go ahead and command her to stand, then repeat the "wait" command. After a few tries your dog should catch on to freezing in position.

Now you are ready to start stepping away. Ask for a "wait" then try to put one foot back. Do not actually take the step yet. Bring your foot forward again, reward-mark and treat. If your dog seems steady and does not respond to your foot moving back then actually take a step back after you give the command "wait." Quickly, before your dog can follow you, step back in front of her, reward-mark and treat. Repeat this exercise a few times until your dog is comfortable with you moving back. Make sure you release your dog after each exercise.

After a few successful practice sessions you can go to the next step in your training. Use your hand signal and verbal command "wait," take your usual step back and instead of stepping back right away, wait for one second. Move back to your dog and wait for a few seconds more, then reward-mark and treat. Begin building up your time while standing back from your dog gradually just as you did while standing close. When you are up to ten seconds or so you can take three steps back but go back to waiting only one second again. Build up the time at this distance as before. Continue to increase distance but always start with a short wait time then build more time gradually at each new distance.

After several days of training you should be able back up several paces, perhaps ten to twenty feet, and have your dog wait for twenty to thirty seconds. At that point, after giving your "wait" command, try turning your back on your dog to take one or two steps. If your dog breaks her wait when you turn away start again but try just partially turning away. After a few successful waits try turning away completely again. During this exercise you will loose eye contact temporarily but you should regain it upon turning to look at your dog. Once again build on the exercise slowly until you can take several steps with your back turned. Each time turn towards your dog and wait for a few seconds. Always return to your dog before you reward-mark and give her a treat. You can then begin increasing the amount of time before returning to your dog.

The next step is to increase distractions. As with any new criteria do this slowly and build on success rather than failure. Try to add mild distractions, like having someone stand near your dog while you practice. Go to other locations. At first practice in familiar places where your dog has been before but you have not tried any training. Gradually, work up to going to novel locations with many new distractions.

Remember to back up in your training anytime your dog makes a mistake. Build each step slowly and do not rush your dog. You must go at your dog's pace and avoid as many errors as possible. Your dog will learn more rapidly by her successes than by her failures. It is up to you to set your dog up for success by progressing slowly.

At the beginning of this section I mentioned that another command always follows a wait. Be sure that you always release your dog or give another command after asking for a wait. Now that your dog knows the "wait" command you can use it in a variety of practical situations. At meal times, make your dog wait for you to put her food down. Make her wait while you unlock and open your car door before giving her permission to get in. Make her wait before you hand her a favorite toy. A reliable wait is great for practicing recalls. You can command your dog to "wait" while you walk away and then call your dog to you. When you do these things you will no longer need to provide a treat for a reward. Getting to do something after the wait will be the reward. You will probably find the "wait" command one of the most useful behaviors that you can teach your dog.

One final attention exercise that I like to teach my dogs is the "leave it" command. Most dog owners will find this one useful. The idea is to be able to command your dog to move away from something and look at you whenever you say, "leave it." It often comes in handy when you are walking your dog and she finds something on the ground of interest but you do not want her to pick up, e.g. discarded chicken bones or other trash. It can also be used to direct your dog's attention away from a passing nervous pedestrian on the sidewalk or even another dog.

The easiest way to start off is by putting a food treat in your open hand and showing it to your dog. When she tries to take it, immediately close your hand. Hold your hand still and let the dog try to figure out how to get the treat. Usually, they will nose and lick your hand in an attempt to get at the treat. Say nothing and watch your dog closely. The instant she gives up and turns away from your hand for any reason, reward-mark and give her a treat **from your other hand**. Repeat the exercise until your dog turns away automatically each time you close your hand.

You can begin adding the command "leave it" as soon as your dog starts to understand that she must turn away from the treat in order to get a reward. Now it is time to raise the criteria. Each time you say, "leave it" wait for your dog to look at your face before reward-marking. This is taught almost exactly like the "wait." The difference between the "wait" and "leave it" command is that your dog does not have to stop or "freeze" in position on a "leave it" command. If you have already taught the wait exercise, getting your dog to look at you should not take long at all. If your dog consistently looks at you each time you say, "leave it" then you can move to the next step in this training.

You must be very alert and quick for this step. Place a food treat on the ground in front of your dog. As soon as your dog goes for it slap your hand over the food and command, "leave it." If your dog turns away, reward-mark and treat with the other hand. If your dog tries to get the food under your hand just wait until she turns away and reward-mark as you did in the beginning of this exercise.[42] If you have progressed step-by-step in this training exercise, your dog should learn very quickly to look at you when you say, "leave it."

It should be possible to put a treat on the floor and say, "leave it," and your dog will not move but simply look at you. You can start adding time before you reward-mark and treat as you did with the "wait." You can also start letting your dog take the treat on the ground instead of from your free hand. Give a command like, "free" or "take it." A good time to practice at this stage is at mealtime. When you start to put the food bowl down command, "leave it'" and be prepared to pick the food bowl back up immediately if your dog does not comply. If she does comply, wait a few seconds, making sure she is looking at you, and then give her a release command so she can eat.

The final stage of this training is to "bait" your dog. Set one or two food items along the ground in advance where you walk your dog. Make them obvious so your dog will not miss them. You will need a leash on your dog. As you approach the food tell your dog, "leave it." If she complies then reward-mark and give her a treat from your pocket. If she tries to sniff the bait prevent her from touching it with pressure on the leash. **Do not allow your dog to get the bait.** Continue to walk past the bait. The instant she looks away from the bait, reward-mark and give her a treat from your pocket. Practice until you get reliable compliance from your dog every time you use the "leave it" command.

I strongly encourage dog owners to work on all attention exercises, the "name game," "wait" and "leave it." They are easy to train and you develop a good foundation for maintaining your dog's attention, which will have carry over value in all aspects of training and control of your dog. Your dog will not obey you unless she is paying attention to you. The attention exercises help promote this habit.

---

[42] Many dogs are so quick that owners have trouble getting the food on the ground. To solve this problem just pull the treat away from your dog quickly even if you have not been able to put it on the ground. Attempt to put the treat down again but pull your hand, with the treat, away if your dog dives after it. Keep repeating this over and over. Eventually, your dog will stop going after the treat. Now you can proceed as described in the main test. **Warning: Never** allow your dog to snatch or steel the treat before you give permission. If this happens, your dog will learn to be fast, faster than you. Do not let that happen, so stay alert while training this exercise.

May I Have Your Attention Please?

Right: The author demonstrates an attention exercise with his dog Pepper. A treat is in his right hand but Pepper's attention remains on her owner's face. She has learned that she will get the reward but only by keeping her attention on her owner. This basic and important principle is at the root of the Follow The Leader training method.

Left: The author's dog, Pepper, "waits" for permission to cross the street. The author feels that the wait command is one of the most useful commands that an owner can teach their dog, especially while the dog is off leash. Note how Pepper is paying *attention* to her owner as she waits for the next command.

Stay and Place

The commands "stay" and "place" are related but have slightly different meanings. I will give you a definition for each command and how it is used. Then, I will explain how you can train your dog to perform each of these behaviors. Also, "stay" and "place" differ fundamentally from a "wait." In a "wait" your dog is expected to look at you and wait for another command. When your dog is in a "stay" or "place" he does not have to pay attention to you at all. He simply has to remain where he is without moving. He can completely relax and go to sleep for all you care.

The command "stay" is given after some stationary command has first been given. You may give a verbal command "stay" or it can be taught as a silent command or an automatic response, i.e. if you tell your dog to sit you do not have to say anything further if you train your dog to automatically remain in the sit until you say otherwise. The choice is yours but **you must always use a release word to end the exercise**. I will explain how to teach the "stay" as a verbal command but if you prefer automatic "stays" then the technique is exactly the same, just leave out the command or signal.

The stay is usually broken into two or sometimes three types, "down stay," "sit stay" and less often "stand stay." To issue the command you must first put your dog in a particular position, usually either a sit or down, and you say, "stay." This means your dog must remain in that position and not move until you "release" him. In theory, a trained dog should be able to maintain a "stay" indefinitely. Of course even the very best trained dog would have a limit to how long it would maintain a "stay." We may reasonably expect a "stay" time of twenty to thirty minutes or more with adequate training.

We use "place" to tell our dog to go to a previously defined area or location and remain there in any position until released from the command. Defined areas or locations can be a particular place in a room, a mat, bedding, crate, chair, etc. Dogs going to "place" have the option of lying down, standing or sitting. Owners may want their dogs to automatically remain in "place" until released or a secondary command of "stay" may be given (if the stay command is given then the dog must first be placed in a particular position).

Stays are useful when you want your dog to remain in one place for a few minutes while your attention is on other things. For example, the family decides to go to the park for a picnic and take the dog. You may want to put your dog in a "down stay" in a shady area while you are unloading things from the car. Your dog can relax and need not pay any attention to you but must remain in place without moving from that position. Once you are settled you could release your dog then allow her to run about under your supervision.

Place is most convenient at home but could be used in other situations. If we continue with our hypothetical park adventure there may be a point, say when it is time to eat, when you want your dog to settle down in one place for awhile. You can have your dog trained to lie on a mat (it can be a towel, large ring, pillow or most any comfortable object) so that when you are ready you simply show your dog the mat and say "place." Or, you can simply point to a spot and your dog would go and either stand, sit or lie down where you indicate.

The difference between stay and place is that with a stay you must put your dog in a location and choose a position (sit, down, stand) you want your dog to remain motionless until released. With the "place" command your dog goes to a pre-determined location (or object) in no particular position (dogs can decide for themselves) and remains until released.

Before you teach these commands, decide exactly what your needs are going to be. If you plan to compete in obedience trails with your dog then you will need to teach all three variations of the "stay" command. Whether or not you plan to compete with your dog, not everyone will find it necessary to teach both stay commands and place. Some find it adequate to have just a "stay" where others prefer to have just a "place." It will really depend on the level of discipline or obedience that you expect or need from your dog. I will explain how to teach each exercise individually.

Teaching The Stay

Teaching the "stay" is very similar to the "wait." You will need to teach each variation of the stay separately ("sit, down" and "stand"). Except for the position itself, all variations are taught in the same way. If you plan to teach a stand stay it is best to begin by teaching a sit or down stay first. Rewarding your dog in either a sit or stand will require that you bring the food directly to her mouth but in the down the food can be placed on the floor between the front feet.

Start your training in a quiet familiar place. Command your dog into a position, either sit, down or stand. Give the command "stay" and wave your hand, fingers together, in a short chopping motion in front of your dog's nose. As long as your dog remains in the position reward her with treats at various intervals. In the beginning give treats often but gradually lengthen the amount of time between treats as your dog learns. If your dog moves or changes positions, command her back into position again and start over. **Do not get angry or rough with your dog** if she breaks her "stay." Simply start over.

At first do not expect your dog to stay for a long time, especially active puppies. Two or three seconds is plenty of time for the first couple of trials. Gradually increase the amount of time you expect your dog to stay over several weeks working once or twice a day. End each exercise with your release word such as "free" (review The Release). You can use any word you want but I do not recommend the word "okay." This word is used too much in our daily speech and you may accidentally release your dog from a stay.[43]

There is no reward-mark for this exercise. Your dog will simply learn that as long as she remains in one position she will get treats. However, you will want to gradually increase the amount of time between treats as well as the overall length of the stay. Eventually, treats can be phased out altogether during the stay and the release becomes the only reward that the dog gets. Always make the release an exciting and worthwhile event for your dog. This makes the release itself a reward. After a rather dull and

---

[43] I am speaking from personal experience on this point. I used to use the word "okay" to allow my dog to get up from a stay. One day, while I had my dog at work with me, I was conducting an important meeting with several people in my office. They were completely unaware that I had a dog in the room. He was quietly lying hidden from view. He was in a down stay next to me behind my desk. The meeting was winding down after about thirty minutes and I said "okay" intending to mark the conclusion of our discussion. My dog (a Belgian Malinois) suddenly leaped up, thinking we were going to do something. There were several shrieks and screams from my guests (by the way only one was a woman!) when my sixty-pound dog came bounding into view. He simply looked at me waiting to see what we were going to do while I made hasty assurances to everyone that he was friendly and that they could evacuate the office in an unhurried and orderly fashion. From that day forward I always found them carefully peering over my desk each time they came in my office to see if I had my dog.

disciplined stay, an exciting release with lots of praise and laughter is going to be very appealing to your dog.

As you increase the amount of time your dog remains in a stay, begin stepping away and adding distance. Train this in the same way described for the wait at the beginning of this chapter. It is okay to repeat the "stay" command to remind your dog what she is doing during this early training but repeated commands should be phased out with time.

As your dog becomes more reliable in the "stay," teach the exercise with more distractions. Increase distractions slowly because you want your dog to be successful. You can be inventive about your distraction work, creating them yourself. You or an assistant can try walking past your dog, tossing a ball, walk by with another dog or make noises. Take your dog to unfamiliar locations. Work up to doing stays on busy city sidewalks with people, cars and other dogs walking by (a leash should always be used for safety). Of course, all of this is done gradually in a step-by-step fashion.

If you intend to teach only one position I would recommend the down stay. Dogs can remain in a down stay for the longest period of time because it is the most comfortable position. There are numerous ways for your dog to be in a down position. One is in the "sphinx" position (technically called sternal recumbency) where the dog is in a very high alert pose. Another is a lateral recumbent position where the dog is entirely on its side. A combination of sphinx (sternal) and lateral recumbency is a common down position where your dog is on its side in the back and in a sternal repose in the front.

Encourage your dog to relax in the down by learning to turn to the side either in a lateral recumbent or combination sternal/lateral recumbency position. You can do this by gently pushing the hip to one side. If your dog resists, do not force her into the position. Any down position is acceptable as long as she is willing to stay. Your dog should be allowed to change down positions as long as she does not actually get up. Under these circumstances you could reasonably expect and train your dog to remain in a down for as much as an hour.

Once your dog is performing reliable stays for a few minutes at a time a more advanced stay can be taught where the owner can be out of site of the dog. Put your dog in a stay and then try stepping behind a barrier, such as a door or fence, where your dog cannot see you. Only step out of sight for a second or two at first. Continue to work for more out of sight time in a gradual way just as you did to increase time in full sight of the dog. It is often helpful if you can use a barrier that allows you to surreptitiously observe your dog for any breaks in the stay. Any breaks in a stay should be corrected quickly (by calmly restarting the exercise). As always, try not to progress too fast.

Whether you are doing in sight or out of sight stays, remember to make releases exciting and a jackpot reward would be most appropriate after a particularly long stay. Stays are very difficult for a dog. To the dog stays are boring and it prevents them from being with you. Good, reliable stays always deserve a great reward after the release.

Do not forget to release your dog or accidentally exceed your current training level. For example, do not give your dog a command to stay and then fall asleep watching television. Always monitor your dog and release before she decides to terminate the exercise herself. This is another form of errorless learning.

Teaching Place

Teaching a stay first can facilitate learning the "place" command but it is not necessarily required. I will describe how to teach "place" with or without a "stay" command.

The first thing you will need to do is decide where you want your dog to go when you say, "place." I do not recommend that it be an isolated area. Dogs are social animals and like to be near their owners. Usually place is a spot in the same room the owner frequently inhabits, such as the family room or living room. You can teach a separate place in several rooms if you want. For example, whenever someone comes to the front door of my house, I tell my dogs to "place" and they go to a location a few feet away from the door. If I am in the family room and I want my dogs to go to "place" they go to a special spot in that room.

One of the easiest ways to teach place is to use a mat (or a dog bed if you prefer). You can move the mat to any location or have several of them distributed in special locations throughout the house. For instructional purposes I will tell you how to teach "place" to your dog using a mat but the procedure is the same regardless of where you decide to "place" your dog. It can be a special corner of a room or just wherever you point.

Take your mat and lay it in a desired location. Stand a short distance away, perhaps only three or four feet, and get your dog's attention by saying your dog's name. Point towards the nearby mat when she looks at you. Of course your dog will have no idea what you want so use a treat to **lure your dog to the mat**. It is important that your dog walks to the mat without you pushing or pulling in any way. Be sure to **keep pointing** at the mat with one hand as you lure her with the other.

Once you lure your dog to the mat, reward-mark and give her a treat. Secondarily, you may give a sit or down command if you wish but make sure you have rewarded the initial behavior of going to the mat first. If you have taught a "stay" command you can also give that command as well but it is not necessary that your dog know the "stay" command prior to teaching this exercise.

If you have your dog in a stay then release her after a few minutes and repeat the exercise. If you have not taught a stay then just have your dog sit or down on the mat and continue to offer treats as long as your dog stays in place. If your dog moves away, repeat the exercise after a few seconds. If your dog voluntarily stays in place, release her after a few seconds with a "free" command and allow her to move away. Then repeat the exercise.

Staying in place is not the most important part of the exercise at first. You want to teach your dog to go to "place" first and then later you will teach her to stay there until you release her. Always start the exercise from the same spot each time and point to the mat after saying your dog's name. When your dog begins to anticipate going to the mat, it is time to change the criteria.

Surreptitiously place a treat on the mat. Go to your starting point, say your dog's name and point to the mat. If desired you can now begin giving the simultaneous command "place." Try to hang back just a little allowing your dog to take the lead if she is willing. If not, then you must continue to lure her but try to fade this out as soon as you can. The moment she gets to the mat reward-mark and let her find the treat (point it out to her if she does not see it right away) as a reward rather than giving her one from your hand. Proceed, as before, keeping her in place for a few seconds but you may want to increase the amount of time slightly before the release. Repeat the exercise several times until your dog is anticipating the reward being on the mat by going to "place" quickly and as soon as you give the command.

When your dog is responding reliably to your command it is then time to add more criteria. Point and give your dog the "place" command but do not have a treat waiting on the mat. As soon as she arrives on the mat reward-mark and give another command such as "down." Reward-mark the correct response then quickly give her a jackpot reward.

From this time forward you should always give a "down" command. You could ask for a sit or stand but these positions are difficult to maintain for long periods. You may want your dog to remain in place for longer periods of time so a down is the most comfortable position. If you always tell your dog "down" when you send her to place she will eventually begin to anticipate the command and lie down automatically without being told.

Up to this point you should have been doing all of this training from the same location each time. It is now time to increase your distance or change your starting location. Make only slight changes, nothing drastic to avoid confusing your dog. Help reassure your dog that she is doing the right thing by temporarily going back to placing a treat on the mat in advance. You may also want to follow close behind your dog at least back to the original starting point. If your dog is comfortable about going to the mat on her own you can reward-mark after she is in place. Again, go slowly in a step-by-step fashion to avoid any errors along the way. Continue to change your location and distance from the "place" until your dog will go to it from anywhere in the room or even from a different room.

When your dog is going quickly to place each time she hears the command and/or sees you point, you can then start to work on requiring even more time before the release. Do this gradually just as described for a stay. If your dog already knows the stay you still may want to re-train an automatic stay whenever you send your dog to her place rather than having to give multiple commands, i.e. "place, down, stay." The choice is entirely up to you.

Just as your dog will anticipate the down each time she can also learn to anticipate the stay each time. But, because the stay is a slightly different exercise than place you want to use the word "place" to differentiate it from "stay." To teach an automatic stay in place follow the instructions for the stay except use the word "place" instead of "stay" once your dog is in the down position. At first, you can repeat the command "place" as often as necessary to remind your dog where she should be but you should soon phase out these extra commands just as you would with a simple stay. Eventually your dog will learn to go to place on command and simply wait there until released in the same way your dog learned the stay.

You should now have a dog that will go to her mat and stay when given the command "place" from any location in the room or even other rooms if you train her that way. You can stop your training at this point or continue, depending on your expectations. You may want to have a different place in other rooms for example. To train, put the mat in each of the different rooms and start your training all over again in each novel location. You may need to back up a bit in your training at first to get your dog to respond correctly in each new location. If you have trained the "place" command thoroughly, you probably will not have to start from the very beginning. However no matter where you have to start, she will most likely be able to progress through the steps much more rapidly than before.

If you want to phase out the mat and just use a location, teach with the mat first then remove it but send your dog to the exact same location. Back up in your training when you remove the mat because your dog will most likely be confused at first. When your dog is really proficient at going to place, try going to a different location or room and just point to a spot on the floor when you give your command. If your dog does not respond, lure her to the place while you continue to point. You can teach your dog to go to place at any spot that you point to. This is convenient if you are in a strange building or room and need your dog to lie quietly in a particular location.

Stay and Place

Left: The stay signal. A chopping motion with the hand in front of the dog is frequently used as a standard "stay" signal. Other trainers may bring the palm of the hand close to the nose. The actual signal that is used is unimportant as long as it is consistent. Always release your dog from a stay and **reward well**. Stays are not much fun for the dog so we need to provide them with some incentive.

Right: Going to "place." Sending your dog to "place" is fairly easy to train but requires some patience. Training proceeds slowly in a step-by-step process. With time, the trainer gradually increases the distance from where he sends his dog to "place." Providing a clearly defined "place" with a mat or pillow facilitates this exercise.

Getting Down

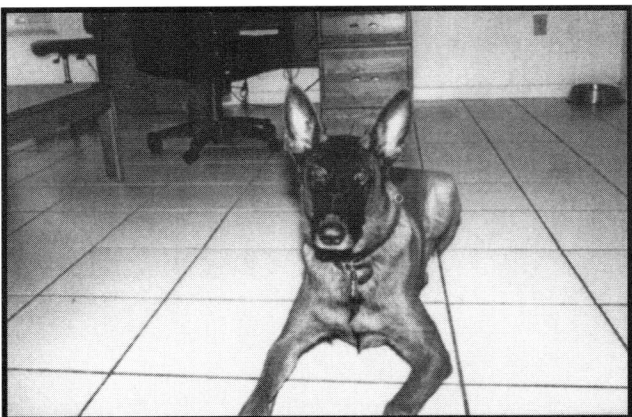

Left: The author's dog, Pepper, demonstrates the down position technically known as sternal recumbency. It is the most alert pose of the down positions. The author teaches this position to his dogs as a "drop" command. Upon hearing the command "drop" (or seeing a hand signal) Pepper will quickly go to this "sphinx" position and stay alert for another command, which always follows after a short time.

Right: Pepper is now in a more relaxed position known as sternal/lateral recumbency. She goes to this position when given the command "down." She can remain in this position for long periods of time and it is used for the "down, stay" command. Pepper can lay her head down between her front paws and be comfortable that way or turn completely on her side as seen in the next photograph.

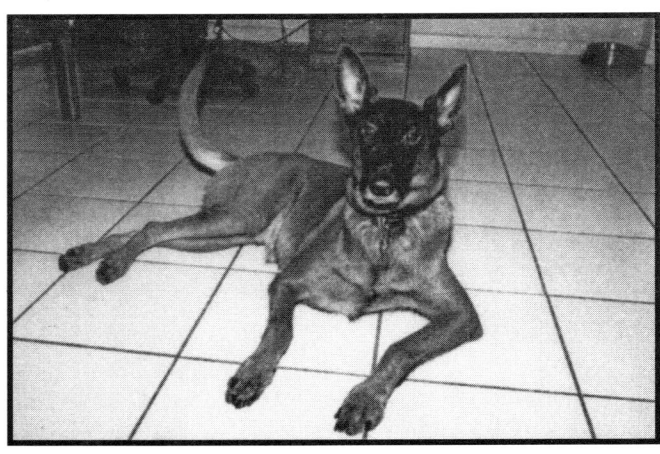

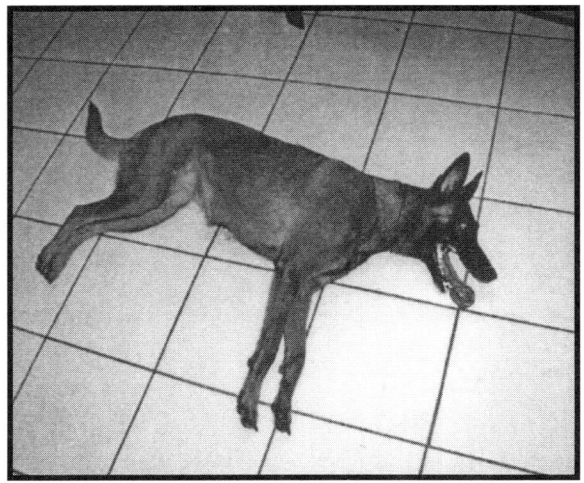

Left: Lateral recumbency is one of the most relaxed positions for a dog. The author recommends teaching this position to your dog when doing "down, stays." Because the dog is in such a relaxed pose they are less likely to get up and can remain comfortable for longer periods of time.

Part 4

Adjunct

Chapter 14
The Dog Whisperer

- Behavior Modification -

Young puppies arrive with pretty much a clean slate as far as behavior goes. If you raise your puppy properly using the principles outlined in this book, you can expect to have relatively few problems. However, older puppies and dogs may come with a number of built-in problems. Most of these problems are relatively easy to solve if you simply re-train, again using training principles from this book. Some problems are not so easy to resolve and may require professional help from a qualified pet behaviorist.

If you have a particular problem with your dog, you should first carefully analyze the behavior before deciding on a course of action. Always look at the problem from your dog's point of view. Try to set aside all anthropomorphic interpretations and be objective. This is not always easy for a dog owner to do. Pet behaviorists are able to look at the problem with more objectivity and should always be consulted in difficult cases.

Basically, owners have four options to handle any given behavior problem:
1. The owner can just live with the problem.
2. The owner can use management techniques that will either cure or at least prevent the problem.
3. An active re-training or behavior modification program can be implemented.
4. The owner can get rid of the dog (surrender to a shelter or euthanize).

Obviously, we would not like to see owners use this last option. Many owners do simply live with the problem but it is usually not necessary. Often management techniques are the simplest and sometimes even the most effective way to take care of a problem.[44] Re-training or behavior modification is most often the best solution of all but it can be the most technically difficult resolution, depending on the exact nature of the problem.

A successful behavior modification program hinges on an accurate diagnosis of the problem. Diagnosis can be very difficult. I often get clients who ask me, "How do I stop my dog from barking?" This seemingly simple question is actually quite complex. I can think of at least ten different reasons that a dog may bark. Each reason would have its own solution. It is critical that I find out much more about the problem before giving any advice of how to stop a dog from barking.

I would strongly recommend that owners solicit the help of a professional pet behaviorist if they have any serious problems with their dog. Ask your veterinarian for a

---

[44] There is a very old joke about the patient that goes to his doctor and says, "Doctor, doctor, my arm hurts whenever I do this!" The doctor replies, "Well, don't do that!" Management techniques for dogs involve this very principle. The owner simply prevents the dog from doing it. This might mean using a crate at certain times or just locking the garbage pail behind a closed cabinet door. The result is that the problem is resolved through management, which may or may not result in an eventual change in the dog's behavior. For example, if your dog always likes to chew on shoes you could teach him not to chew on shoes by saying "no" and giving him an appropriate object to chew and then praise. This would be behavior modification but management would probably be a more effective solution in this case. Management would be to simply keep shoes away from your dog by always keeping them in a secure location. Months or years later, your dog may not chew on shoes even when they are left out as a result of the management program.

referral. Be aware that good dog trainers are not necessarily good pet behaviorists. But then, pet behaviorists do not necessarily have to have a Ph.D. or even a college degree to be a good pet behaviorist. Referral from a veterinarian is the best way to find a qualified professional but if that is not possible be sure to at least get some references and ask about their experience.

If you feel that the problem is not serious and would like to find a resolution yourself, you may be able to use the following troubleshooting chart to help you isolate the exact nature of the problem and decide on a remedy. The chart is by no means complete but I have tried to cover the most common problems. If the chart does not seem to cover the particular problem that you may be experiencing with your dog, check *Miscellaneous Problems* at the end of this chapter. Use the chart below by starting at number one, find the answer that fits best to your dog's problem and go to the next number as instructed until you reach a possible diagnosis. Then refer to the section in this chapter dedicated to that particular problem.

1. Is this a sudden problem or one that has been developing slowly?
    A. Sudden problem (go to #3)
    B. Slow developing problem (go to #4)
    C. New dog so you do not know (go to #2)
2. Take your dog to your veterinarian for a thorough examination to eliminate any medical causes.
    A. Medical cause found (follow veterinarians instructions)
    B. No medical cause found (go to #4)
3. Does the start of the problem correspond to any sudden change in the dog's routine or environment? (e.g. children starting a new school year, new pets or people in the house, construction in the house or nearby, new furniture, etc.)
    A. Yes (go to #4)
    B. No (go to #2)
4. How would you characterize the problem?
    A. Destructive behavior (read *Destructive Behavior*)
    B. Aggressive behavior (read *Aggression*)
    C. House soiling behavior (read *Housetraining Problems*)
    D. Fearful behavior (read *Fearful Dogs*, end of chapter 11)
    E. Barking behavior (read *Excessive Barking*)
    F. Escape behavior (read *Escape Behavior*)

Destructive Behavior

If your dog is destructive important clues that may reveal the causes for the behavior can be found by analyzing exactly what is being destroyed and when. The first question to ask yourself is, "Does the destructive behavior occur only while you are not present?" If so, does it occur within thirty minutes or so of your departure? Is the destruction directed primarily at or near exit doors, windows or objects that may have a strong scent of the owner, such as chair cushions or clothing? If the answer is yes to any of these questions your dog is exhibiting signs of separation anxiety. Read the next section on *Separation Anxiety*.

If the answer to any of the above questions is no, then the problem could have other causes. It may be normal investigative or play behavior (see *How To Stop Your Puppy From Chewing,* chapter 11 for re-training). Or it can also be attention solicitation. Make sure you are providing your dog with enough exercise and social stimulation. Dogs do not exercise on their own. They need participation by the owner. To an under-stimulated dog, even negative attention (punishment) is better than no attention at all, so they will do anything that will produce interaction from the owner.

Related to this is environmental depravation. If a dog is left alone a lot and his environment provides little or no suitable stimulation, destructive behavior is quite common. If you have to leave your dog alone a lot, provide some play and chew toys (caution: make sure they are safe for your dog). Be sure to give your dog plenty of attention during the time that you do have together.

As a general rule, a well-exercised dog is a well-behaved dog. Providing your dog with plenty of physical, mental and social stimulation will invariably reduce or even eliminate many destructive behaviors.

Destructive behavior due to fear is usually a phobic reaction (typically associated with certain sounds, especially thunder, but may be an object). Phobias are extreme fear that can cause a dog to become destructive. Simple fearful behavior ordinarily does not result in destruction. Phobias are treated in the same way as fearful behavior but of course phobias are going to be much more difficult to overcome. Read *Phobias* for more information on how to treat this kind of extreme behavior.

Sometimes destructive behavior can result from territorial behavior. Destruction will be secondary as the dog is attempting to chase away people, dogs or other animals that it can see from a window or fence. The best solution for this is to block the view or access to the area where your dog might see perceived threats. Sounds can often trigger territorial aggression, e.g. a knock on the door. Only behavior modification techniques will work to eliminate this problem. Read the section on *Aggression.*

Nesting behavior is another cause of destructive behavior. Some dogs will like to scratch at carpets or cushions in an attempt to make a more comfortable bed. Training is the key to stopping this kind of damage. If your dog likes to "nest," simply train your dog to stay off of vulnerable furniture or areas. Provide your dog with his own bedding. This may have to be replaced from time to time if your dog is a really determined nester but it is better than having to replace the couch. The nesting behavior itself is instinctive and it is unlikely that you will be able to train it out of your dog. The most resonable solution is management, which involves controlling access to items that are at risk of being damaged.

Separation Anxiety

Separation anxiety is a condition where dogs become severely distressed when they are left alone. Dogs with separation anxiety may whine, bark, howl or become destructive when the owner leaves the house or even the room. In the most severe cases, the dog may actually injure themselves as a result of their destructive activities. It is also one of the most common reasons dogs are surrendered to animal shelters.

As usual, the best "cure" for separation anxiety is prevention. Owners should practice leaving their dogs for short periods of time, even while they are home. A dog should be able to remain in another part of the house or in the yard separate from the owner. To practice this, just put the dog someplace that is **safe** but where he is prevented from seeing or getting to you. Crates are good for this kind of training. If your dog is calm and does not bark, whine or scratch at the door, you can allow your dog out after a few minutes. If your dog is not calm and begins to make noise and tries to scratch at the door, do not allow your dog out. Wait until he does calm down. If he remains calm for at least one minute let him join you once again. Repeat the session several times for a few days until your dog learns to remain calm whenever he is separated from you.

To help your dog adjust to being alone, provide him with some chew toys or a raw bone. Let your dog have these items **only while you are absent from the area**. Soon your dog will associate pleasant things with your leaving.

If your dog is showing mild to moderate signs of separation anxiety it is important to take corrective measures right away and not let the behavior escalate. There are a number of other things that owners can do to reduce or eliminate separation anxiety.

Reducing the amount of attention that an owner gives their dog can help alleviate separation anxiety problems. Owners who constantly lavish attention on their dogs should discontinue this practice. Instead of constantly petting and talking to their dog, the owner should try to go for periods where they basically ignore their dog. When the dog solicits attention he should be ignored. This will help reduce some of the dependence the dog has on the owner.

If the dog is laying quietly somewhere, the owner can try to slip out of the room for just one or two seconds and then return without saying anything. If the dog learns to remain quiet, the time can gradually be increased, perhaps one second at a time. Another way the owner can reduce the anxiety for their dog is to stop providing cues of the departure in advance. Cues that dogs commonly pick up on are putting on shoes, picking up the keys, always leaving from the front door.

To eliminate the cues, the owner can put his shoes on well in advance of leaving or even practice putting on the shoes at various times during the day and not leaving at all. Keys can be put in a pocket or purse in advance. Exiting through a different door than usual can also help. Anything that the owner can do to reduce the routine of leaving will help reduce some of the anxiety for the dog.

A common "solution" is to get a second dog. I would not advise this. Many times the plan backfires because the first dog teaches the second dog to be anxious and you end up with "double trouble." One dog rarely improves the behavior of another dog. In fact it usually goes in the opposite direction. The lowest common denominator rule seems to take effect. Each dog sinks to the lowest level exhibited by the other.

If your dog is already exhibiting more advanced signs of separation anxiety the task can be more difficult. Locking your dog away in a crate or room may result in the dog injuring itself. A more tedious and lengthy therapy program will be required. Procedures for such a therapy can be complicated and go well beyond the scope of this book. Owner's who want to cure their dog of separation anxiety should seek out the services of a qualified pet behaviorist.

Even with the aid a pet behaviorist, the problem is going to be very difficult to eliminate. A management approach could be more practical. Management may be accomplished by taking the dog to a "dog daycare" facility or even a good boarding kennel. Perhaps friends or other family members could care for the dog. Some owners may be able to take their dog to work with them.

Aggression

Aggression is a common and sometimes serious problem in pet dogs. There are many different ways in which aggression is exhibited by a dog. A precise treatment program will depend on exactly how the aggression manifests itself. The subject is further complicated by the fact that a scientific definition of "aggression" has not yet been agreed upon by professional behaviorists. Furthermore, an aggressive type behavior exhibited by a five-pound Yorkshire Terrier may barely get noticed, or might even be considered humorous, whereas the exact same behavior from a one hundred-pound Rottweiler will earn it the term "vicious."

Any dog, no matter what the breed, can be aggressive. There is no such thing as an "aggressive breed." Even labeling individual dogs as "aggressive" can sometimes be difficult. Have you ever seen a news report about a dog that has just been impounded for having bitten someone but the owner has pictures of the same dog playing with his children? Is that dog aggressive? Obviously, it all depends on the circumstances.

It is doubtful that any dog can be aggressive all the time. A dog can exhibit aggression but that is in a response to something. Many animals will respond with aggression under certain circumstances. When I was just a young boy, I learned that my otherwise peaceful pet gerbil could be aggressive when I reached in to pick her up one day without knowing that she had just given birth to several pups. She put a nice hole in my finger. Was my gerbil "vicious?" I do not think so. Her aggression was simply a response to the particular circumstances.

Any dog can respond aggressively under certain circumstances. Each will have a different level or threshold at which aggressive behavior is exhibited. The degree of aggression also has a threshold and can vary from dog to dog, circumstance to circumstance. For example, some dogs may behave aggressively by merely growling at a specific level of agitation but others might respond to a higher degree and actually bite at the same level of agitation.

Aggression is undoubtedly a survival behavior that is inherited by almost all animals, including human beings. Aggression is a permanent trait that could never be bred out of dogs completely but the mechanism that controls aggression thresholds may well be influenced by genetics to some degree. On the other hand, it has been convincingly demonstrated that socialization and training will always have a far more important and significant impact on aggression thresholds.

So lets forget about banning so-called "aggressive breeds" and get to the real root of the problem, socialization and training. It is the responsibility of dog owners to train and socialize their dogs. Because dogs live in a human society they must be taught to behave according to the standards that are established by human beings. Dog owners must watch for signs of a low aggression threshold under normal circumstances and take action that would either raise the threshold to acceptable levels or use a management approach that would prevent any possibility of the dog being exposed to the stimulus that elicits an aggressive response.

Treatment for aggression should always be done with positive reinforcement. Only appetitive methods can actually raise thresholds that hold back aggressive behavior. Negative or punishment methods may sometimes provide a temporary means of inhibiting aggression but does not actually raise the threshold. In fact, there is good reason to believe that it may even lower the threshold. Punishment never truly resolves the problem and often exacerbates it.

I have already given some hints in some earlier chapters on dealing with aggression in dogs. The most common techniques are known as "counter conditioning" and "desensitization." These techniques are utilized to treat nearly any kind of inappropriate aggressive behavior. Although scientists have yet to agree on exactly how to categorize different types of aggression (or even if there are truly different types), it is agreed that there are definitely different motivations for the behavior. Fear motivated aggression is by far the most widespread. Many owners do not believe that their dog is fearful when it is behaving aggressively but that is frequently the case.

Barking at strangers is a sign of fear. Barking at anyone or anything that is in the dog's territory is fear. Aggressive lunging at another dog on leash is almost always triggered by fear. Maternal aggression (a mother dog protecting her pups) at its root is fear based. The mother gerbil that bit me was fearful that I might harm her pups. Some mother dogs will behave in a similar fashion.[45]

When a dog is fearful, it has three ways to react. It can run away, freeze in place or fight. Just because a dog is moving forward does not mean that it is not afraid. It is simply one way for the dog to deal with its fear, by attacking. We could train our dog to run away or freeze when they are afraid. Basically, that is what an aversive trainer does. The problem is, fear can quickly turn to panic. A panicked dog will react defensively. No amount of training can overcome panic. A far better approach is to train your dog not to be afraid so that panic is avoided altogether.

If you have a dog that behaves aggressively under certain conditions, you must take measures to eliminate the problem. I would strongly urge owners to seek the services of a professional pet behaviorist for any serious or potentially serious problem. Prevention, through proper socialization of puppies and young dogs, is the best way to combat inappropriate aggressive behavior. However, if the problem does come up, the responsible dog owner must take measures to curb or eliminate the behavior.

Professional help is strongly advised not only because of the technical aspects of behavior modification but also due to the danger element in treating aggression. But, if owners decide to treat the problem on their own, it is important that a veterinarian first examine the dog to eliminate any possible physical causes. This is an important first step and should not be ignored. Second, an accurate diagnosis of the aggression must be made, i.e. what exactly triggers the aggression and why. Then, if the aggressive behavior is motivated by fear, a very specific counter conditioning and de-sensitization program will have to be designed and implemented. Safety should be of paramount importance

---

[45] Mother dogs can teach her puppies to be fearful and therefore aggressive towards people. This occurs with females that are overly protective of their young and will behave aggressively towards almost anyone coming too near. The aggressive behavior is usually directed only towards unfamiliar people and gradually disappears as the puppies get older. If the mother displays fear and aggression during the socialization period the puppies will learn to fear humans as a result.

Although a mother dog could be trained through counter conditioning and de-sensitization to accept strangers, it is easier to just manage the situation. The best way is to allow only those people the dog will trust near her and the puppies during this time. Puppies can still be socialized but only in the mother's absence. Usually, mother dogs become less protective as the puppies get a little older so more interaction with less familiar people is possible.

during a treatment program. The basic principles for counter conditioning and de-sensitization were outlined in Chapter 11 under *The Fearful Dog.*

Aggressive behavior can be elicited for reasons other than fear. Predatory drive can cause some dogs to act aggressive under certain circumstances. Usually prey aggression is directed towards smaller animals but in some extreme cases it can involve people, especially children. If the problem is limited to small animals, management techniques could be employed, i.e. keeping the dog restrained or even muzzled during those times when it may be exposed to vulnerable animals. Re-training may be possible but usually it is very difficult.

If prey aggression is exhibited towards people, the owner must seek professional advice from a qualified pet behaviorist. Only a pet behaviorist can make this kind of diagnosis and evaluate any possible solution.

So-called "dominance aggression" towards human owners is quite common. Even the smallest dog will sometimes exhibit this particular genre of aggression. Aggression in this form is generally thought to be motivated by the dog's desire to achieve and maintain a higher status in the social hierarchy. Dominance type aggression can have a number of manifestations; "possession aggression," "food bowl aggression," "personal space aggression" and "challenge aggression" are labels for various typical problems.

Dominance type aggression towards people can be treated through a combination of counter conditioning, desensitization and a technique known a "rank reduction therapy," which leads me to question whether the behavior is really dominance or simply learned.[46] Rank reduction therapy methods are effective regardless of whether the behavior is motivated by dominance or a learned response. The idea behind rank reduction therapy is for the owner to control all the resources. The dog is only allowed to have access to them when the owner gives permission (this should sound familiar since it is one of the underlying principals of the Follow The Leader training philosophy). This means food, toys, petting, bedding, the couch, etcetera are all strictly controlled by the owner.

Possession and food bowl aggression are essentially the same although some dogs will display one but not the other. The treatment for the problem is essentially the same. If your dog guards his food bowl from people you can either manage the problem or make behavior modifications.

The behavior can be managed if only adults live in the household and your dog can be fed in a secluded area where he will **never** be disturbed while eating. This is not a good option for free fed dogs that do not eat their food right away or for families that have children.

Behavior modification can be accomplished with little difficulty but it will require the participation of everyone in the family. Adults and older children should participate first and younger children can help later with close adult supervision.

---

[46] What may appear as dominance behavior could actually be learned, e.g. if an owner tried to take away a toy and the dog growled, the owner might back away. The dog gained by growling, so the next time the owner tries to take away the toy the dog is more likely to repeat the behavior. Each time the dog growls and the owner does not take away the toy the more likely it becomes that the dog will continue to growl. (**Note:** This does not mean that an owner should forcefully take the toy away. For safety reasons this would not be prudent.) It calls into question whether this is true dominance or learned behavior. Fortunately for dog owners, it is not necessary to differentiate between the two. Rank reduction therapy methods are appropriate regardless of the true motivation behind the behavior.

For safety, put a collar and leash on the dog. One person is in charge of restraining the dog by holding the leash firmly as a second person places the bowl with a **small** amount of food in front of the dog. The food should **not be of high value**, perhaps dry kibble. As soon as the dog finishes the food the second person can take away the bowl and put in some more kibble but include just a **few pieces of high value food**, e.g. left over steak. The person in charge of restraining the dog should keep enough tension on the leash to prevent the dog from biting the person taking the bowl.

If the dog growls or snaps at the person, do not say anything. Ignore the behavior but keep the dog securely restrained. Pull back on the dog only enough to maintain a margin of safety for the feeder. Continue to feed in this way until the dog has eaten its full ration of food for that meal. The idea is that each time the person takes the food bowl away it comes back with something special. The same procedures should be used every time the dog is fed for the next several days. With time the dog should stop the aggressive behavior and actually look forward to the person taking the food bowl away because he will expect that something really good is going to end up in the bowl.

Each person in the family should take a turn feeding the dog. Adults and older children (supervised) should do the training first. When the dog seems reliable small children can be involved but in a slightly different way. Instead of taking the food bowl away a small child (directly accompanied by an adult) should be allowed to toss high value treats into the food bowl. The dog should be kept retrained as before during this time.

With some time the dog will change the association of someone approaching his food bowl from a threat to a pleasant experience. Possession aggression is handled in a similar fashion. As always, adults should be in charge of this type of training. And, just as you did with food, dogs that show possession aggression should be started off with a low value possession.

Give your dog a toy. Command your dog to "release" or whatever word you want to use for relinquishing the object. At the same time produce a high value reward. Treats are usually best. As your dog goes for the treat he should automatically drop the toy. Reward-mark and give the treat as you pick up the toy. As soon as your dog finishes the treat, give the toy back and repeat the procedure. After doing this sequence a few times put the toy away. It can be brought out later or the next day for another session.

Once again you want to change your dog's association with someone taking away a toy. Your dog will eventually learn that giving up a toy often results in a treat and it usually gets the toy back anyway. Your dog no longer feels threatened and will gladly relinquish the toy upon command. Again, all members of the family should do this training but small children should train at later stages and only when directly supervised by an adult.

Personal space aggression is where a dog will aggressively defend a particular area or large object such as a chair or bed. A typical example is when a dog is resting on a sofa and will growl or otherwise menace the owner when approached.

The solution for this behavior is the use of classic rank reduction therapy. Whenever you want the dog to move from the couch or any other place he is protecting, you simply need to give him some counter command (a command that asks for a behavior that is not compatible with the present behavior). For example, if he is on the couch you may want to say "off." Have a treat with you and if necessary lure him off the couch. As soon as he is off the couch, reward-mark and treat. You can ask for some more behaviors at that point like sit or down. Reward each time your dog complies.

You should discontinue luring as soon as possible and use random reward schedules as the dog learns to respond to your command "off." The solution is really as simple as that. There are a few words of caution here; never back away when your dog threatens you but at the same time do not meet his aggression with your own. Backing away will reinforce the aggressive behavior. Aggressive action may be met as a challenge but even if you win it will not necessarily solve the problem.

Challenge aggression is when a dog behaves aggressively towards someone when they are being physically forced to do something. For example, the dog may not like it when a trainer tries to force him to lie down and the dog responds by becoming aggressive. Aversive trainers will often meet this challenge with a challenge of their own. The old fashion way is to "string up" the dog. This is where the dog is lifted off the ground by the leash and choke collar and held there for a certain length of time.

Obviously, appetitive trainers do not use this method. In fact, appetitive trainers never even see challenge aggression. Challenge aggression will only manifest itself when force is involved. Since force is contrary to appetitive training, it simply never becomes a problem.

Phobias

Phobias are extreme versions of fear behavior. The best cure for a phobia is prevention. It is important that the owner does not unintentionally create a phobia in their dog from a fear. This is a common way for phobias to develop.

Owners must watch their dog carefully for signs of fear of particular events, sounds, sights and even smells. If a dog shows fear of anything, let's say thunder, it is vitally important that the owner does not try to comfort the dog while fear is being exhibited. The same thing happens at the veterinary office. The dog shows signs of fear, shaking, rapid breathing, etc., and it is only natural for you to want to comfort your dog by petting and talking in reassuring tones. What you are really doing is rewarding the fearful behavior. You are telling your dog that he is correct for being nervous.

Sometimes phobias develop for no apparent reason. Perhaps your dog has a bad experience during your absence or it could have occurred before you owned your dog. Unfortunately, a phobic dog can present a danger to itself and others. Phobias can produce such intense fear that a dog may jump through screens, closed windows, chew through doors or exhibit other extreme forms of behavior. They may even attack and severely bite someone.

A treatment program for phobias can be quite complicated and tedious. Without the help of a professional pet behaviorist the average owner will have little chance of success and may even exacerbate the problem if it is not handled properly. A professional pet behaviorist will design a very specific counter conditioning and desensitization program. In addition, appropriate psychotropic drugs will most likely be prescribed. Given enough time and effort, the combination of appropriate drug and behavior therapy can cure a phobia. The drugs can usually be reduced and even eliminated by the end of the treatment period.

Since phobias require highly specialized professional care I will not describe treatment programs here. However, because thunder phobias are so very common I thought it would be worth describing how to **prevent** fear of thunderstorms from developing into a full phobia.

A fear of thunderstorms is very difficult to overcome because thunderstorms are so difficult to simulate for standard counter conditioning and de-sensitization programs. Many behaviorists have tried using sound recordings to simulate an approaching storm. The recorded thunder is played on the stereo at a very low level so as not to overly alarm the dog while classic counter conditioning and desensitization techniques are employed. The volume is gradually increased over many sessions until the dog is able to tolerate the full volume. The method has been successful but only in a limited number of cases.

There are many thunderstorm factors that cannot be simulated using a recording. The sound of thunder may not be the only or even primary stimulus that elicits fear. There is some evidence that perhaps many dogs experience an unpleasant sensation due to static electricity in the atmosphere. These dogs often seek shelter in bathtubs or next to the pipes under the sink. Presumably, the zinc tub or metal pipes under a sink can help "ground" the dog, thus preventing a static build-up. Other theories propose that dogs may sense drops in the barometric pressure or perhaps detect the smell of ozone in the air (a by-product of lightening), which becomes associated with an unpleasant event.

Not only is it difficult to simulate a thunderstorm, but also it is impossible to prevent a real thunderstorm from occurring during the training program, which may take from weeks to several months to implement. It is imperative that the dog not be subjected to a full thunderstorm until a full recovery has been achieved. Controlling the weather is simply not possible so weeks of progress can be suddenly erased with a single real thunderstorm event.

Obviously, it is better to prevent a thunderstorm phobia because the difficulties in curing them are sometimes insurmountable. Fortunately, prevention is not quite as problematic so watch your dog closely for any signs of anxiety at the approach of or during a thunderstorm.

If your dog seems nervous at the approach of a storm it is a good idea to start playing with your dog or get out some treats and do some fun training. Act happy and completely unconcerned about the thunder, even going to the point of acting completely silly. Don't worry; your dog won't ridicule you for acting silly but I cannot necessarily say that about the rest of your family! To avoid ridicule from the rest of your family, get them to join in. Your dog will love it. If you always make the approach of a thunderstorm a fun and exciting event for your dog, you will change the association from something stressful to one that your dog will actually look forward to.

Excessive Barking

There are many reasons for a dog to bark. It is important that you determine exactly why your dog is barking before any behavior modification is attempted. You can quickly narrow the possibilities by asking yourself a few questions:

1. Does problem barking occur while you are present or usually in your absence?
   - ➤ If your dog barks only while you are absent he may have separation anxiety. For more information, read *Separation Anxiety*.
   - ➤ If the barking occurs while you are present, read question #2.
2. Is the barking directed at a person, object, sound or another animal?
   - ➤ If your dog barks at person skip ahead to question #3.
   - ➤ If your dog barks at object you probably have a fearful dog. Review *The Fearful Dog* chapter 11.
   - ➤ If your dog barks at sounds you probably have a fearful dog. Review *The Fearful Dog* chapter 11.
   - ➤ If your dog barks at another animal there can be any number of causes. Fear, territorial and play behaviors are the most common. If you suspect fear then you should read *The Fearful Dog*, chapter 11. If you suspect that the behavior is territorial or play motivated, management techniques are probably the best choice, e.g. prevent your dog from seeing or hearing the other animal.
3. Does your dog bark at unfamiliar people or at you or family members?
   - ➤ If your dog barks at unfamiliar people the cause is most likely territorial or simply fear motivated. Both can be treated in the same manner. Review *The Fearful Dog* chapter 11.
   - ➤ If your dog barks at you or family members the cause is usually play or social solicitation. This can be the result of two extremes; either the dog is not getting enough attention from the owner or the dog has learned how to get attention simply by barking. Under stimulated dogs will bark to get social interaction from their owners even if the attention is punishment. Be sure you are providing your dog with enough social, mental and physical stimulation. If your dog has learned to bark simply to get attention, the answer is just the opposite. Ignore your dog when he barks. When your dog finally does go quiet, wait for at least one minute then reward your dog with some play or a treat.
4. Does your dog seem to be barking at nothing in particular?
   - ➤ If your dog seems to be barking at nothing in particular it may be caused by boredom. Make sure your dog is getting plenty of exercise, social interaction and mental stimulation, i.e. training and play.

Escape Behavior

Escape behavior can have consequences ranging from a nuisance to disastrous. Responsible pet owners never allow their dogs to roam free but sometimes it is difficult to keep certain dogs from escaping. Stopping or preventing escapes is important. There are numerous reasons that motivate dogs to escape. The most common causes are boredom, bad manners, exploration drive, territorial instincts, reproductive drive, predatory drive, separation anxiety or fear (including phobias).

It is important to have an accurate diagnosis before attempting to solve the problem. If the reason for the behavior is separation anxiety or fear (especially phobias) it is important to use appropriate treatment protocols and not simply try to manage the behavior. If bad manners are the problem, (running out an opened door or gate) review *Door-Manners* in chapter 11.

Boredom is probably the number one reason for escape behavior. The average healthy dog needs at least thirty minutes of vigorous exercise each and every day. They do not get this exercise by themselves. The owner must provide the stimulation. A simple walk around the block is not going to be adequate except for the smaller toy breeds. Most dogs need to run, chase balls, swim, jump or romp with their owner in order to get an adequate aerobic workout.

Remember, the general rule of thumb, "A well-exercised dog is a well-behaved dog." Many owners underestimate the amount of exercise their dog needs. Training is also good exercise but cannot take the place of aerobic activities. Most dogs will require at least one hour of your time everyday. A typical breakdown of that hour would be thirty minutes exercising, twenty minutes training and at least ten minutes of play and grooming (petting, scratching, brushing, etc.) activities. These activities do not have to be done all in one block of time. It is surprising how many escape problems can be solved simply by giving a dog more attention.

Besides providing more personalized attention, the owner should also try providing the dog with a more stimulating environment. This can easily be accomplished by giving your dog a couple of chew items such as raw beef bones or safe chew toys. Even hiding treats around the yard is a good way to keep your dog busy while you are away (just make sure your dog can easily reach them without damaging property).

Other motivations for escape behavior can usually be managed, although some dogs are very determined. Certain modifications can be made to fences that will make escape more difficult. Burying large rocks or extending the fence well below the ground can stop dogs that dig their way out. This must be done everywhere or a determined dog will find the "weak" place and make his escape.

Adding three or four feet of chain link fence to the bottom of an existing fence will stop dogs from digging out. The secondary piece of fence is attached a foot or two above the base of the original fence and curves downward laying flat on the ground along the inside perimeter. In this way, the dog can no longer dig at the base of the fence. This solution can often be temporary. When enough time has passed and plenty of activity is provided, many dogs will no longer try to dig and the additional fence can be removed.

If the dog is jumping the fence, the solution is rather obvious; make a higher fence. If that is not an option then putting secondary barriers around the area, such as a hedge can make jumping more difficult for the dog.

Climbing a fence is actually more common than jumping. Putting a ninety-degree extension around the top of the fence can usually thwart climbers. Often there is some particular location that a dog climbs out because the local topography or some object aids in a successful climb. Owners must watch closely to see if this is the case and remove anything that helps the dog climb out or put the ninety-degree extension at that location.

Miscellaneous Problems

It would be virtually impossible to cover every single behavior problem that a dog might exhibit. Dogs are living creatures with diverse behavior patterns. Dog behavior can be predicted only to a certain degree. Obviously, dogs are capable of a broad range of behaviors. Genetic differences not withstanding, exposure to varied social and environmental influences will affect each dog in an individually distinct way. One of the things that I have learned as a dog trainer and behaviorist is that you can never "see it all" when it comes to dog behavior.

However, few (if any) problems are truly unique. The uniqueness is only in the way the problem manifests itself. Problems always fall into one of several standard categories. Careful analysis of the problem is paramount. Once we identify what is at the root of the problem an appropriate remedy may be formulated. Be aware that sometimes multiple problems exist, which complicates matters. Nevertheless it is important find the root cause or causes of the problem before action is taken.

Because the manifestation of a problem may be unique it is not possible to write a specific protocol or set of procedures that will correspond to every situation. Each problem has to be analyzed, identified and labeled so that it fits into a generalized "pigeon hole." I have outlined a number of standard protocols for a variety of the most common problem behaviors but owners will need to adapt these standard protocols to fit their particular circumstances.

The following are just a few examples of problems that are representative of how dog owners need to make a deeper analysis of seemingly unexplained behaviors. The examples are intended to help the owner look at a problem from a dog's perspective and recognize the basic motivations for behavior, which can ultimately lead to the appropriate procedures for behavior modification.

Carsickness

Experts say that dogs do not actually suffer from carsickness. Carsickness is really a form of motion sickness and dogs are physiologically "immune" to the malady. Yet dogs occasionally develop symptoms that resemble carsickness, such as heavy drooling, vomiting and appear quite miserable. These symptoms are apparently stress related and can become a learned response. This is actually good news because a learned response can be un-learned. It is also possible to reduce and eliminate stress.

To start, you will need to change the association that your dog has with the car. Exactly where you start will depend on how willing your dog is about entering your car. I will start by assuming the worst-case scenario but you can begin wherever it is appropriate for your dog.

If your dog will not even voluntarily get in the car you will need to start by offering all daily meals next to your car. Once your dog is accustomed to being fed by the car start opening the doors and leave them open while the dog is eating. Later try to lure the dog to eat his meal inside the car, even if it is just to put his head inside the open door and eat from the bowl on the floor.

Eventually, your dog should be readily going inside your car for his meals. Practice closing the doors while he eats but let him out as soon as he is finished. Start using a command like "car" or "lets go for a ride" each time you lure your dog inside the car for a meal.

Next, put a crate in your car and continue to feed your dog in the crate. If your dog is not crate trained, do so by following the crate training instructions in Chapter 11. Begin using treats instead of a full meal. Get your dog to go in the crate, close the door and give him a treat or two before letting him back out.

If your dog is comfortable with this have someone help you by feeding your dog treats while you start the engine and go down the driveway and back again or have them drive. If this is not a problem try going around the block. Continue to make trips longer. If possible go someplace that is not far away but fun for your dog, like a park or "grandmas" house. **If your dog shows any signs of stress during the training you are proceeding too fast**. Back up in your training and proceed slowly.

If you have progressed slowly you will change the entire association that your dog has with the car. You may even find that a new problem will crop-up; every time you open the car door your dog will jump in. To correct this problem, see *Door-Manners* in chapter 11.

A final word of caution; **do not leave dogs in a parked car for any length of time, especially during the summer**. Dogs can over-heat and die in a remarkably short period of time. If you must leave your dog in a car for a few minutes make sure it is parked in the shade and the windows are open enough to allow fresh air to enter the car. Do not underestimate how hot it can get in a car on a warm or even cool but sunny day.

Involuntary Elimination Problems

Most elimination problems will be avoided if the owner carefully follows proper housetraining procedures. Errorless learning methods work best but require vigilance and persistence on the part of the dog owner. I am often asked how long it takes to housetrain a dog. It is a difficult question to answer. Some dogs seem to catch on within two weeks whereas others may take two or three months before being completely reliable. However, the most important factor is the owner. Some simply do not have enough time to housetrain so there are a lot of mistakes. This will extend the training period considerably.

Normal elimination problems aside, there are still some problems that have nothing to do with housetraining.[47] The most common is *submissive* or *excitement urination*. Puppies do this more than adult dogs but it often occurs when owners first return home or the dog gets overly excited. Normally only small amounts of urine are involved. This type of eliminative behavior is triggered by the dog's attempt to be submissive.

Getting angry or annoyed will only exacerbate this problem. Owners need to avoid any kind of postures or movements that might be interpreted as threatening. Examples of threatening postures or movements are bending over the dog (even to pet her), directly approaching or reaching for the dog, hugging and making direct eye contact. Also facial expression can be important. If you are annoyed because your puppy has urinated on the floor again while you are greeting her she may react by becoming more submissive and urinate again.

Most puppies probably will grow out of it but simply changing your greeting routine will curb the problem in a shorter time and will ensure it does not become a learned response. Although emotionally difficult for many owners, the best thing to do is **ignore** your dog when you first come home. Your dog will run around and try to get your attention but the owner must withhold all interaction.

---

[47] There can be medical explanations for elimination problems. Have a veterinarian examine your dog to rule out this possibility. It makes no sense to try training methods when a medical condition is the real cause. Training will not work and the dog is in need of medical attention.

After several minutes the dog should calm down. You can then calmly sit on the floor or on a low chair and allow the dog to approach (do not call your dog). **Keep your hands close to your body and let the dog solicit contact**. Slowly and gently reach under the chin to pet your dog or pat the chest while using a soothing voice. Keep the entire greeting very low key and avoid any movement, gesture or posture that might be interpreted as threatening by your dog, such as leaning over or placing your hands on top of the dog.[48]

Continue this routine each day until your dog stops all signs of eliminative behavior. Once your dog does well at this routine then a slightly more enthusiastic greeting can be used the next time but make very gradual changes. Back up in your training if your dog begins to eliminate again. Provided you proceed **slowly** to ever increasing excitement levels of the greeting routine, you will eventually (at least several weeks in most cases) be able to greet your dog with all the exuberance that you want.[49]

Elimination on Undesirable Surface (Preference or Avoidance)

Most dogs prefer to eliminate on soft surfaces such as dirt or grass but many have other preferences. Studies have shown that early experiences can strongly influence eliminative behavior in terms of surface type. For example, some dogs will only eliminate on grass or dirt and have difficulty when boarded at a kennel with cement floors. In some extreme cases the dogs have actually developed medical problems because of their refusal to eliminate on the kennel floor. These problems are usually rare but good kennel operators will recognize the problem early on and simply take the dog out frequently for elimination on a more suitable surface.

On the other hand, some dogs do not like to use the grass, particularly if it is long or wet from rain. This is especially true of short legged or toy breeds. These dogs will often use the sidewalk to eliminate which is most often not desirable to the owner. In some cases, the weather may actually be the problem. Some dogs do not like the rain or heat on a hot summer day.

These problems can be very difficult to solve. Usually it will take a combination of management and training to correct the problem. Management consists of making inappropriate areas inaccessible to the dog. Also grass should be cut very short or alternatively an easily accessible area could be cleared of grass. Depending on the dog the cleared area may need to be hard packed dirt, pea gravel or even sand.

Training would involve taking the dog to the desired location, bringing plenty of treats. If the dog eliminates in the area a jackpot reward would be in order. The idea is to change the association with the area from being uncomfortable to a place where good things happen, especially if the dog eliminates there.

If rain is a factor perhaps a more sheltered area can be found. Although many people do not like to do it, the fact is, dogs should be encouraged to go out in the rain. It is entirely possible to change a "fair weather" dog's association with rain by enticing him outside during rainy conditions. Of course this is difficult to plan but it is best to start

---

[48] Keeping your back turned to the dog as it approaches is also a less threatening position. Face to face encounters can be intimidating to an extremely submissive dog.

[49] **Caution**: I am not a big proponent of exuberant greetings with any dog. I feel it is okay for dogs to greet their owner with enthusiasm but also with appropriate self-control. Exuberant greetings often encourage dogs to jump up or exhibit other undesirable behaviors.

with light rain and work up to heavier rains. If you use an umbrella, try using one that is extra large so that it provides at least some shelter for your dog. The methods are the same as any desensitization program. Just proceed slowly and use lots of rewards. It also helps if you "get silly" in the rain to make it fun for your dog.

If hot weather is the problem then a different approach will be needed. Long coated breeds may not be able to tolerate the hot weather and want to remain in air-conditioned homes. Training them to tolerate the heat is unlikely. However, it may be possible to make them a little more comfortable by shaving off their hair for the summer. Talk to a professional groomer for advice.

For heat sensitive dogs, choose shaded areas for elimination and do not make the dog stay out any longer than it is necessary to do his business. A healthy adult dog should be able to control eliminative functions well enough that he could be allowed out in the morning and again in the evening when it is cooler. Regular schedules for feeding and elimination can be timed to correspond to the cooler periods.

Cold weather can bother some of the short-coated breeds. Again, try to find easily accessed and sheltered elimination areas. If snow is a problem, clear an adequate section on the lawn so that short-legged dogs can easily walk in the area. Also, do not make the dog stay out any longer than what is necessary.

Grooming Aversions and Husbandry Training

Too many dogs have problems when it comes to normal grooming or regular husbandry treatment (i.e. standard health examinations). Prevention is the best approach to this problem. Good breeders will handle young puppies, trim their nails, give baths and inspect ears and teeth on a regular basis. The puppies will be completely used to this kind of handling and will accept it without a problem.

New owners should continue this practice once they get their puppy or start it right away if it has not been done. Husbandry training is a standard part of all my puppy classes. Owners are taught to "play doctor" and do thorough mock exams of their puppy. Puppies are also passed to another person in the class to perform a mock exam to get the puppy used to strangers. Owners are encouraged to make mock exams a part of their daily interaction with their dog. If they take time out to pet their dog, they can do a quick mock exam. It takes less than one minute.

For dogs that are already fearful of being handled in this way, they will have to be desensitized. Standard fear desensitization programs were discussed in chapter 11 under socialization. Aversions to grooming can be treated in the same way. A brief example might be the dog that is sensitive about his feet and does not like to have his nails trimmed.

Start off by touching the dog on his leg just above the feet. If he does not mind that reward him with a treat. Do this several times. The next session you can try touching his leg at a location much closer to his feet. As long as he is not reacting negatively reward him with treats. Eventually you should be able to touch his feet just briefly, then for longer periods and finally hold them in your hand. At any point in the training the dog shows sensitivities to the handling you will need to back up in your training to the level where the dog does not react and proceed more slowly.

If your dog is fearful of the nail clippers themselves you will have to work with these as well. Get your dog used to seeing the clippers by the fact that every time you bring them out he gets a treat. Then start working at getting them close to his feet. When you get to the point where you are actually going to trim his nails, cut only one nail in each session and trim only a very tiny amount. Reward well, jackpot if there is no reaction at all.

The same procedure will work for cleaning ears or teeth, cutting hair, taking baths or any other husbandry treatment. Start at a point that is not threatening to your dog and move slowly forward. You must be very patient and avoid rushing the process. Whenever you take your dog to the groomer, leave some of your dogs favorite treats for the groomer to give him during his stay. If you are at the veterinarian's office for regular exams, bring favorite treats for your dog. Most vets will have some treats available, which are fine, but it is best to have your dog's favorite.

I do one other thing in my puppy classes that is related to husbandry management. I encourage owners to dress up their dogs in all sorts of clothing. This may seem like a silly thing to do, and actually it is sometimes quite hilarious, but there is a very practical value to the lesson. The best time to get dogs used to bandages is while they are well, not after they have been hurt.

Hopefully your dog will never be injured and require bandaging but you can never be sure. Most dogs that are not used to clothing will chew on bandages. To stop them, all sorts of contraptions can be used such as muzzles or Elizabethan collars but it is much easier and less stressful for the dog if he is already accustomed to bandages. I encourage my clients to put bandages on their dogs all the time in the form of children's socks, bandanas, tight fitting shirts or sweaters, etc.

Dogs that are sensitive to wearing clothes should be desensitized in the usual way. In addition to bandages and clothes, it may be useful to get your dog accustomed to a muzzle. Some veterinarians may require your dog to wear a muzzle for certain exams, especially if your dog were to be seriously hurt. It would be far less stressful if your dog were already used to the muzzle in advance.

Rough Play With Other Pets

Some dogs, especially puppies play too rough with other pets in the house. Usually an older dog will set a puppy straight with little effort. Two dogs or puppies of the same approximate age will generally work out the problem on their own by establishing a mutually agreeable hierarchy. Owners should respect the hierarchy structure that is established and not try to change it by favoring the lower status dog. That would only create problems. If your dogs have settled things between them always "favor" the dominant dog by giving him treats first or allowing him to have a better position or whatever the situation calls for. The dominant dog should always be allowed to be dominant with respect to the other dog.

This is sometimes difficult for some owners because they feel sorry for the subordinate dog. Remember human thinking and canine thinking are not the same. If you "favor" the subordinate dog the dominant one will feel that his position is threatened and will only become more assertive. This will in turn stress out the subordinate dog because he is not really challenging.

There are times when human intervention is necessary. For example, sometimes a puppy or young dog may become too rough with an older dog that is not in good health. If the older dog is in danger of injury then the human owner can step in. Use a "time out" method by **calmly** placing the offending youngster in an isolated area (e.g., safe room or crate) for a short time. Do not get emotionally involved in any fight by shouting or hitting your dog. Be sure to **reward the young dog heavily for good behavior** in the proximity of the infirmed dog.

If no clear hierarchy has been established the play aggression between two dogs could start to escalate to the point where serious aggression may break out. In these situations there is a risk of injury to one or both animals so once again human intervention is required. It is very dangerous to physically try to break up a bona fide dogfight. You can be seriously bitten no matter how good your relationship is with either dog. The important thing is for you to remain calm. Shouting often exacerbates the problem. The dogs simply think you are joining in the fray. It is better if you use a loud noise such as rattling a soda can with coins in it or squirt water at them using a garden hose. I have broken up fights by grabbing one or both dogs by the tail and lifting their hind legs off the ground but this is very risky and I do not recommend it.

Prevention is the best approach. If play tends to escalate to dangerous levels the human owner should anticipate this and intervene early by either using a counter command or "time out" measures. Counter commanding, i.e. giving commands that are not compatible with the undesirable behavior is one way of cutting off the aggression if you have trained your dogs well. Command the dogs to sit or down when play fighting first starts to escalate to a higher level. Some physical restraint may be necessary to initially get their attention. Using treats as rewards, try to redirect activities toward less volatile behaviors, like chasing a ball or some parlor tricks.

Another alternative is the time out method. The dog that is getting too excited and out of control can be placed in isolation for a few minutes to allow him time to get his emotions under control. If the behavior persists when he is allowed out, do another time out. Do as many as necessary to get compliance. Having to repeat the exercise is actually beneficial since your dog will learn by the repetition.

Eventually, your dog will learn that every time he looses control and becomes too rowdy that the fun ends. He will learn self-control in this way. As always, the owner will need to be patient and maintain his self-control by not becoming emotionally involved in this training process. A calm but persistent approach by the owner will get results.

If fighting continues to occur and there is a real danger of injury then a professional behaviorist should be consulted. Management techniques can be used as a temporary solution, i.e. keep the dogs physically separated, but behavior modification will be safer in the long run.

Chapter 15
Food For Thought

- What Should I Feed My Dog? -

I get this question all the time. At first I was surprised how often people ask me what to feed their dogs. After all, I am a dog trainer, not a nutritionist. I have never actually kept track but I would estimate, conservatively, better than 50% of my clients ask me about feeding their dog. Obviously, there is considerable confusion on the subject. Because I am asked so frequently, I decided to include a chapter on feeding dogs.

B.A.R.F.

I have to start off with a *caveat*; as I said, I am not a nutritionist, nor a veterinarian, nor have I ever taken any courses on animal nutrition. All I have is my experience and that of others that I know. Having said that, I am convinced that I know the answer to the question, "what should I feed my dog?"

Actually, veterinarian, Dr. Ian Billinghurst gave me the answer, author of the book *Give Your Dog A Bone*. I had the opportunity to hear Dr. Billinghurst speak on the subject of feeding your dog at a dog training conference in 1998. His talk and book inspired me to try his approach.

Dr. Billinghurst's approach resonated well with me primarily because of his "natural" view of the dog and its diet. Dr. Billinghurst looks at the evolution of dogs, especially as it pertains to their feeding habits. He also considers their wild counterparts. Of course dogs are descended from wolves and most likely they became specialized scavengers of human refuse. For a few hundred thousand years dog have eaten this way. They are still with us today, so the diet must have been adequate.

Ironically, during the last two or three decades, dogs have come to be in perhaps the poorest health ever. Veterinarians all over the country are treating dogs afflicted with maladies such as skin problems, dental problems, anal sac problems, bone or joint problems, just to name a few. Dr. Billinghurst believes that the vast majority of these problems could be nutrition related.

Outside of having some difficulty keeping my dog's teeth clean, I did not think I was having any real health problems with my dogs. Nevertheless, I found Dr. Billinghurst's arguments for switching to a more natural diet compelling, so I switched. After only a few weeks on this diet my dogs actually seemed in even better condition than they were in before. Their coats were shinier and my dogs seemed more vigorous than ever. I realize that this is a very subjective testimonial and would be considered anecdotal evidence at best.

One thing did improve measurably. My dog's teeth became really clean. I have not brushed their teeth once since starting on the new diet and yet their teeth are just about as white as they can possibly be. This is still anecdotal evidence but it is not as subjective as judging the shininess of the coat or overall vitality. I have since met and have heard from others using the same diet and without exception hear of similar or even better results.

The diet is called by many names. Most often it is referred to as the "raw diet." It has also gotten some rather humorous nicknames like the acronym "B.A.R.F." diet, which stands for either "Biologically Appropriate Raw Foods" or "Bones And Raw Foods."

Sometimes those of us using the diet are called "B.A.R.F.'s," which stands for "Born Again Raw Feeders." This stems from the perception by some that the enthusiasm of those of us who use and endorse the raw diet resembles a religious fervor. Perhaps the reader has gleaned as much from my writing on the subject so far! I believe the "fervor" comes from the revelation that a complicated problem (a myriad of nagging health problems) appears to have such a simple solution (the raw diet).

The raw diet consists of meats, crushed vegetables and bones, lots of bones. **All of these items are raw, never cooked.** Some supplements are also given but essentially raw foods are the basis for the diet. I could not begin to do the subject justice in one short chapter. Nor am I really an expert. But then, that is one of the great things about the raw diet. You need not be a great expert to make it work.

Anyone interested in the raw diet should get a copy of Dr. Billinghurst's book, *Give Your Dog A Bone* and/or his second book *Grow Your Pups With Bones*. Both of these books are listed in the suggested reading section at the end of this book. After reading the books you should talk to your veterinarian before you embark on a new diet for your dog. Even though thousands of dog owners use the raw diet, including some of the top show dog breeders in the world, I have to tell you that some veterinarians do not endorse this method of feeding. I suggest you read Dr. Billinghurst's books then talk to your veterinarian before making a final decision.

The Obese Dog

While the raw diet may not be embraced universally among pet professionals, the problem of obese dogs certainly is. Obesity is one of the leading health problems in dogs. Part of the problem seems to be that many owners think a fat dog is cute. Fat dogs are not only socially acceptable they are often preferred. I personally have difficulty with this concept because I feel that if an owner really cares about their dog, health should be the number one priority.

Another problem that contributes to obesity is the ability of dogs to manipulate their human owners. Of course dogs readily learn to beg and can teach their owners to give them a lot of extra food in this way. They also learn how to "boycott" their regular dog food and get their owners to give them all sorts of less nutritious but tastier high calorie foods.

For a moment, let us look at the natural feeding habits of the dog. Dogs are designed to be "gorgers." They, like their wolf relatives, are physiologically designed to be able to gorge on a big meal but go for long periods (two or three days) without food. In the wild, food does not come along very often. When it does, it is important to eat as much as possible to make it to the next meal.

Domestic dogs usually have access to food on a regular basis but most still have the "gorge instinct." I often hear owners say that they feed their dog more because their pet still seems hungry. A dog is genetically programmed to eat as much food as it can when it is available. When a dog is being fed on a regular basis, this can become a problem. Owners actually have two choices; feed their dog a lot of food at once and wait a day or so before feeding again or just feed smaller portions on a regular basis.

The bottom line is that the owner is responsible for regulating the amount of food their dog receives each day. If a dog is fat, the owner is feeding too much (there are some very rare medical conditions that could cause obesity). It is really that simple. If you are not sure, ask your vet what is the ideal weight for your dog, then regulate the amount of food you give to keep your dog at his optimum weight. I merely look at my dogs and judge whether they are looking thin or heavy and adjust the amount of food I am giving them accordingly (You can learn to feel for the ribs on dogs with heavy coats). It is not difficult to do.

When your dog refuses to eat his regular meal, put it away after five minutes or so.[50] Do not offer the food again until the next mealtime. Unless your dog is experiencing medical problems (always check with your veterinarian first) he is probably just trying to get tastier treats from you. As long as you know you are feeding your dog a healthy diet, and your dog refuses to eat it, you do not need to panic and go about trying to find something else to feed him. Remember, a healthy dog is easily able to go without eating for a day or two (rare) if necessary. It will not harm them.

After fasting for a day, or just a few hours, most dogs will eat their next regular meal with great pleasure. Be mindful that you are the leader and have responsibilities. You must control when and what your dog eats. Do not be fooled by a dog's natural abilities to manipulate you into feeding them on their own terms.

Commercial Dog Food

Finally, if you are going to feed with commercial dog food, it should be a high quality food (yes, it is more expensive). You can use kibbled or canned food as long as it is of the highest quality. Many owners buy cheap dog food hoping to save money but end up spending more on veterinary bills because of the effects of poor nutrition. Allergies, skin problems and even bone problems, to name just a few, can often be attributed to poor diet.

As a general rule of thumb, do not buy your dog food at the grocery store. To the best of my knowledge, grocery stores only carry the cheaper brands. Higher quality dog foods can be purchased in specialty stores, such as pet shops or even most veterinary clinics. If you are not sure which brand to buy, ask your veterinarian for an opinion.

Commercial foods have the advantage of convenience but do not be fooled by the extravagant claims that many dog food manufacturers make about the suitability of their product. Their claims and commercials can be very convincing. Keep in mind that the industry does not have to comply with the same strict standards as human food manufacturers. They can easily make a variety of claims that may sometimes be misleading. For example, just because a product is "veterinarian recommended" does not necessarily mean that veterinarians actually did any scientific testing of the product.

---

[50] Many dog owners will "free feed" their dogs. This is where food is put out in a bowl and the dog can take their time eating the food. I find that most dogs that are at normal weight will eat their food immediately. Free fed dogs are more often over weight. Owners believe that they are just slow eaters so they like to leave the food out for the dog. If your dog is over weight, you should not free feed your dog. If your dog is at a normal weight, your dog will most likely eat all the food offered at once. Most dogs will not be able to eat in moderation. They will continue to eat even when they do not need to. It is up to the owner to control the amount of food a dog gets each day.

Canine Nutrition

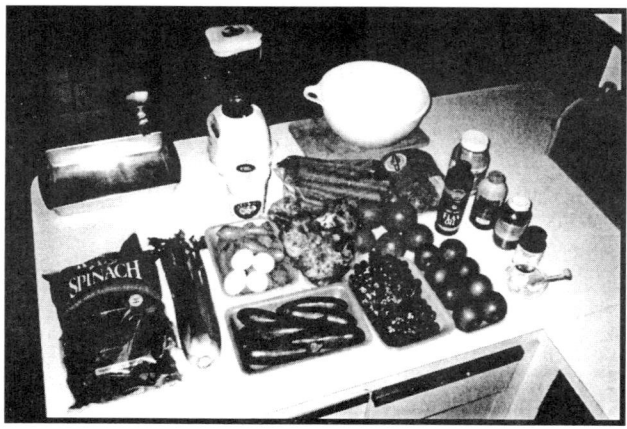

Top Left: The author prefers to feed his dog "Biologically Appropriate Raw Foods" or a "B.A.R.F." diet. This photograph shows just some of the fresh vegetables, fruits and supplements that go into making the raw food diet. Typically, spinach, celery, squash, zucchini, cauliflower, carrots, tomatoes, apples, grapes and other raw plant matter is ground up and blended. Raw eggs, yogurt and some ground turkey or beef is also mixed in. Supplements include cold pressed fish and flax oils, brewers yeast, kelp tablets, vitamin C and raw honey. Raw chicken necks and backs are fed almost everyday as well as raw beef bones. Raw chicken livers or gizzards are fed two or three times each week. Anyone interested in the B.A.R.F. diet should read *Give Your Dog a Bone*, by Dr. Ian Bilinghurst first and then consult their veterinarian before switching to the raw diet. It should be noted that some veterinarians do not approve of this diet.

Above: Wide load! Most dogs have a "gorge" instinct and will eat as much as they can whenever food is offered. It is important for owners to control how much (and what) their dog eats. Obesity, and its consequences, is one of the leading health problems facing the modern dog. The problem is completely under the control of the owner. Spaying and neutering **does not** contribute to obesity. Over eating causes obesity. Owners must feed their dog properly to ensure good health and longevity.

Chapter 16
Dynamic Training

___

- Doing The Same Thing, Only Different -

I always encourage my clients to employ what I call "dynamic training" techniques with their dogs. Dynamic training is teaching your dog to do something but then training the same behavior in a different context. An example should make this clearer. Let us say you have taught the sit just as outlined in this book. Your dog sits, right in front of you, in your family room, where you trained him, virtually every time you give the command with no problem.

Everything is fine as long as you are in your family room but when you take your dog to a new location, say the local park, he seems to forget how to sit. Or if you want your dog to sit at your side instead of in front of you, you may find your dog is unable to comply with your command. He might seem confused or just ignores your command or perhaps he will walk around and face you before sitting. What is going on here?

One of the more remarkable things about human beings that most of us take for granted is our ability to understand a concept. For example, as a small child we can be taught the concept of "chair" and quickly learn to recognize almost any chair, without ever having seen that particular type of chair before. Dogs do not do so well in this kind of thinking. To a dog, a chair may essentially be the same as a table, bed or maybe even the kitchen counter. Their *perception* of the world is different from ours because they do not *conceptualize* as we do.

Dogs tend to be "picture oriented." That is to say that dogs perceive the world in pictures. When you teach your dog to sit, the command "sit" has a somewhat different meaning to him than what you have in mind. When you say, "sit" to your dog you just want him to keep his front legs straight while the back legs are tucked underneath the body until the hindquarters touch the ground. Nothing else matters to you. To your dog the word "sit" may mean that there is an opportunity to gain a reward by facing you when your hand rises above his head at the same time you are bending over and in a particular location; your dog believes the only way to reach the reward is to position himself with his front legs straight and hindquarters on the floor. This is a very complicated picture to us but if this is how you taught your dog to sit, all of those factors and more may need to be in place for your dog to execute a sit. This is the mental "picture" that the dog has memorized through dozens of trials in the past. If anything is out of place it may confuse your dog.

Dogs do not have language and cannot truly understand language. It is only through our ability to use language that we as human beings are able to conceptualize. We can perceive the world with our senses but are also capable of perceiving it completely through conceptual means.[51] Dogs cannot conceptualize because they do not have the

___

[51] For example, I could describe something to you and if I did a good enough job you would recognize it when you saw it. Let us say that you lived a very isolated existence and had never seen a television before but I describe one to you. I would only have to give you a general description. Things such as the exact size, the number of control buttons or the color of the housing would not matter. Later, if you saw a television, whether it was a big screen TV, had remote control or the housing was red, you would probably

capacity, mental or physiological, for language. When you say, "sit" to your dog, he does not have a real concept of the word as we do. Rather, the sound "sit" has been associated with a mental picture of how and where he should be in relation to many other things in order to gain a reward. Factors that we may regard as irrelevant to a sit, such as facing us, may in fact be one of the more important features of a sit to your dog. He does not truly understand the concept of the isolated act of sitting.

When you train your dog to sit under many different circumstances and conditions, you are really helping your dog to narrow his mental picture through the process of elimination to its minimal criteria. With practice, your dog's mental picture begins to look more and more like your concept of a sit. Eventually, the specific behavior that you want, in this case a sit, can be performed in a variety of situations.

If dogs really understood language and could conceptualize we could just teach them to read, then give them a book on dog obedience and say, "This is how I want you to behave."

The point of all this is that if you always train your dog in the family room and only show your dog how to sit while in front of you, your dog will only know how to sit in that specific context and may have difficulty performing well under new conditions. It is important to change venues when training so that the mental picture that your dog gets is more refined. If you want your dog to be able to sit in different positions in relation to you, for example at your side or at a distance, you must teach this separately.

In order to get your dog to simply sit, no matter where he is or in what position relative to you or what his own current position is (i.e. standing or lying down), you must train under many different circumstances to help your dog refine his mental picture of a sit. He can start to eliminate certain aspects of the mental picture such as location or relative position and start to zero in on just the mechanics of sitting. Eventually your dog will be able to sit under almost any circumstances upon hearing the command as his mental picture becomes closer to our concept of the sit.

There is another aspect of dynamic training. That is the command itself. You may need a different command for each variation of the same behavior. To continue the example of sit, let us say you want a special command that would tell your dog that you want him to come to your left side and sit; differentiating it from an immediate sit. For example, in AKC competition the dog is called to a sit position in front of the handler, then upon command, goes directly to the handlers left side in a sit position. To your dog these are two totally different behaviors.

Not only that, in AKC obedience there are two acceptable ways for your dog to get into the position, called a finish. There is an outside finish and an inside finish. An outside finish is accomplished when the dog goes to the handler's right then passes behind the handler and ends up in a sit on the left side. For an inside finish the dog goes directly to the left side without passing behind the handler and makes a sharp "U" turn to get into a sit position. A variation of this it the "military" finish where the dog hops into the air, performs a 180-degree pirouette, and ends in a sit at the left side of the handler. Trainers have the option of training any of these behaviors.

Just for fun, I teach my dogs another method for finishing. I spread my legs apart slightly so they can go between my legs, around the back, and end sitting at my left. My

---

know what it was solely from my description. You had a concept of what a television was based on my verbal description and when you saw something similar you recognized it. A dog cannot do this.

dogs know three ways to get from a sit in front of me to a sit at my left side. Each method has its own command. I use "finish" to mean run around me to a sit on the left side. "Swing" means to pirouette to a sit on my left. And "through" means to go between my legs to get to the sit on my left.

The practical value of this is that dogs must think in order to get rewarded. This helps prevent anticipation or an automatic finish before being commanded. In competition, the judge tells the handler when to finish the dog. If the dog anticipates and finishes before told the team would loose points. But, dynamic training also benefits owners who do not want to compete in obedience because dogs learn to **pay attention**. Attention is beneficial whether the owner is competing or just walking his dog in the park.

Other examples of dynamic training are "downing" at a run, either at the handlers side or from a distance (often called a "drop"). Healing or walking in various positions, like right side, left side, follow directly behind, walk in front or even between the legs of the handler. Your imagination is really the only limit to dynamic training.

Dynamic training is both practical and fun. I believe that one creates a thinking dog by employing dynamic training. Thinking dogs are easier to train, control and they adapt more readily to changing environments. It can also be a lot of fun for both you and your dog by making training like a game rather than a routine chore.

Training need not always be serious. I often train behaviors just for fun. I also like to watch my dogs for behaviors that they do naturally and I put it on a command by rewarding each time the dog performs. This is called "capturing" a behavior. Sometimes my dogs invent things on their own. The finish between my legs was actually invented by my dog when he was trying to figure out what I wanted when I was trying to teach him to stand between and legs and walk backwards (another whimsical behavior that he also eventually learned). When he went through my legs and ended at my left side I just rewarded him and got him to do it again. Soon he was doing it every time when I would stand with my legs apart. Eventually I was able to put a specific command word to the behavior.

Routine training can sometimes become boring and too repetitious. Teaching your dog other behaviors helps liven up training sessions and maintains the interest of both the owner and the dog. The owner has a better attitude and the dog is more enthusiastic. Mix lots of play with your training and train your dog to play. All dogs know how to play but they do not always know how to play according to our rules. The next chapter covers both play and trick training.

Doing The Same Thing Only Different

Left: A competition "finish" begins with the dog in front of the handler in a sit position, and upon command, the dog quickly goes around the handler to a sit position at the left side of the handler. In this photo the author's dog, Pepper, can be seen performing an outside finish.

Left: The author's dog, Pepper, demonstrates a military finish. The military finish is one type of inside finish where the dog goes from a sit in front of the handler and then upon command jumps up and pirouettes or twists into sit position at the left side of the handler. Pepper must pay attention and listen for the command before knowing which way to finish.

Say What You Mean

Left: Pepper is in a sit position but she would not sit this way if given the command, "sit." For her to sit in this position the author must give one of three commands. If Pepper were directly in front of the author the command to sit on the left is either, "swing," or "finish," as seen on the previous page. If Pepper is in any other position, even several feet away, then the command, "get it in," will prompt her to a sit on the left. To Pepper, none of these commands translate to "sit," which would elicit an entirely different response.

Right: Now that is a sit according to Pepper! She would quickly sit any time and any place upon hearing the command, "sit." However, she will also run to the author and sit automatically if she hears the command, "front." If she ran ahead of the handler and heard the word, "halt," Pepper would turn around and sit immediately at that spot. As you can see, a simple "sit" is not just a sit to a dog. A dog will only respond to the word "sit" in the right context. When the context changes, so does the command.

Chapter 17
Exercise, Play Training And Parlor Tricks

- Exercise -

Few modern dogs get adequate exercise. The amount of exercise a dog needs will vary according to breed, age and physical condition but the average dog needs **at least thirty minutes of aerobic exercise every day**. A walk around the block is simply not enough exercise for most dogs. The activity can be done all at once or broken up into two or three quick sessions. Short sessions can involve vigorous exercise, longer ones can be more moderate.

The most common ways of providing enough exercise for your dog are jogging, bicycling, roller-skating and ball playing. If you jog, take your dog with you. You can teach your dog to run with you nicely using the same techniques as described for loose leash walking. Bicycling or skating with your dog are excellent ways to provide a good aerobic work out. However, both activities have inherent dangers even without a dog. If you want to exercise your pet while bicycling or skating please take all necessary safety precautions. You should be sufficiently practiced at these activities so that you can avoid injury to both yourself and your dog. Ball playing, or retrieving any thrown object is probably the easiest way to exercise your dog but he must have natural retrieve drive (see Play Training below).

I have frequently been able to solve behavior problems for clients either partially or entirely by prescribing a regular exercise regime for their dog. The general rule is; a well-exercised dog is a well-behaved dog. Many problems such as digging, excessive barking and destructive behaviors may be curbed or eliminated by regular exercise.

Caution: It is important that you provide your dog access to plenty of water after each aerobic activity and if you live in particularly hot areas do not over exert your dog. Also, the above exercises are for *adult*, healthy dogs. If your dog has certain health problems check with your veterinarian before embarking on a regular exercise regime. If your dog is not used to a lot of activity work up to a thirty-minute exercise program slowly. Dogs can get sore muscles and sport related injuries the same as human beings.

Finally, puppies should be excluded from these kinds of exercises except for short retrieves of a ball or object. Vigorous exercise should be limited to normal "puppy play" until your dog has reached his full adult size. Growing bones and muscles can be damaged and result in serious medical conditions such as hip and elbow dysplasia later in life. Puppies need exercise but in smaller segments and they should never be pushed to go farther than they want. If you are walking your puppy and they just stop walking do not encourage them to keep going. Pick them up and carry them if your have to and do not try to walk so far the next time.

Some appropriate exercise for your puppy or alternative exercises for your adult dog can be found in the examples given in our next topic Play Training.

- Play Training -

As I mentioned in the previous chapter, training does not have to be all practical and strictly business. In fact, as training gets more advanced one of the most effective ways to get optimum performance from a dog is to mix plenty of play and lighthearted training in with the more serious behaviors.

Some dogs do not know how to play, at least according to our rules. That is okay. We can teach them. The kind of games you play will depend on your dog's natural tendencies. For example, some dogs like to retrieve a ball, whereas others are not interested. Some dogs are enthusiastic about playing a lively game of tug-of-war but some refuse. Chasing, jumping and wrestling are more examples of "natural" games that some dogs like to play.

The natural games can be used as great motivators. When your dog has just performed some difficult training exercise it is often a good idea to reward the effort and relieve the tension with some play or just as part of a regular exercise program. However, before you can play games with your dog you must first establish the rules. As leader it is your job to set limits and control games. Here are examples of some typical natural games and their associated rules:

1. **Retrieve** – The dog always returns the retrieved object to the owner.
2. **Tug-of-war** – The dog always releases when commanded.
3. **Chase, or tag** – The dog always comes when called.
4. **Jumping** – The dog never jumps on the owner unless invited.
5. **Wrestling** – The dog has a very "soft mouth" or does not bite at all and stops when told.

If your dog enjoys any of these activities then all you have to do is teach her the rules. Your dog must enjoy the activity itself and do it without being taught.[52] The only things that are taught are the rules. Teaching the rules is not difficult but they must be reinforced consistently. In some cases it is best not to engage in the game until the rules are established first.

Retrieve

If your dog likes retrieving a ball the easiest way to establish the rule that the dog always returns the ball to the owner is to have two balls. Throw one and when she returns with it, entice her close with the second ball in your hand. Hold the second ball right next to her nose if necessary. When she releases the first ball to grab the second do not let her have it. Reward-mark the release immediately and quickly throw the second ball. You can put a command to the release such as "give," "out" or any other word of your choice.

Of course, any retrieve object can be used. You just need two so that you can distract and throw with one in order to get your dog to release the other. A rope tied into a "monkey's fist" knot is favored by my dogs and me. It has a handle so it is easy to throw a long distance and my dogs love the texture for gripping. It can also be used as a "tug" for tug-of-war games, which is described next.

An alternative method of teaching your dog to release an object is to offer a food reward. Show your dog the food reward and wait until she releases the retrieve object. Again, you can put a verbal command to the release. As you reward your dog with the food pick up the object and throw it again.

---

[52] It is possible to teach some of these activities to your dog even if she does not do them naturally. However, if we want to use play as a reward or part of regular exercise your dog must derive enjoyment from the activity itself. Dogs that must be taught the activity do it primarily for a secondary reward, i.e. food or praise.

If your dog is still a puppy do not throw the object very far. Short runs are better for young growing dogs. Regardless of whether your dog is a puppy or fully grown it is important to always end the game before she gets bored with it. In other words, always leave them wanting more. This will ensure that your dog will be willing to play the game again the next time. Keep all reward play games exciting.

Tug-Of-War

Teaching your dog the tug-of-war game is sometimes controversial. Some trainers believe that tug-of-war is a dominance struggle and that your dog may become aggressive towards you as a result of the game. I do not feel that this is true. Tug-of-war is a natural pack activity. It has little or nothing to do with dominance. It appears to be a group activity that is enjoyed by just about any pack member regardless of status in the hierarchy.

If it were really a show of dominance, the "alpha" would simply give a convincing growl and subordinate would drop the object. In fact this sometimes happens if a subordinate tries to take something from a dominant pack member. Either subordinate or dominate pack members can initiate the tug-of-war game but all members seem more than happy to play along. There could be a good deal of growling but it is merely play growls. Tug-of-war may also have practical value. In some cases it is a means of dissecting killed prey into small, more manageable pieces.

The rule for tug-of-war is that the dog always releases when commanded. This is one of the cases where the rule is taught before the game is played. Owners should train their dogs to give them objects on command. Start by encouraging your dog to take things in her mouth and then give it back to you.

Treats are the best way to train a release. Get your dog to take something in her mouth then put a treat close to her nose. When she releases the object, reward-mark and give her the treat. Begin putting a command to the release just as described in the retrieve. Repeat this exercise over and over. If your dog ever picks up something voluntarily and brings it to you, have her release but then give it right back to her after reward-marking or give her a treat if you have one available.

Once your dog is releasing objects reliably you can begin to play a very abbreviated and low intensity version of tug-of-war. Just tug on the object slightly for only a second or two before giving the release command. Slowly work up to more time and intensity as your dog responds appropriately.

Always practice the release several times during a game. **Do not get into the habit of playing tug-of-war with your dog and doing a release only at the end of the game.** Your dog will learn not to let go because she knows that it will be the end of the game. If you always have her release at random times she will not know if you are going to end the game or continue.

Treats can be eliminated after a while because the game itself will be rewarding. Always let the tug go slack just before you command your dog to release. If your dog will run away with the tug or not stop pulling, hold on to her collar but do not struggle with the tug. The tug toy will become somewhat boring at this point to your dog. She will learn to let go when commanded because she knows that the game will only get exciting when you start the game again. (If your dog is really good at releasing when commanded then you can see if she will release while there is still tension on the tug toy. This is for more advanced training.)

Once again we must use caution when playing this game with puppies. If your puppy is teething the tug-of-war game can be painful. It is best to play the game gently or avoid it altogether during the teething stage, usually between four and six months of age. Also, never lift your dog off the ground with a tug toy. If they let go they may land badly and injure themselves.

A spirited game of tug-of-war can be great exercise for a dog (and owner!). However, it is imperative that the dog is first taught the rules of the game and releases the tug upon command.

Chase or Tag

Some dogs like to be chased. They will run around in tight circles and come very close to the owner as the owner pretends to grab the dog by making sudden lunges. Once again the owner should be the only one who initiates this game and decides when it should end. You do not want to teach your dog that she can run away from you anytime she wants.

The game is usually not very difficult to end because the dog will stop as soon as the owner discontinues lunging. The game just isn't fun unless the owner is actively involved. The owner should never call the dog and lunge. Recalls should be taught separately and reaching down to touch the collar should be quite different from making pretend lunging motions.

Normally, only dogs that do this naturally can be trained. Initiating the game usually just involves getting the dog excited and making lunging motions toward the dog. You can put the game on command by using a word like "chase" or "let's play tag" in a very excited, high-pitched voice while initiating play.

Jumping

Jumping games can be fun and good exercise if done in moderation. There are a few other rules of caution that should be observed. Larger dogs are more likely to land badly attempting vertical jumps, which could cause serious injury. Also, larger dogs are more prone to accidentally bumping into people and other objects in the area when they get exuberant, jumping up and down. Generally, I would not encourage larger dogs to jump up and down, only the smaller breeds should be taught to make these vertical jumps.

Young dogs or puppies should not be encouraged to jump. Only dogs that have achieved their full growth should be encouraged to jump to avoid any skeletal problems.

The owner can use a treat or toy to lure the dog to jump. If you are teaching your dog to jump up and down, wait until your dog is in a very animated mood then encourage her with a treat and an excited voice. Associate a verbal command or signal with the behavior plus practice a counter command such as a sit or down to end the jumping.

Larger dogs do better if they jump over some appropriate object or barrier.[53] A broom or mop handle held in the owner's hand makes a great object for your dog to jump. Start with the handle on the floor then gradually lift it higher and higher as your training sessions proceed.

If you want to teach your dog to jump into your arms, start by sitting on a short stool or crate. Invite your dog to jump into your lap. Gradually use a taller stool or chair. As the behavior becomes more reliable upon command, eliminate the chair and simply bend at the knees in a squat position. Catch your dog in your arms and stand up straight.

Eventually, depending on the size of your dog and how high she can jump, you should be able to catch her while standing straight up or with just a minimal squat. I would only recommend that smaller dogs be taught this trick. A large dog can knock you flat on your back!

The author taught his dog Pepper to jump over his extended leg upon command. He first taught her to jump over a broom handle then gradually started to extend his leg with the broom handle still in place. Eventually, the broom handle was eliminated and just the extended leg was used. As a reward Pepper gets to catch the "monkey's fist" which is thrown as soon as she makes her jump.

---

[53] Jumping is an activity that certain dogs enjoy but it can cause serious injury if done improperly. Always start off with very low jumps and never attempt to have your dog jump excessively high, even if they seem physically able. Jumping is good exercise but only when it is done in moderation.

Wrestling

Some dogs love to wrestle. Most well socialized dogs like to wrestle with each other. If you watch dogs wrestle there is a lot of biting, especially around the neck area, during the skirmish. The biting does not cause any damage and it appears not to bother the dog participants at all. However, the same bite on human skin would be quite painful.

This game should not be taught to nipping puppies or dogs that do not have good bite inhibition. I also do not recommend that small children ever engage in the activity. One must be very sure of their dog before allowing any mouthing. In fact, mouthing may not be allowed at all if desired.

Be very sure that your dog does not misinterpret your behavior during this activity. Start off slow and never intimidate or frighten your dog. Only dogs with the proper temperament should be encouraged to wrestle with the owner. Your dog should be willing to roll onto her back when you first initiate the wrestling. If your dog does not like to roll onto her back, do not try this game.

Once your dog is on her back grab the loose skin around her neck and playfully tug on it while rubbing her belly with your other hand or gently rocking her back and forth. Have an excited voice but keep the session low-key, especially at first. If your dog tries to play bite you (or bite too hard if you do not mind a little mouthing) use the same method as teaching a puppy not to bite. Over react by shouting "ouch" and end the game immediately. Try again after a minute or so but be prepared to end the game at any time it gets too rough. You set the limits. Your dog can easily learn what they are.

Never allow children to play this way with any dog. Adults should be very familiar with the dog and able to know when or if the dog is afraid. Obviously, this kind of play could have some risks if the wrong dog or person is involved so I do not normally recommend it unless the owner is very sure of their dog and has established a really good relationship.

- Parlor Tricks -

Parlor tricks are usually whimsical behaviors. They are just fun for the dog, owner and onlookers. Many are easy to teach and while the tricks themselves may have no practical value the exercise and process does. Teaching and performing parlor tricks helps keep your dog mentally and physically active. It promotes the development of good training skills for the owner and teaches the dog to pay attention. It also facilitates the formation of an even deeper bond.

Parlor tricks range from the extremely simple to the very complex. A few of the more simple tricks are described here. You can also use your own imagination. Watch your dog for natural behaviors that can be modified or trained on command. For example a dog that naturally "throws" its paw when in a sit can readily be taught to "shake hands."

Nose Games

All dogs have a superior sense of smell. Dogs explore their world with their noses all the time. One of the easiest nose games to play with your dog is hide-and-seek. Have a friend or family member hold your dog while you show him a treat. Tease him with it a little and run away into another room and hide the treat. Once the treat is hidden have your assistant let your dog go and tell him to "find it." Your dog should start sniffing around for the treat. If your dog does not immediately start looking for the treat try to encourage your dog by showing him where it is hidden.

The first few times you do this the treat should placed in an area where it is very easy to find, even in plain view. Once your dog starts to get the idea you can begin placing the treat in a little more concealed spot. At first you may just want to place it on the floor somewhere with a piece of paper over it. Later you could use a pillow or article of clothing. Start putting it up a little higher, for example on a low stool, so your dog does not always expect it to be on the floor.

Before long your dog will become very good at the game and you will be able to send him to search for a hidden treat simply by giving the command. You can also use toys as search objects or even people. People can hide in different rooms, closets or behind doors. When finding people a treat or toy should be given as a reward.

Object Discrimination Game

If your dog likes to retrieve you can teach him how to discriminate between different retrieve objects. For example, you could place a ball, a dumb-bell and a tug-rope on the floor. You could then specify which object you want your dog to bring. Eventually, you could even combine the hide-and-seek game with the object discrimination game by sending your dog on a search for a specific object in the house.

To start out you should just use two objects that your dog likes to retrieve. Place them a foot or so apart and ask your dog to bring one of them. If your dog picks up the wrong object just ignore him. If he brings the correct object you should reward-mark and either give a treat or play with him and the object. If your dog brings the wrong object and does not go back for the other when you ignore him, take the wrong object away and place it back with the other and send your dog again. Eventually, your dog should pick up the correct object. After numerous trials your dog will learn to discern which object you want from your command.

Once your dog is discriminating between two different objects and you want to add more you may. Just add one object at a time and train until your dog is consistently picking up the correct object before adding another. Be sure to switch positions of the objects. Remember, your dog is very picture oriented and may think that "ball" means whatever object is on the left if that was where it was always placed during training. Also, make sure the name you use for each object has a distinctly different sound so your dog can easily recognize the command.

If you want to combine the hide-and-seek game with the discrimination game you should train each exercise separately first. Later put a "decoy" or incorrect object in plain view when you send your dog. If he brings the wrong one, do nothing and send him again for the correct object. I know some owners who have a toy box for their dog. They bring it out when it is time to play and they give their dog a command to bring a certain toy. The dog will root around in the toy box until it finds the correct object.

The Classics

Some of the more classic parlor tricks are *sitting pretty (or beg), roll over, walk on the hind legs, bow, play dead* and of course many more. I will briefly explain how I teach these six parlor tricks. Owners who want to teach more can get more information by referring to the suggested reading section of this book.

Most of these parlor tricks are taught by lure training methods. For example, to teach your dog to *sit pretty* ask your dog to sit first. Then hold a treat in front of her nose, raise it just above her head at nose length and towards the back. As your dog's head goes back to follow the treat the front paws should come off the ground. Reward-mark at the moment this happens and give your dog the treat.

If your dog jumps up or moves out of position simply start over. Make sure your dog is sitting in a good square sit prior to luring, otherwise her balance will be off. You can also try placing your dog in a corner with her back to the wall to help train the behavior initially. The command can be put to the behavior once your dog starts to respond to the luring.

A *roll over* is usually very easy to teach. Your dog must have a good down first. Ask your dog to down and then put a treat in front of her nose with your hand. **Slowly** bring your hand to the side so that she has to look back along her side for the treat. Now move your hand up and across. If you keep the treat right in front of your dog's nose she should roll onto her back and then to the other side.

Do not worry if your dog does not make the entire roll. Many dogs are confused or uncomfortable at first. It is important to reward your dog for any attempt even if it is just a shift of her weight to one side. As your dog becomes more comfortable with the maneuver and gets better at it you can gradually increase the criteria, trying to get her to roll a little further. This is a classic "shaping" technique where you reward for an approximation of the behavior at first but work towards improvement until the entire behavior is in place.

The biggest mistake owners make is luring too fast and expecting too much of the complete behavior. Move your hand slowly so your dog has no trouble following the treat and increase criteria gradually. Make sure you hold the treat in the right position, which should be right by her chest as you rotate to the other side. In other words, your dog should be looking down towards her chest as she rolls. It is okay to give a little physical help by pushing your dog gently if she seems to be getting stuck but keep this physical contact to a bare minimum. Your dog needs to learn to do this on her own.

Eventually, she should be able to make a complete 360-degree roll. You can add a command, such as "roll over" as soon as your dog does the complete behavior. Fade out the luring by being less precise as your dog becomes more proficient at rolling over. In time you can just use a hand signal, a circular motion with your hand in front of you, to get your dog to roll over.

Getting your dog to *stand or walk on the hind legs* is another simple behavior to teach. Once again lure training is the method of choice. Get your dog to rise up on his hind legs by enticing him with a treat held above his head. Do not reward for jumping. Always wait until your dog simply stands on his hind legs before reward-marking then treat.

Once your dog is standing on his hind legs in front of you, then you can get him to walk by slowly stepping back, luring the dog forward towards you. Only expect one or two steps at the beginning. You can encourage more as the training progresses. Once your dog is performing you can add a command, such as "walk."

The *play dead* trick is another popular parlor trick. It must be taught in stages. Your dog must have a good down. From the down you will need to teach your dog to lie on his side. Do this in the same fashion that you would teach the first step in the roll over. Use a different command such as "dead dog" or "bang" (a lot of people like to pretend that they shoot their dog). If your dog knows it, a second command of "wait" can be used to cue your dog that he should lay still.

Teaching the sequence goes like this: First command your dog to down. Then get your dog to lie on his side by luring and use "dead dog" or some other command to differentiate it from a roll over. To get your dog to lie still, try using a "wait" command. The instant your dog stops moving, reward-mark and treat. You may have to hold the treat on the floor near your dog's nose to get him to put his head down (or teach your dog to lay his head down on command separately).

Once your dog learns that he must lie still to get rewarded you can begin increasing the amount of time in slow increments, just as you would teach a wait. Use whatever hand-signal you want but many people like to pretend they are using a gun. As soon as your dog responds to the hand signal, secondary commands, such as "down, wait" or "head down" can be phased out.

A *bow* can be taught while your dog is in a stand position then quickly luring the dog's nose downward toward the chest then between the feet. Your dog should begin to go down chest first. The instant the front of your dog is down and **before the hindquarters can follow,** reward-mark and treat.

Bowing is a natural behavior for dogs and they should catch on quickly but if your dog simply lays down each time you may have to give him some help to get started. Try using your free arm to hold up his belly. Alternatively, get your dog to stand over a narrow barrier of a suitable height (like a low dog jump, or a board turned on edge supported with stacks of books) that can keep the hindquarters from reaching the floor.

As always, the command can be added as soon as your dog begins to understand the behavior. If you want your dog to bow while standing at your side you will have to teach this by moving your body into position gradually as you train. The picture your dog has of the behavior will be with you in front. Gradually begin turning your body while you ask for the bow.

Your signal for a bow can be a bow from you. You have to bend over to give your dog the treat anyway. This can become your signal for your dog to bow. Just link the command and your bow together. This way, after you and your dog have just performed some parlor tricks for your friends, you can bow to their applause and your dog will respond in kind.

Of course there are many other tricks and games that can be taught to your dog. The tricks mentioned here are merely small samples of the ones that can be taught to your dog. The possibilities are mostly limited by your imagination. Dogs seem to be capable of learning as many things as you can come up with and are willing to teach.

Just For Fun

Wave!
The wave is the same as "shake hands" except the command is given at a distance. This classic trick can be easily taught to almost any dog. The easiest way is to *capture* the behavior by waiting for the dog to naturally lift its paw, then reward-mark and treat. The command is added later.

Sit Pretty!
Another classic, the "sit pretty" or "beg" is taught by luring a dog into position the same way as the sit except the lure simply goes back a little farther. Most dogs can learn this trick. A good square sit is a prerequisite. Teaching your dog to respond to a command at a distance makes the trick even more impressive.

Take a bow!
A perfectly timed reward-mark helps when teaching the bow. Lure your dog down and reward-mark the instant she is in a bow position. Start using a separate command to distinguish it from a down. You can keep the hind legs up by having your dog straddle some obstacle or gently use your hand to support her belly just in front of the hind legs.

Just For Fun

Hands up!
Pepper demonstrates how she does a "hands up" command. When the author points his finger at her in this position and says, "bang!" Pepper drops down into a "dead dog" position as if shot by a gun. The behaviors have to be taught separately and then "chained" together.

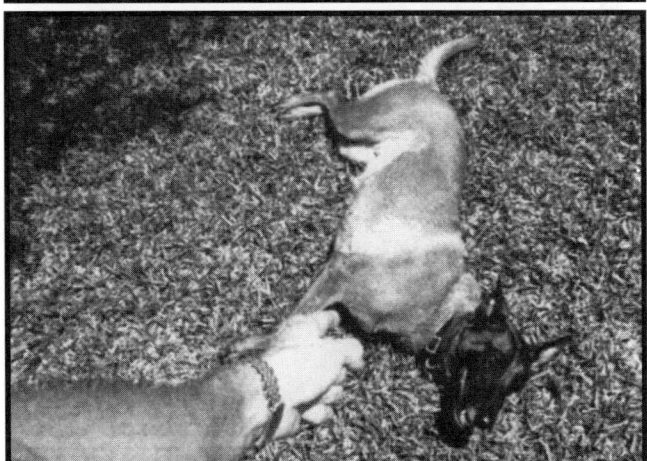

Dead Dog!
Pepper shows off her best "dead dog" impression. A finger point and the word "bang" will induce Pepper to drop to the ground. Parlor tricks like this one are fun to train and help build a good working relationship between the trainer and dog. Not all training has to be serious.

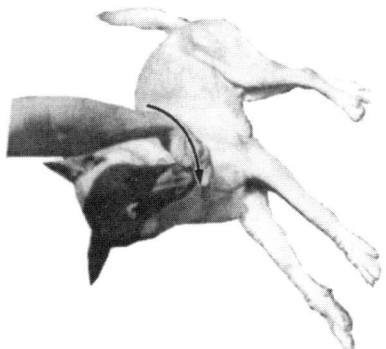

Teaching the roll over. From a down position put a treat in front of your dog's nose with your hand. Slowly bring your hand to the side so that he has to look back for the treat. Now move your hand up and across. If you keep the treat right in front of your dog's nose he should roll onto his back and then to the other side. Reward-mark and treat. The lure is gradually faded and a circular motion becomes the hand signal.

Chapter 18
Final Words

- Some Final Hints -

Always remember that training should be fun. It should be fun for you as well as your dog. If it is not, then you are not doing it right. Appetitive style training provides a means of making learning fun for your dog. It also provides an opportunity to reinforce and build on the four key elements for effective training, which are bonding, leadership, communication and understanding.

It is easy to see how bonding is strengthened through reinforcement training. Praising, petting, playing and even feeding are all excellent ways of bonding with your dog. This bond will continue to grow as time goes on.

Leadership is easily established with appetitive training. Always be generous with your rewards for good behavior. If you are generous with rewards for desired behavior the lack of a reward as you ignore bad behavior will provide a very powerful contrasting message to your dog. Always maintain control of all the resources that your dog wants but give them generously as rewards for acceptable behavior. It is your kindness and generosity that will leave no doubt in your dog's mind as to who is the leader.

Be consistent in the way you communicate with your dog. Communicate at your dog's level and watch your dog carefully for signs of what he is trying to convey to you. Avoid inconsistencies in your behavior and expectations for the behavior of your dog.

Understanding of your dog will only come from being objective. Always try to look at things from your dog's point of view. It will almost always be different from yours. Allow your dog to be a dog. Do not try to make them into something that they are not. A dog must behave like a dog but one of the remarkable things about them is that their natural dog behaviors can be easily shaped by us to be compatible with human society.

- Patience Is A Virtue -

Training takes time. I realize that modern society moves at an ever-increasing pace. We want to travel faster; we want our meals faster; we want news and information faster; we want our computers to go faster; we want everything faster because in spite of our technological advances that are supposed to save us time, we seem to have less and less of it. Many probably would like their dog to be trained faster too but that is not going to happen. There are certain things that cannot be rushed. Certainly, training our dogs is one of those things. Always proceed at your dog's pace not yours.

I do not consider that a bad thing. With our hurried and rushed lives we need to slow down once in a while. Time with our dog actually provides us with an opportunity. We should really enjoy the process of watching our dog learn and slowly grow into the kind of companion animal that we want. There is a great deal of satisfaction in shaping the behavior of our pets into something that will make us proud as owners.

- A Final Philosophical Look At Dogs –

My dogs make me laugh and smile every single day. Not one day goes by that my two dogs, Jack and Pepper, cannot lift my spirits and bring joy into my life, if only for a moment. That is a rare talent but it is not unique to only my dogs. All dogs can do this for their owners. In case you have not been reading between the lines throughout this book, I have great respect and admiration for all animals but most especially dogs. This book was written in the hope that all dog owners can experience, as I have, the special joy that comes from owning a well-mannered dog.

I hope I have convinced the reader of this book the value and effectiveness of appetitive training. Becoming your dog's leader should be a fun and rewarding experience for both you and your dog. Build a relationship with your dog that is based on cooperation and trust not contention and domination. Think of time spent with your dog, including training, as therapy for combating the stress and pressures of our modern day life. Scientific studies have shown that the simple act of petting your dog will help lower your blood pressure and that pet owners tend to live healthier, longer lives than non-pet owners.

There can be a kind of symbiotic relationship that develops between you and your dog. Dogs are social animals and require social interaction. We, as human beings, require social interaction. I find it amazing that dogs are one of the few animals that can relate to us on a social level. Arguably, our mutual social needs are probably more similar than any other two species on this planet.

In the beginning of this book I mentioned how attitudes have changed toward dogs in recent years. I think I know at least part of the reason. As urban sprawl rapidly takes over and isolates us from the natural environment, perhaps the dog serves as an important vestigial link to nature. As a species we have traded the challenge of surviving in the wild for the rigors of surviving in our manufactured urban environment. We have brought our dogs with us and we need them as much as they need us.

Part IV

Addendum

GLOSSARY OF TERMS

Aggression, *Dominance* – Hostility motivated by the desire to increase or assert status in a hierarchy.

Aggression, *Possession* – Hostility motivated by the desire to retain or gain an object.

Aggression, *Food* – Hostility motivated by the presence of food.

Aggression, *Personal Space* – Hostility motivated by the close proximity of a person or other animal.

Aggression, *Challenge* – Hostility motivated by outside physical force, e.g. leash correction.

Alpha Position – The top or dominant member in a hierarchy.

Anthropomorphic – The assigning of human characteristics to non-human animals.

Appetitive Training – A training method that employs a reward system for eliciting a desired behavior.

Applied Animal Behaviorist – A psychologist specializing in animal, rather than human behavior.

Attention Training – Training a dog to look at the owner.

Aversive Training – Any kind of training that requires force or punishment.

Bite Inhibition – A learned behavior that prevents a dog from biting or biting too hard.

Calming Signals – The various postures or body language of the domestic dog that indicates the desire to avoid conflict without showing weakness or submission.

Canids – A scientific name that refers to the dog family, which includes foxes, jackals, wolves, coyotes, wild dogs and domestic dogs.

Correction Training – See Aversive Training

Counter Commanding – A command that is in conflict with a behavior, e.g. the command sit to keep a dog from jumping up.

Counter Conditioning – Changing the association of a learned response to a stimulus.

Desensitization – The result of counter conditioning that eliminates anxiety towards a stimulus.

Dominance Theory – The theory that assumes that dogs see humans as "pack members" and that the dominant pack member controls the pack.

Drive – Instinct or strong urge to exhibit a certain act or behavior.

Dynamic Training – Authors term for training dogs to do variations on the same behavior so as to promote a more attentive dog.

Ethology – The scientific and objective study of animal behavior.

Fear Aggression – A term often used to describe a dog that behaves aggressively (e.g. growls or bites) because it is frightened.

Finish – A command that instructs the dog sitting in front of a handler to go to a sit position by the handler's side.

Force Training – See Aversive Training.

Free Feeding – The practice of putting out essentially an unlimited amount of food to allow the dog to eat whenever it wants.

Gorge Instinct – The natural tendency of a dog to consume large quantities of food whenever it is available.

Head-halter – A device that goes around the dogs muzzle and allows a leash to be attached for control.

Heeling – A formal and rather precise position taken by the dog while walking with the owner, usually at the left side. Used mostly in competition obedience.

Jackpot – A larger or more desirable reward, usually reserved for the best behaviors.

Lateral Recumbency – A dog that lies on its side.

Lure Training – Using a treat or reward to bait a dog into a position before actually giving the reward.

Mark – See Place

Marking Behavior – Urinating in certain locations or on certain objects to "mark" territory. More common with male dogs but some females will mark too.

Morphology – The outward appearance or structure of an animal.

Motivational Training – See Appetitive Training

Negative Training – See Aversive Training

Opposition Reflex – The natural tendency of a dog to resist physical force or restraint.

Place – A specific spot or area where your dog will go upon command. Sometimes called a "mark."

Positive Training - See Appetitive Training

Puppy Mill – A business that breeds dogs primarily for profit.

Rank Reduction – A behavior "therapy," according to dominance theory, that lowers the dog's status in a hierarchy.

Raw Diet – A "natural" diet of mostly raw meaty bones and raw crushed vegetables.

Recall – Calling a dog to come to you.

Rehearsal Behavior – The offering of a variety of behaviors by a dog in an attempt to see what earns a reward.

Release – A word, sound or signal that tells the dog that it is no longer required to perform a command.

Reinforcement Training - See Appetitive Training

Rescue Dog – An abandoned or abused dog that has been placed in a good home.

Reward – Anything a dog wants or that provides a positive motivation to perform a behavior. Payment for performing a desired behavior.

Reward-mark – A sound linked or associated with a reward that tells a dog the exact moment it has done something to earn the reward.

Reward Training - See Appetitive Training

Shaping – Breaking a training behavior down into smaller components or less precise movements and rewarding for the best attempts in an effort to "shape" the behavior into a more exact or complex behavior.

Socialization – Exposure and acclimation of a dog to a wide variety of environmental elements, especially other people but also other dogs, novel objects, sounds, smells and situations.

Sphinx Position – A "down" position where the dog has its chest and abdomen centered and touching the ground.

Sternal Recumbency – Sphinx position.

Stimulus – Any outside influence that elicits a reaction.

Targeting – A trained behavior where a dog touches his nose to a specific spot, usually the end of a stick or the palm of the trainer's hand.

Temperament – The disposition or mental character of a dog in the environment, especially how it interacts with human beings.

Variable Reward Schedule – Rewarding at random intervals to reinforce desired behavior.

SUGGESTED READING

General Information on Dog Breeds

The Complete Dog Book, Official Publication of the American Kennel Club
Macmillan, Inc., New York, NY
The Encyclopedia of the Dog, Bruce Fogle, D.V.M.
DK Publishing, Inc., New York, NY

Dog Behavior and Learning

The Culture Clash, Jean Donaldson
James & Kenneth Publishers, Berkeley, CA
The Dog's Mind, Bruce Fogle, D.V.M., M.R.C.V.S.
Macmillan, Inc., New York, NY
Excel-Erated Learning, Pamela J. Reid, Ph.D.
James & Kenneth Publishers, Oakland, CA

Training

Purely Positive Training, Sheila Booth
Podium Publications, Ridgefield, CT
In Tune With Your Dog, John Rogerson
The Northern Centre for Animal Behaviour, Durham, England

Games

Fun and Games with Dogs, Roy Hunter
Howln Moon Press, Eliot, ME
The Trick is in the Training, Stephanie J. Taunton and Cheryl S. Smith
Barron's Educational Series, Inc., Hauppauge, NY

Nutrition

Give Your Dog A Bone, Dr. Ian Billinghurst
Ian Billinghurst, P.O. Box WO 64, Bathurst, N.S.W. Australia 2795
Grow Your Pups With Bones, Dr. Ian Billinghurst
Ian Billinhurst, P.O. Box WO 64, Bathurst, N.S.W. Australia 2795

* Indicates books that are highly recommended. Yes, I know all of the above books have an asterisk. Think about it!

Dog Sport Organizations

For those dog owners who may be interested in getting involved in dog sport activities I have compiled the following list. It is by no means complete but represents the best data that I could find at the time of this writing.

Obedience

American Kennel Club (AKC)
    51 Madison Avenue
    New York, NY 10010
    www.akc.org

United Kennel Club (UKC)
    100 E. Kilgora Road
    Kalamazoo, MI 49002
    www.ukcdog.com

Agility

United States Dog Agility Association (USDAA)
    P.O. Box 850955
    Richardson, TX 75085-0955
    (214) 231-9700
National Club for Dog Agility (NCDA)
    401 Bluemont Circle
    Manhattan, KS 66502
    (913) 537-7022
AKC   (See above)
UKC   (See above)

Flyball

North American Flyball Association, Inc. (NAFA)
    P.O. Box 8
    Mt. Hope, ON LOR 1 WO

Protection Sports

French Ring –
    North American Ring Association
    23341 Two Mile Road
    Newaygo, MI 49337
    (616) 856-8973
KNPV –

    American Dutch Police Dog Association
    19123 Yontz Road
    Brooksville, FL 34601
    (352) 796-4715

Protection Sports (cont.)

KNPV America
Rt. 9 Box 241-B
Harlingen, TX 78552
(210) 428-5976

NAPD –

National Association of Protection Dogs
798 Hillborn Court
Suisun, CA 94585
(707) 422-5095

Schutzhund –

United Schutzhund Clubs of America
3810 Paule Ave
St. Louis, MO 63125
(314) 638-9686

Miscellaneous
Herding, Tracking, Frisbee®, Sledding, Carting, Freestyle, etc.

www.workingdogweb.com (links to many dog sport sites)
www.dogpatch.org (herding)
www.isdra.org (sledding)
www.dog-play.com (freestyle)
www.coursing.com (lure coursing)
www.nordkyn.com (weight pulling, carting, etc.)

REFERENCES AND ADDITIONAL READING

Abrantes, Roger: The Evolution of Canine Social Behaviour. Wakan Tanka Publishers, 1997.

Beaver, Bonnie V: Canine Behavior: *A guide for Veterinarians*. WB Saunders Company, 1999.

Billinghurst, Ian: Give Your Dog a Bone. Ian Billinghurst, 1993.

Booth, Sheila: Purely Positive Training. Podium Publications, 1998.

Booth, Sheila: Schutzhund Obedience, Training in Drive, with Gottfried Dildei. Podium Publications, 1992.

Donaldson, Jean: The Culture Clash. James and Kenneth Publishers, 1996.

Donaldson, Jean: Dogs Are From Neptune. Lasar Multimedia Productions, 1998.

Fogle, Bruce: The Dog's Mind. Howell Book House, 1990.

Fogle, Bruce: The Encyclopedia of the Dog. DK Publishing, Inc., 1995.

Fox, Michael W.: Behaviour of Wolves Dogs and Related Canids. Kriege Publishing Company, 1971.

Hetts, Suzanne: Pet Behavior Protocols. AAHA press, 1999.

Payne, Joan: Flying High: *The Complete Book of Flyball*. KDB Publishing Company, 1996.

Pinker, Steven: The Language Instinct. HarperPerennial, 1995.

Reid, Pamela J.: Excel-Erated Learning. James and Kenneth Publishers, 1996.

Rugaas, Turid: On Talking Terms with Dogs: *Calming Signals*. Legacy By Mail, Inc., 1997.

Rogerson, John: In Tune With Your Dog. The Northern Centre for Animal Behaviour, 1997.

Scott, John Paul and Fuller, John L.: Genetics and the Social Behavior of the Dog. University of Chicago Press, 1965.

Serpell, James, editor: The Domestic Dog. The Cambridge University Press 1995.

Wendt, Lloyd M.: Dogs, A Historical Journey. Howell Book House, 1996.